"Finally a practical and actionable guide on how to make sense of sustainability for brands. *Brand Valued* defines a new currency for brands that is urgently needed in today's socially networked world. Every brand marketer who has more than three years to retirement should read this."
Matthias Kurwig. Co-Founder and CEO, Green Decisions. Formerly COO Worldwide, Neo@Ogilvy

"*Brand Valued* is an inspired and timely gift to business leaders concerned with building enduring trust in their companies. Guy Champniss and Fernando Rodés Vilà powerfully demonstrate how social capital presents a remarkable opportunity to build corporate brand value in ways that accelerate the transition to sustainability. *Brand Valued* is a roadmap for business to enhance its social license to thrive in the 21st Century. The 'Era of Social Capital Rising' has arrived! Read this book and then join the conversation."
Chris Coulter, SVP, GlobeScan.

"In *Brand Valued*, Guy and Fernando address an essential but much overlooked aspect of the role businesses and brands can play in creating a more sustainable world beyond dealing with resource constraints. They remind brands of their responsibility as aspirational role models for consumers. Brands can and should play a key role in (re)building the social capital which underpins long-term viable sustainability. Without it, it is doubtful that we can reach a world in which 9 billion can live well within the limits of one planet. I would recommend any brand owner to take note of the *Brand Valued* concept and make the thinking an integral part of their strategy."
Peter Paul van de Wijs. Managing Director, Business Role Focus Area, World Business Council for Sustainable Development.

"Brand valued? The answer to this singularly profound question will determine not only the future of brands and the brands of the future, but it will also define the social capital – the lifeblood of brands – in which they trade. *Brand Valued* engagingly arms us with the arguments and tools to answer this question."
Ron Vandenberg. Co-Founder, FutureBrand & Merchant

"A refreshing new approach to how brands can become part of the solution rather than the background noise of the mindless consumerism and GDP growth damaging our wellbeing and our planet. The age of consumers bombarded by advertising created 'wants' is ending and a focus on the 'citizen', real human needs and wellbeing beginning. The economy of the future will be one in which the successful, valued, brands, products and services focus on maximising outputs of wellbeing per unit of planet input. In *Brand Valued* Guy and Fernando give us a valuable insight into this new world."

Jules Peck. Author www.citizenrenaissance.com, nef Trustee and creator of the 'Flourish' wellbeing innovation process.

BRAND VALUED

HOW SOCIALLY VALUED BRANDS

HOLD THE KEY TO A SUSTAINABLE FUTURE

AND BUSINESS SUCCESS

GUY CHAMPNISS AND FERNANDO RODÉS VILÀ

A John Wiley & Sons, Ltd., Publication

Registered office
John Wiley & Sons Ltd, The Atrium, Southern Gate, Chichester, West Sussex, PO19 8SQ,
United Kingdom

For details of our global editorial offices, for customer services and for information about how
to apply for permission to reuse the copyright material in this book please see our website at
www.wiley.com

Library of Congress Cataloging-in-Publication Data
Champniss, Guy.
   Brand valued : how socially valued brands hold the key to a sustainable future and business
success / Guy Champniss and Fernando Rodés Vilà.
      p. cm.
   Includes bibliographical references and index.
   ISBN 978-1-119-97667-7
   1. Branding (Marketing)–Social aspects.   2. Social responsibility of business.
   I. Rodés Vilà, Fernando.   II. Title.
   HF5415.1255.C476 2011
   658.8'27–dc22

                                                                        2011013531

ISBN 978-1-119-97667-7 (hardback), ISBN 978-1-119-97777-3 (ebk),
ISBN 978-1-119-97801-5 (ebk), ISBN 978-1-119-97799-5 (ebk)

A catalogue record for this book is available from the British Library.

Typeset in FF Scala 10/14.5 pt by Toppan Best-set Premedia Limited
Printed in Great Britain by TJ International Ltd, Padstow, Cornwall, UK

To Ness, Frederick and Leafy.
Valued beyond words.
G.C.

CONTENTS

ACKNOWLEDGEMENTS

The idea for this book sprang from a trip we made to Stanford Graduate School of Business at the end of 2009. Between then and now there have been a number of people who have helped to shape the ideas into the pages that follow.

Firstly I would like to thank my co-author, Fernando Rodés Vilà, for his invaluable point of view, his unwavering interest in the area and his belief in the concepts that make up the book. Thanks must also go to Hernán Sánchez Neira for his support during the writing period. Nick Ceasar, at Ashridge, and Jon Alexander, formerly of Fallon, were instrumental in getting the premise straight in my head (even if they didn't realize they were helping at the time). David Wood proved vital as a sounding board and head-scratcher when certain ideas needed polishing. Thanks also to Nico Muñoz, for his friendship and belief in this and other ideas. Thanks must also go to Prof. Hugh Wilson of Cranfield School of Management for his interest and support. At Wiley, I am extremely grateful for the constant and professional support of Claire Plimmer, Michaela Fay and Tessa Allen, and to Helen Heyes for her extraordinary eye for detail. Thanks also to Liz Draper for meticulously – and doggedly – sorting out all permissions and ensuring references were complete. Finally, I'd like to thank my family: Ness, for her constant support, belief and interest in the idea; Frederick for not managing to delete the entire manuscript with a single keystroke; and Leafy for coming into the world right in the middle of the project. Not only did her arrival alongside her brother offer a compelling distraction, it also brought back into sharp focus how we must all redouble our efforts to make tomorrow better.

Guy Champniss
London, March 2011

LIST OF FIGURES

INTRODUCTION

Brand Valued?

'Brand Valued? Don't you mean Brand Value?'

That's the response we've had from a fair few people with whom we've shared the title of this book before laying out our arguments.

'No,' we say. 'Brand Valued is exactly what we mean.'

For several years we've been watching with growing interest how brands have a growing interest in the nebulous, contradictory but compelling area of sustainability. Yes, we know, probably the last thing we need now is another book with the words brand and sustainability in the title. Not a week seems to go by without another report or book extolling the virtues of connecting with consumers in this emerging, complex and highly ambiguous space, and the subsequent benefits that then stream towards the business. It's invariably painted as a virtuous circle, where brands lead from the heart, trust is restored and we all inch that little bit closer to what is positioned as a more sustainable lifestyle. It seems sustainability for many represents the mother of all 'win-wins'.

Our take on this is a little different. Yes, we agree with the enthusiasm and energy with which many of these reports hit the market, and cannot fault the belief that this represents an opportunity for some sort of brand renewal. But we struggle with sustainability. Whilst sustainability is, of course, incredibly important, we don't believe it's what brands should be focusing on. For a start, sustainability tends to be abstract, reactive and apologetic. And it focuses, more often than not, on zero: zero emissions, zero impact, zero to landfill, etc. Admirable though it is in purist terms, aiming for zero is never going to be a compelling platform upon which to build stories for widespread engagement.

But we struggle with sustainability for another, more fundamental, reason. Because we believe sustainability – or rather 'unsustainability' – is a symptom of our current situation (albeit a big one) masquerading as the cause. For us – and this is our core argument in this book – the real cause of our woes today is a collapse in social capital. And if we want to find solutions – genuine solutions – then we need to focus on the underlying cause. We need to take a long hard look through the social capital lens. And by the way, we're talking about solutions not just to the wider sustainability debate, but the very brand-specific sustainability debate – how brands can survive and thrive today.

At first glance, the very term 'social capital' can appear like a piece of sleight copy, trying to appease increasingly vocal and empowered critics of unfettered capitalism, by tethering this problem child to a concept usually considered an antidote to raw market mechanics. In doing so, it may look as if the last unsullied aspect of our lives is now beholden to market forces in a final bid to retrieve some sense of legitimacy. That would be grim, and thankfully it's not the case. Social capital – as a means of describing the strength and inherent value in our societies through qualities such as dialogue, shared thinking and widespread trust – has been around as a term certainly since the mid-1800s, when France's Alexis de Toqueville toured the US and studied the burgeoning sense of cohesion in new American communities. Quietly and discretely, social capital has been at work since day one, acting both as 'engine bolts' in keeping us connected and 'engine oil' in removing friction in new connections within our personal, collective and professional lives and networks.

Only now we believe we've reached a crisis point, where the bolts have worked loose, or have been overtightened in some cases, and where the oil has become too glutinous or indeed too sheer in others. Social capital has reached a point of such instability and decay that we are collectively pining and striving to re-establish a sense of equilibrium.

When we talk about social capital from the brand perspective (and in all honesty, we think we're the first to do this), we're talking about the process by which brands engage in rich, diverse and frequent dialogue with constituents, the shared thinking and engagement that can spring from that dialogue and the subsequent trust that flows from these interactions: trust between the constituents and the brand, and between the constituents themselves. And whilst some may say this model confirms the way brands already operate, we believe it highlights just how *restrictive and shortsighted* this behaviour has been to date, and how *destructive* it will be going forward. The social capital perspective reveals the complexity and dynamism of how a brand should now interact with all those around it – not just for the brand's benefit, but society's as well. In an increasingly complex environment, the social capital perspective offers the opportunity to apply rigour and theory to what is often reliant solely on intuition.

For us, the link between social capital and sustainability is straightforward and elegant. Where social capital is low – with patchy dialogue, low involvement and little trust – the ability and propensity to externalise costs and marginalise voices is high. Low social capital, then, allows the two most pressing criteria of 'unsustainability' to flourish. Conversely, where social capital is rich and balanced – so plenty of dialogue, swathes of engagement and an abundance of specific and generalised trust – the ability and desire to marginalise 'dissenters' and externalise costs falls away. In short, social capital is the route to sustainability that is more intuitive, engaging and durable. Sustainability that is, dare we say it, more sustainable.

Looking at brands through the social capital lens is crucial for a number of reasons. Firstly, the social capital lens throws into sharp focus how brands have interacted with society up until this point, and what they clearly need to do from this point on. We'll lay out our argument that the proliferation and ever-widening reach of brands go hand in hand with the long inexorable decline in social capital in western Europe and the US. It's a period we call the 'Era of Social Capital Waning': a period when brands have almost hedged against, or shorted, the long-term health of society with low quality and often toxic debt (examples are knowingly unhealthy eating options, disruptive forms of entertainment and, at a higher level, the enduring idea that consumption in itself can bring wellbeing and happiness).

But we're adamant that the Era of Social Capital Waning is now behind us, and that we're witnessing the transition towards what Philip Pullman calls a 'wakefulness' amongst us all. It's what we've chosen to call the 'Era of Social Capital Rising'. And whilst social media may be playing a key part in the emergence of this Era of Social Capital Rising, this is most certainly something that transcends pure technology. This is something more fundamental. It's changing who we 'are', and it's challenging business and brands to re-evaluate their broader role and purpose too.

The second reason the social capital lens is so important for brands is that we're convinced a commitment to building rich, abundant and balanced social capital is the route to enduring brand value for the firm. In other words, social capital is fast becoming the *technology* of brand value.

Our rationale here is that the principal driver of brand value is brand equity, which, in turn, is dependent on trust in the brand (in fact we'd go as far as to say brand equity *is* trust). On the other side of the equation, we also know that trust – and opportunities to demonstrate trustworthiness – is the crucial outcome of social capital development (after dialogue, shared thinking and engagement). Combining these two, we can see that the most efficient and effective way for the firm to enjoy brand value is for the brand to build abundant and balanced stocks of social capital. In other words, the route to long-term and self-sustaining brand value is via becoming a brand that is enduringly *valued*:

$$B^{\dot{\uparrow}\uparrow\uparrow} \rightarrow B^{\text{🤝}} \rightarrow B^{\$\text{📈}}$$

Brand Valued	Brand Equity	Brand Value
(Bvd)	(Be)	(Bv)

As well as social capital being the most intuitive and efficient way for us to collectively nudge a little closer to a sustainable future and build long-term value, building social capital is also something brands are uniquely qualified to do. As we'll set out, the crucial stepping stones towards higher and more balanced social capital are dependent on key qualities held by many a self-respecting brand. The fit could not be better. Brands have the potential to be excellent engines of social capital.

So it seems we're sailing perilously close to the 'win-win' scenario we were critical of in the opening paragraphs. But whilst nurturing social capital should be well within the grasp of most brands, we do not, for one moment, think the process will be easy or painless. In this emerging Era of Social Capital Rising, the focus has to shift not to brute levels of social capital as a means to increase trust, but to high and *balanced* levels of social capital. As we'll show in detail, social capital comes in many flavours, and brands have really only shown an ability, to date, to get behind one type, much to our, and ultimately their, detriment. The route to deep and lasting trust is now far more complex and dynamic, and we're betting these early years of the Era of Social Capital Rising will witness many a brand's demise, through not making the grade in terms of being valued.

To reiterate, it's our core thesis that durable brand value relies on becoming a brand that is valued. And becoming the latter through building rich, vibrant and balanced stocks of social capital ensures the brand is enduringly salient, timely and authentic for its myriad constituents. It's time for the brand to move beyond being a shrill cheerleader for corporate CSR efforts, and become instead a trusted ambassador for social capital.

In terms of layout, the first part of this book is descriptive: descriptive in that we've charted the rise of brands from the social capital perspective. What really caught our attention with this exercise was just how complex – how compromised – the relationship has been between brands and balanced, healthy stocks of social capital. Drawing on consumer, social and cognitive psychology, along with sociology, behavioural economics and long-standing brand strategy approaches, we think it's fair to say that the route brands have taken to today has been rocky and, at times, ugly. But, ever the optimists, we believe there's a lot we can learn from the journey so far in terms of where we go from here.

This takes us to the second part of the book, which is unashamedly prescriptive in mapping out what we think a brand needs to become in this Era of Social Capital Rising. In these chapters we'll detail our approach to building a brand that is truly valued. Drawing on research on more than 120 brands across nine markets, and conversations with more than 25 000 consumers, we'll present what we believe is a brand archetype in this new era. We call this brand a 'Social Equity Brand' in recognition of the way it approaches and engages with society. More specifically, we've identified what we believe is the anatomy of a Social Equity Brand: ten Social Equity Traits (SETs) that determine the personality, vision and outlook of this new breed of brand.

From there, we set out our thoughts on how to leverage these SETs and position the Social Equity Brand in order to create a brand that is genuinely and enduringly valued by all who experience it. We call this brand management strategy a 'Social Capital Strategy' (SCS).

Placing it within the panoply of existing approaches to brand strategy, our Social Capital Strategy is predicated on five commitments (the '5Is'): Interconnectedness, Inclusiveness, Ignition, Interest and Imagination. Again, we offer a detailed breakdown of each, and how they individually and collectively support the creation and maintenance of rich and balanced social capital. We believe the Social Capital Strategy approach to strategic brand management represents a key contribution to – and extension of – the wealth of theories on how best to build and maintain a brand.

With these prescriptive components in place, we can extend our earlier expression of how we believe brand value will be derived from a Social Equity Brand (B_{se}) in this Era of Social Capital Rising:

| Social Equity Traits (SETs) | Social Capital Strategy (SCS) | Social Equity Brand (Bse) | Brand Valued (Bvd) | Brand Equity (Be) | Brand Value (Bv) |

Finally, we tackle the thorny issue of measurement: of understanding how the brand is contributing to social capital stocks, and how the brand is benefiting from being credited with those long-term, authentic and intrinsically motivated investments.

Actually, that's not the final part. The final part – Part V – is currently empty, bar a few opening remarks. This is the part of the book that we would like to invite you to write. It's the part of the book for agreements, challenges, reflections and case studies from anyone who'd like to engage in the conversation, hopefully making this a living discussion rather than a traditional closed book. Within and around the communications and marketing industries, it's our way to start building some social capital around the concept of social capital. We've placed a few fledgling case studies to kick off the dialogue at www.brandvalued.com, and you can contribute directly. We hope you will.

To sum up, exploring and understanding brands – their creation and management – through the social capital lens throws into sharp focus the complexities and opportunities facing brands today. Complexities and opportunities shaped by more diverse audiences and their demands for the crucial outcome and feedback loop of social capital, and the core tenet of the brand: trust.

Despite some early detours, we're profoundly pro-brand. We have no doubt in their ability to become pivotal sources of value for the business, through supporting and enabling all those who experience the brand to explore, understand, shape and share approaches to the myriad challenges and opportunities that lie ahead.

The social capital lens reveals the uniqueness and vulnerability of the brand in this Era of Social Capital Rising. In this new era, the brand that is truly valued – the Social Equity Brand – does not treat society as its most important customer to be targeted. Instead it recognises society as its principal *supplier*, to be protected and nurtured for the long term.

We firmly believe that an unswerving commitment to social capital is the route to more lasting and engaging solutions to our collective sustainability challenges, the route to creating a brand that is appreciated, respected and welcomed within the increasingly rich and dynamic networks that swirl around it, and the route to long-lasting brand value for the firm.

So, you see, it's not a typo. We do mean Brand Valued.

Our arguments for the importance of being valued

1. When business and brands talk about sustainability, what they're really addressing is nothing more than a symptom of our current condition (albeit a major one). To really get to the heart of the issue – to really start creating innovative, durable and valuable solutions to the myriad issues we face – we must focus instead on the root cause: the undermining of social capital. We define social capital in the context of business and brands as:

   'The quality, depth, breadth and frequency of brand-inspired dialogue, exchange and interaction that occur within a community. It is the benefits – both private (to the brand) and public (to the community) – that are generated as a result. And it is the resultant collective ability to maintain and enhance these processes and benefits.'

2. The link between balanced social capital and sustainability has always been there: when social capital is high and balanced, so the propensity to marginalise voices and externalise costs diminishes (through higher awareness, greater collaboration and increased innovation). When social

capital is low, however, it becomes all too easy to squeeze out 'dissenters' and offload costs in order to meet the demands of narrower and more exclusive audiences. In short, social capital drives sustainability.

3. For more than half a century and the best part of a generation – and since the arrival of brands en masse – we've been chipping away at the levels of social capital, to the point that our current stocks are chronically low and perilously out of balance. We may not know it, but we've been in a prolonged period we've labelled the Era of Social Capital Waning.

4. With dialogue and trust as central tenets of both, brands and social capital are intricately wrapped around each other, which is good news and bad. It's bad, in that historically brands have always been obsessed with building one form of short-term social capital – bonding capital. Bonding capital can only exist in tight-knit, homogenous relationships, and left to its own devices (without the balancing effect of other forms of capital), bonding capital becomes intoxicating. This is the cutthroat – and increasingly redundant – world of bare-knuckle brand competition for consumer loyalty – striving to create bonding capital at all costs.

5. We are now entering a new period, one where the pendulum has begun to swing the other way, where the value placed on exclusivity is diminishing, and the value in connectivity and inclusion is rising. With an awakening desire to restock and rebalance levels of social capital, it's a period we call the Era of Social Capital Rising.

6. In this new era, brands need to reinvent themselves and renew their purpose if they want to have a constructive, pivotal role (which we believe they should). Today, brands delight in cajoling us into 'maximising' our decisions around 'sustainability', blasting us with intricate facts and exhaustive data in the name of full-frontal transparency. We're forced to stare blankly at the myriad trade-offs and opportunity costs around more sustainable options, with the result being we blink, swallow and look elsewhere to make our purchase decisions less stressful. Despite pledging their unswerving commitment to the cause, most brands' behaviour when it comes to sustainability could not be less sustainable.

7. Brands that will thrive in this Era of Social Capital Rising will be brands that turn their backs on the traditional practice of offering society short-term, crippling debt wrapped up as the next best offer or exclusivity.

Instead they will genuinely invest in society, with long-term equity contributions via collaborative, constructive experiences that drive rich dialogue, deep thinking and widespread trust. These are what we call Social Equity Brands: brands that invest *with* society instead of hedging *against* it; brands that are not tolerated by society, but truly valued.

8. Social Equity Brands are identifiable by a series of traits – what we call Social Equity Traits (SETs). We've mapped ten of them into the process, and they include: Celebrating emotion; Exploring the citizen; Striving for 'assessability'; and Understanding 'value-in-use'. As a thread that runs through many of these SETs, this new breed of brand understands that rich social capital doesn't demand 24/7 full-frontal transparency. Transparency simply removes secrets, yet trust – the crucial endgame of social capital and tenet of brand equity – evaporates not with secrets, but with *deception*. As such, Social Equity Brands recognise not to predicate their efforts on total transparency, but on the permanent eradication of acts of deceit.

9. In order to leverage these traits, Social Equity Brands must embark on a brand-building strategy that places the development of social capital at its core. It's what we call a Social Capital Strategy. A Social Capital Strategy is predicated on what we've labelled the '5Is': Interconnectedness, Inclusiveness, Ignition, Interest and Imagination.

10. In this new Era of Social Capital Rising, to create long-term value for the business, irrespective of sector or market, the brand has to be genuinely valued. In this new era, it is not enough to ask ourselves; 'What is our brand value?' . . . Instead, we have to begin by asking 'Is our brand valued?'

Part I

Setting the Scene – The Tangled Worlds of Brands and Social Capital

Brands are everywhere, it seems. Everything that embodies or represents any service, function or form of utility feels as if it has been 'branded'. There's a terrifying statistic regularly paraded to new recruits in advertising agencies, that the average UK consumer is subjected to more than 3000 commercial messages a day: messages that are made pithy and ballistic by their use of brands, branding, tight copy and arresting visuals. The statistic is trotted out to make all the new recruits realise the importance and challenge of establishing 'cut-through'. In other words, how your message can make the cut to being in any way registered amongst those 3000. But wait – 3000 a day? It's a wonder we have time to do anything else. Colleague Jon Alexander[1] offers a novel way to look at this number. He points out that the Koutoubia in Marrakech calls the city's Muslims to prayer five times a day.

Five times a day to prayer – that seems quite a lot.

But brands – if we position them as some similar glue from which millions also get meaning in their lives every day – call their faithful to pray 3000 times a day. Now that is a lot. And what's more, it's not even a case of asking the faithful to be complicit and engage in the process – nope, the messages get preached directly to you, wherever you are, whatever you're doing.

And of course it's not just the usual stuff we consume – from a strawberry yoghurt at breakfast to a fortnight in the sunshine in August – that falls under the purview of brands. No, brands appear to have extended their influence even into the heart of our political system and the election process. As numerous commentators have noted, the least spotted beasts in these campaigns have become the policies themselves. As such, the UK has followed the US into an era of personality-led elections, where ideology-lite parties, increasingly huddled together in the middle ground, compete on brand positioning and propositions, tightly packaged and delivered to laser-accurate targets across the country by media-trained spokespeople. Policy debate seems to have been replaced with impassioned pleas of personal ambition and aspiration, all in an attempt to make the party 'brand experience' more engaging.

In politics, as in so many other parts of life, the seemingly unstoppable rise of brands is frequently met with derision, frustration and scepticism. So how did brands get to be so disliked and mistrusted?

Chapter 1

B rands first made an appearance in the nineteenth century,[2] pretty much at the same time the Industrial Revolution started to radically change the way we worked and lived. This is, of course, no coincidence: rapid industrialisation meant people flocked from rural areas to the cities and the newly created industrial centres. At the same time, an unswerving focus on the novelty of efficiency in process meant most of those taking up these jobs found themselves in roles that were highly specialised and fragmented. Specialisation, efficiency and scale were the watchwords of these burgeoning economies.

Both the mass migration of hopeful workers and the world of specialisation that awaited them had one overriding effect: people became more distant from the products and services they had previously taken for granted and, very importantly, trusted. Suddenly, the local butcher could no longer vouch for the cut of meat, the local greengrocer was unable to defend which vegetables would be best at this time of year, the local tailor unable to run you up a suit, knowing your size and favourite cloth.

Suddenly, no-one knew the quality of anything anymore – there was no-one trusted on hand to recommend, and if there was someone there, chances are they would no longer fully understand the processes and suppliers involved in underpinning their recommendations and guarantees.

In the process of exploding supply, provenance – that key mediator of demand – was being bent out of shape. To put it another way, a major casualty of progress was the ability to establish trust. We call this the 'provenance cost'. And it represents the fundamental spark that ignited the whole revolution in brands.

To try and lighten this provenance cost, to try and restore this level of trust and to try and reduce this enormous search process that now confronted the new consumer, brands were created. In short, these first brands were there to slash search costs for consumers, and attempt to bring them 'closer' to the process in order to gain their trust. Brands were a substitute for personal, trusted sources of knowledge, which meant the brands themselves had to be *perceived* as personal, trusted sources of knowledge.

In the beginning, these brands were very straightforward creatures, attempting to communicate the bare necessities in order for consumers to assuage these provenance costs. Take, for example, P&G's efforts for Ivory Soap in the 1880s, where the product was advertised as '99 44/100 per cent pure'.[3] It went on to list what the soap was useful for (washing laces, infants' clothing, cleaning gloves and '. . . for the varied uses about the house that daily arise'). Not the most catchy piece of writing, but it did the job in terms of slashing search costs and demonstrating provenance (the illustrations that accompanied this copy were equally austere and perfunctory).

For their very existence, then, brands were – and are – dependent upon social capital. Without social capital – the synaptic fluid between the 'brand nerve' and 'consumer receiver' – there can be no connection, reaction or event. Brands and social capital are bed-fellows, like it or not.

To be more specific, in trying to lighten 'provenance costs', brands were trying to compensate for widespread reductions in broad social capital as a result of migration and specialisation, by offering up their own artificial version. But they were not replacing like with like.

Although the specifics of social capital in the context of brands are covered a little later, it's worth sewing some seeds now. Social capital – the health of a society measured in relationships and their strengths – is underpinned by three main constructs: a structural construct, a cognitive construct and a relational construct.[4]

The structural construct refers to dialogue – conversations between people and groups of people, be they your family, neighbours, work colleagues or, in fact, complete strangers on the other side of the country (or world). If we look back at the 'provenance cost' associated with the migration of workers and their more specialised roles (the inability to talk to the butcher, greengrocer or tailor, for example), it becomes clear that brands were there to try and meet this social requirement: to keep a form of dialogue in play – and very specifically, to try and mimic a form of local dialogue, even though parties were far apart. This intimacy is a tactic that brands today still use to great effect, realising that we've never let go of that emotional desire to be close to community, despite the enormous efficiencies of globalisation.

Which leads us to the second undergirding construct – the cognitive construct. This represents the new ways of thinking that emerge when social capital is higher. Think about how your opinions or views on issues can be influenced through discussions with others, or editorial comments or even documentaries on television. Again, brands in their nascency attempted to stimulate thought processes within consumers that allowed them to build cognitive links with the products and services represented by those brands. In particular, even though these consumers were now in new cities and new environments, brands were attempting to assuage that sense of dislocation by presenting a way of thinking that still celebrated 'local'. It didn't matter that the company behind the brand was thousands of miles away, because the *brand* was close to you.

Third, there's the relational construct. Put simply, this construct represents trust. Small word, but long reach and big punch. Trust is the grease in most relationships. Trust underpins whether you accept the inherent risks in entering into a relationship, with past performances an indicator of future performances. Without trust, a promise is useless, and without a promise, a brand has virtually nothing to say. And as we have seen, these early brands were trying to restore trust in that sense of confidence in a contract between producer and consumer. And once again, they were trying to do this by bringing the consumer 'closer' to the producer, with language, design and other devices to elicit intimacy.

As mentioned, we'll look at social capital in much more detail a little later, but we felt it worthwhile seeding these elements at this point, since they provide a novel context within which to view the development of brands. This social capital lens offers a view of how they subtly helped society shift from a local community system to one of mass urban mobilisation by simulating the continuation of a form of social glue that had kept communities together for generations. Brands made a token, but highly visible, contribution to tradition in a world preoccupied with looking forward.

But behind that token was a far more fundamental fillip. In easing this transition, brands were instrumental in adding one more thing to the 'social capital mix': they were swapping a blend of naturally occurring social capital with their own plastic version. As we'll see in the later sections, we'll argue that this switch has had a profound effect on the way brands engage with consumers, and how we as consumers react.

The reason it's important to distinguish between the different forms of social capital at this stage is that brands were trying to always reproduce a form of capital built on intimacy, familiarity and homogeneity. The result is what is often called 'thick trust'[5] (where trust is very localised and determined often by the perceived homogeneity within the group). But what was missing were the balancing devices of other forms of social capital, built more on heterogeneity and 'thin trust'. Put another way, there was too much glue to stick us together and not enough oil to remove friction.

This pseudo capital process had clear benefits for the producer. By offering up this fillip for capital, firms were able to scale their operations and reach immeasurably, for one simple reason: as the brand was all about being close to the consumer, it didn't matter where the operations were, or how long their distribution chains, because ultimately the brand was always next to the consumer – and the consumer liked this cosy homogeneity.

Brands, then, became a vital link between increasingly efficient and scaled business, and increasingly mobile and disconnected consumers: a link that represented a guarantee of quality and consistency from the producer to the consumer. And to this day, this guarantee, or promise, in the form of an implicit contract between these two parties persists. Brand equity is built largely upon this trust[6] in delivering on this promise.

So, it is fair to say that during this era of brand emergence, brands represented a win-win for producers and consumers: they guaranteed quality, consistency and accuracy. They presented consumers with a short-cut to making the right choice along with a level of protection, and they presented producers with a device with which they could establish themselves in markets far from home, and in categories or industries in which they had no previous presence. Everyone was happy. This was when foundations were laid for some of the most enduring brands.

Take Kellogg's, for example. Today, the company boasts an impressive portfolio of cereal brands. In fact, in many households, Kellogg's *is* breakfast cereal. Back in the early 1900s, Kellogg's was a striking example of how brands tried to mimic 'cosy' and intimate social capital in their positioning and communication efforts.

An example of a campaign that dramatically stimulated this plastic, brand-driven social capital was rolled out in 1907 as the brainchild of Will 'W.K.' Kellogg, and called 'Wednesday is Wink Day in New York'.[7] With no mention of Kellogg's in the advertisement, housewives were encouraged (dared even) to wink at their local shopkeeper. If they duly did this, the wink was the signal for the shopkeeper to hand out a free trial packet of cornflakes. By all accounts it was extraordinarily effective, running on successive Wednesdays and increasing sales in the New York area alone fifteen-fold.[8]

Behind being seen as a progressive, innovative marketer and bringing cornflakes to millions more American homes, Kellogg's was leveraging its own version of bonding social capital (as opposed to linking or bridging capital). Implicit in its message was an invitation to feel comfortable and playful with your shopkeeper, in maybe the way you would have been when you knew he was the son of the guy your father used to buy groceries from. It was a great way to foster stronger immediate bonds within what was probably an already homogenous, but recent, transient community. Except, of course, that level of intimacy and informality could not have developed that quickly had Kellogg's not intervened. The Kellogg's brand, then, was a mediator of this rapid replacement of social capital.

Procter & Gamble (P&G) is the fourth most profitable company in the world, and the fourth largest company in the US by market capitalisation, behind only Exxon Mobil, Microsoft and Walmart.[9] It's also the largest advertiser on the planet, with a staggering portfolio of twenty three 'billion dollar brands' (brands with annual sales of one billion dollars plus).

We've already mentioned P&G for its early work on Ivory Soap in the 1880s. But it was also early to get on the bandwagon of reproducing a form of social capital for its consumers in a novel way.

It's fairly common knowledge that the term 'soap opera' was coined because of the fact P&G, and its leading detergent brands, were behind many of these most successful shows in the US. Starting on radio in the 1930s and then moving to television from the 1950s, P&G delivered more than a dozen popular daytime dramas. What links all of these efforts – from 'Another World' through to 'Young Doctor Malone' – is the fact that they presented tight community antics to disparate audiences. They were, once again, a fillip for a form of social capital: a fix for all those who were far from such communities, as a result of the rapid and continued migration. As it happens, 'As The World Turns', which started in 1956 and takes place in the fictional town of Oakdale, Illinois, is the last of the P&G sponsored shows still airing in the US. So it seems, in the US at least, the appetite for these fillip portraits of high social capital has waned. Could this be a sign of the return of genuine social capital?

So as society underwent seismic shifts in terms of productivity and migration at the tail-end of the nineteenth century through to the early decades of the twentieth century, brands were a means to help people remain connected to forms of social engagement that defined the way things used to be, even if that help from brands involved a certain amount of manipulation. Brands have always been in the social capital game.

And, of course, as productivity rose, so did personal wealth. This was a generation growing up with money in its pocket – and since an increasing amount of social meaning was being shaped by the social capital supplied by brands, it was inevitable that this new generation of consumers would put their hard-earned money to good use and buy into these brands.

Initially these emerging consumer needs were essentially utilitarian: warmth in the form of clothing or indeed heating; security in the form of personal living space and ownership; and safety in the form of safer cars or indeed secure banking. And in each case, brands attempted to deliver on these needs by promising a level of value that would satisfy the consumer: a level of value couched in the context of intimacy and familiarity that can only be achieved through strong 'snug' social capital.

Well maybe. But looking back, the writing was very possibly on the wall at this point. Maybe the obsession with efficiency and an over-reliance on what had become known as 'scientific advertising'[10] allowed an overestimation of what brands could do. Or rather should do.

Efficient and rational – adjectives of an era

Frederick Winslow Taylor[11] (and many others) was hugely influential in progressing not just the mechanics of the Industrial Revolution, but the ideology of the era. Man had conquered the chaotic and whimsical, in terms of nature and the cottage-industry era, to emerge as scientific master of all he surveyed. The Era of Scientific Management and the Efficiency Movement had arrived. Suddenly, the earth was caught unawares, and her riches in terms of resources were laid bare for new scientific man, courtesy of his ingenuity, focus and rigour, to use in whatever way he felt fit to further his dominance in the world. Scale and efficiency were 'in'.

Such was the pervasiveness of this scientific enlightenment in management and business that it determined the way these businesses – and their emerging brands – attempted to engage with their new consumers. As with everything else, consumers could be seen as people striving for efficiency and rational purity. From these origins, what are now seen as the traditional consumer behaviour models were born. These were models predicated on the consumer striving to gain as much pertinent and focused information as possible, systematically sifting through this information over as many iterations as it took to arrive at an unbiased position as to which of the options then appeared to deliver maximum value, i.e. the greatest net benefit with all costs considered. Humans were rational processing and counting machines, systematically and efficiently working through every decision in a precise and formulaic manner.

Described in this way, the models feel woefully inadequate, especially when placed in the context of behavioural economics, aspects of social psychology and, closer to marketing and communications, the work around networks, collaboration, co-creation and value-in-use.

It's also important to remember that this perspective is still extremely powerful today. Whilst emotion is now recognised as a key driver of engagement and consumer behaviour,[12] the vagaries of dealing with such volatile (if effective) processes still push many firms to model their brand communication efforts on what is still, essentially, the traditional consumer behaviour model: communication strategies built on the assumption that the consumer approaches a purchase decision in an essentially linear and rational fashion, in a vacuum without higher or more abstract goals playing a part and without other complementary brand experiences getting involved. The consumer purchase funnel is testament to that persisting scientific management approach to consumer behaviour.

From this 'rational' perspective, the 'good' is the thing, and is primarily shaped by the capture and manipulation of natural resources, to create something with value embedded for the consumer. In other words, what you're paying for is a product already laden with all the value it can possibly deliver: it's hardwired in, before you even get your hands on it.

This dominant logic emerged in this era of rapidly expanding businesses, benefiting from hitherto unheard of levels of efficiency delivered by eager, plentiful and adaptable employees. And whilst natural resources were also plentiful, in this new scientific playground, businesses quickly recognised that controlling the physical raw materials and resources was paramount. Vargo and Lusch[13] describe this separation of physical and human resources as operand resources (those to which changes are made in order to produce value) and operant resources (those who work on operand resources). In a nutshell, early business saw operant resources as limitless, but operand resources as the scarce resources. And so a fixation with product and good was created, spilling into the marketing function, as brands worked to extol the embedded value in the product they represented.

Despite many shortcomings, the rational consumer behaviour models, the focus on raw materials (operand resources) and the conviction of embedded product value, together with the general scientific management approach and all of its extensions, served the burgeoning marketing function and its creation of brands well. As already stated, these new markets of consumers were made up of people often dislocated from what had been their established communities and the various forms of support they offered through social capital (invariably of the bonding variety). Consumers needed to offset these 'provenance costs' by gaining access to trusted mavens of quality. And, as we've also mentioned, in many cases these needs for quality and consistency were in the context of functional, utilitarian aspects of the products in question.

This marriage of utilitarian need and scientific response seemed pretty good, for maybe the reason that both were pretty rational fellows: to go back to the earlier examples, if you want clothing to keep you warm, a heavy fabric, well stitched is what you need, and the process to ascertain which overcoat delivers that can be fairly swift, thanks to the substitute provenance offered by the brands. Consumers could easily weigh up the utilitarian benefits with the associated costs, incorporate the promise proposed by the brand with respect to future performance and chug through the process until a clear winner became obvious. As already shown in the earlier P&G Ivory Soap example, this rational, transparent, ordered decision process was clearly reflected in the style of the brand communication efforts.

But the system seemed less suited to the inevitable evolution of this process; that once these basic, functional utilitarian needs are met, a new wave of 'wants' emerges – wants based on emotion, personal circumstance and a moment in time. Suddenly, a model based on 'scientific making' and 'rational selling', a model based on a solid processor of a consumer, seemed ill-suited for the job.

From utilitarian to hedonic – when needs explode

Common sense says that once utilitarian needs are met, individuals start trying to meet higher-order wants. There are many ways to describe these, but we're going to go with 'hedonic'.

By hedonic wants we refer to the emotional wants of the individual – those wants fuelled by what are labelled 'Three Fs' – fantasies, feelings and fun.[14] So if we go back to the previous examples, we can see how, once the utilitarian benefits have been experienced and expectations have risen, these exact same relationships can evolve into being about hedonic benefits: clothing ceases to be about warmth and function, and becomes about fashion, style and personal statement; housing becomes less about shelter and security, and more about size, location and decoration, all to broadcast a desired image; and cars become less about secure and efficient transportation from A to B, and more about design, speed and demonstrations of wealth. These are in no way meant to represent the sum of all of these hedonic wants with respect to these products, and that is the point: to try and sum all types is impossible, since not only are there (probably) thousands of fragmented types of hedonic want, but they all swirl around in a turbulent sea, whose currents are determined by contextual, relativistic and temporal factors. So the rational consumer type, born out of scientific management, appears woefully inadequate in trying to understand and respond effectively to this new type of want.

And there's one particular facet of this inadequacy that we want to introduce now as a primer for a later discussion. The rational model is based on consumers being able – and willing – to sift through information in a balanced and systematic way until a clear frontrunner appears: acquire, analyse, acquire more, analyse further, etc. Utilitarian benefits, by their very definition, are not abstract or volatile, meaning they remain static and constant long enough for the consumer to go through this iterative process with some degree of effectiveness. But when we get into the realm of hedonic value, those qualities tend to disappear. That's not through any volition on the part of the consumer, but rather the inherent nature of hedonic wants. The result is a constantly moving target, buffeted by a panoply of conflicting wants and needs, meaning any systematic analysis becomes onerous at best, and futile at worst.

The important point to set up here – and one that we will return to in Part II – is this: traditional (but pervasive) models of marketing and brand communication place a considerable – arguably unsustainable – demand on the consumer to reach a decision when it comes to satisfying hedonic wants.

And are these really hedonic wants? Or are they also needs?

On the surface, it's very difficult to accept that a pair of Jimmy Choos, an Aston Martin or a villa in the south of France are 'needs'. Surely these are out and out luxury goods that can only ever be wants?

Well, maybe not.

To argue the want/need distinction, it's worth considering another sociological phenomenon at this point: adaptation. We humans are extraordinarily adaptable. We live, work and play in a variety of environments and circumstances like no other creature on the planet. Whether it's on the Upper West Side in Manhattan or in an impoverished district of New Delhi, we find a way to make it work. We adapt.

Carol Graham[15] cites adaptation as a major reason why people can appear happy in environments as extreme as war-torn Kabul. She does argue, however, that the process of adaptation can be painful for us, which explains why rapid transition towards affluence can be so dislocating for society.

Graham goes on to talk about the paradox she calls 'happy peasants and miserable millionaires'. You probably know them: people who have lots of stuff yet seem persistently unhappy with life. This is also a product of adaptation, in that we adapt to these luxuries increasingly quickly, with the result that the delight they initially delivered wears off faster and faster. But it is not simply the case that delight is more rapidly replaced with nothingness or neutrality. Research shows that delight is replaced by pain. In other words, there is an actual negative hit that is felt when the delight has passed.

Psychologist Richard Solomon[16] calls this effect – where initial euphoria and delight turns to some form of pain – 'affective contrast'. He argues that it exists in even the first experience with the product or service that is attempting to meet this want, when the delight is at its maximum because of the sheer novelty of the encounter. Only at the beginning, the size of the negative after-effect is so small, and possibly so distant from the act of consumption or enjoyment, it doesn't register as linked to that encounter. But from that point on, he argues, the negative after-effect only grows in size and moves closer to the positive until it is simultaneous with the positive effect – and indeed larger than the positive effect. The result is the 'unhappy millionaire' effect. The concept is closely linked to the arguments laid out by Scitovsky[17] in his 1976 book *The Joyless Economy*, where he argues that for hedonic wants to be met with delight, they always have to be novel. Hence our search to consume must constantly find fresh new pastures in order to uncover 'the hit', as these wants morph into needs.

If we head back to the era of 'brand emergence' we can see how these burgeoning hedonic wants, together with the social capital fillip that brands represented, potentially combined to form the perfect storm that exacerbated the onset of what we call the Era of Social Capital Waning.

We've already argued that the emerging brand communication model was predicated on a misplaced, or certainly limited, understanding and appreciation of how the consumer approached consumption decisions, especially decisions influenced by rapidly surfacing hedonic wants. The result was very possibly an increasing focus from consumers on how to make the best choice to meet hedonic desires, given the tools and guidance provided by the brands in question.

It is our argument that this resulted in more time needed, effort expended and souls searched to make increasingly complex decisions. In short, less time being an everyday person and more time trying to be the best consumer they could be (with increasingly little effect). Consuming was becoming hard work.

At the same time, the artificial social capital offered by brands (to replace the trust in small communities) as a remedy for the 'provenance costs', very possibly acted to drive these consumers further towards consumption. Why? Because their most trusted source of social capital, with respect to consumption, were brands that were fundamentally *defined* by consumption, as opposed to the impartial, discrete referees within communities rich in authentic social capital. In other words, this branded fillip for social capital had a pernicious multiplier effect on this transition towards consumerism.

The old social system had included mavens who not only offered discrete and unbiased guidance on purchase decisions that were predominantly utilitarian, but where nascent hedonic wants surfaced, would advise in the context of a sense of natural balance. In other words, individualistic hedonic ambition is tempered by more altruistic concern for others. There is an appreciation and responsibility for the 'commons'.[8]

The 'commons' refers to the communal assets available for use by a group of actors, with the optimal outcome being that these actors use the assets at a rate that is good for them all collectively. The frequent example given is the grazing of livestock on a communal patch of grass, with the optimal outcome being that the farmers don't exceed the grazing capacity of the grass by putting too many cattle on it, since whilst this may produce short-term gains for certain individuals, it produces long-term losses for all of them. A failure to see this long-term, collective view gives rise to the 'tragedy of the commons'.

So, high – and balanced – social capital keeps the 'commons' in good condition for all. And to reinforce the link between social capital and sustainability (or rather 'unsustainability'), it is no coincidence that the expression 'tragedy of the commons' is used most frequently these days to describe the issues around climate change (where the 'field' is our atmosphere) and fishing practices (where field equals ocean, naturally).[19] Sustainability and social capital, to reiterate, are joined at the hip.

Back on our timeline of the evolution of brands, we can also see how brands went through a major shift in how they connected with consumers, as this emergence of hedonic wants and needs became apparent. Brands moved away from the simple, plain, provenance cost assuaging approaches ('announcement' advertising) and instead adopted more spirited and artistic approaches to align themselves with this new 'want set'.

We introduced the P&G Ivory Soap example of 1882 a few pages back, focusing on the perfunctory nature of its communication efforts. But just fourteen years later (1896), the same brand was using strong imagery of beautiful, calm and elegant women and ran with copy that was essentially a wistful poem, appealing to emotions more in line with these emerging hedonic ambitions (Figure 1). We had now entered the brand image era, building powerful associations between ideas and beliefs, and personal and subjective norms for the consumer.[20]

Over the period of a few decades, and as a result of both a rise in hedonic wants and in the context of an artificial form of social capital (accelerated by the arrival of brand image), we'd argue it is pretty easy to see how two key characteristics of modern human behaviour started to make an appearance: in came materialism and individualism. The former, we would argue, was as a result of brands providing an unchecked and intoxicating form of social capital to otherwise dislocated and isolated consumers. And the latter, we believe, aptly describes another character in the tragedy of the commons – the 'free-rider'. The free-rider is the actor who abuses the situation – someone who places their short-term personal gain over the long-term gain of the collective. In this instance, we would argue that individualism per se represents a free-riding mentality towards the wider common that is our overall stock of social capital.

We're not, of course, saying these aspects alone explain the emergence of these characteristics that most agree are antithetical to the solutions we need to find today. But we are trying to present a perspective that we hope is novel in this debate: one of different sources, levels and types of social capital, and brands inadvertently supplying this as a means to meet burgeoning consumer needs. Through recognising that social capital is the 'operating system' for

Figure 1: 'Summer Girl in Yellow' Procter & Gamble's Ivory Soap advertisement, 1896. Reproduced with consent from the Procter & Gamble Company.

society, this novel lens allows us to recognise that brands, in extending what they were set up to do, were in fact tinkering with some crucial code within that operating system.

In doing so, this perfect storm of substitutes in social capital, together with the emergence of wants based around 'fantasies, feelings and fun', initiated a slow but unmistakable alteration process to the basics of modern society. This was the start of the Era of Social Capital Waning. And as the key tenets of social capital (trust, dialogue and shared thinking) started to shudder, so externalities and marginalised voices started to rise. If we stop to think for a moment, these are inevitable consequences of lowering social capital. As trust diminishes, dialogue dries up and shared thinking falls by the wayside. So it's no wonder opportunities to externalise and marginalise not only appear, but appear *attractive* to certain players.

We've already introduced two of the most striking symptoms of this tinkering with society's operating system: materialism and individualism. But recognising the emergence of externalities and marginalised interests, it is easy to see another, profound consequence of this process. This Era of Social Capital Waning brought about unsustainable practices. In other words, it is our view the current crisis around sustainability is symptomatic of the collapse in social capital.

This is the crux of our argument: that social capital – or a lack thereof – is at the root of our problems, not unsustainability per se. The latter is a symptom of the former, and any meaningful solution will need to focus on the former.

We believe this is extremely exciting for brands, since their relationship with social capital – as we've started to show – is deep, historic and dynamic. If we're going to produce meaningful solutions, brands and social capital have to be a part of those solutions.

Before launching into that argument further, there are, however, two more questions that need to be explored in order to fully understand the context within which progressive brands can be instrumental in restocking our levels of social capital.

First, how much are brands to blame for the onset and continuation of the Era of Social Capital Waning? And second, how much do consumers *believe* they are to blame?

Chapter 2

At the end of the first chapter we laid out an argument that at the same time as the explosion in production, migration and wealth, we entered the Era of Social Capital Waning. A combination of reductions in certain forms of social capital and dramatic increases in hedonic needs gave rise to the slow, inexorable creep of individualism and materialism at the individual level, and consumerism at the societal level.

Brands were certainly instrumental in that decline, we believe. We've talked about the fillip brands offered to this new, mobile consumer, and how it became divisive in terms of our overall 'operating system' for society. But were brands really aware of the potential long-term impacts of their actions? Was this a deliberate ploy?

In hindsight, despite the venom that is directed at brands today, there may be a suitably strong argument to say it was not. If we consider for a moment a balance sheet for society, and turn specifically to the liabilities side to see how society was being 'capitalised', it's possible to look back and see brands as supplying what could be described as low quality, very short-term debt for society. Brands contributed by propping up quantitative growth in the short term, pumping the market with staggering sales figures and expansion plans. Brands, on behalf of their corporate guardians, were responding to increasingly shrill calls for quantitative growth in shorter and shorter periods. To efficiency and scale, we needed to add speed to the criteria by which business and its management were being judged.

Avoiding a critique of it just yet, it's worth dwelling on this insatiable thing called quantitative growth, and specifically putting it in the context of consumer behaviour. Most of us probably know the following in our bones: we are the backbone of GDP, and the pivotal cog in the whole quantitative growth machine. To substantiate this 'gut feeling', the World Business Council for Sustainable Development (WBCSD – of which Havas is a member and a core contributor to the sustainable consumption research workstream) has compiled research that shows that more than 60% of national GDP in Western markets is driven by consumer spending.[21] In these markets we – the consumer – are propping up more than half of the economy. That's a lot of responsibility – on us and the brands on which we rely for cues and prompts as to when and how to buy.

And those of us who are in the driving seat when it comes to supporting GDP – the middle class – are increasing at an incredible rate. By 2025 there will be 220 million middle-income consumer households in China alone,[22] and by 2030 it is estimated that 80% of the world population will be middle class (Figure 2).[23]

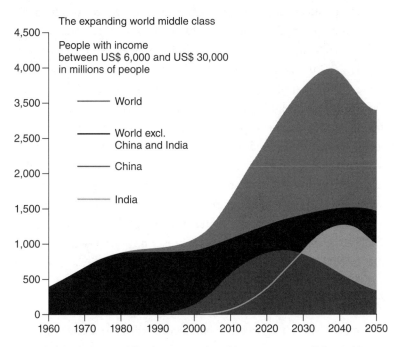

Figure 2: The expanding middle class. Reproduced by permission of The Goldman Sachs Group, Inc.

So even though the responsibility is being shared, overall we are becoming a larger cog in an even larger – and fuel-hungry – machine. The centrality of our role in the stimulation and maintenance of GDP is undeniable. More specifically, our role seems to revolve around one simple instruction: buy more stuff.

Consume! Consume! Consume!

We don't have to look very far to get a pretty clear view of the challenges we face; challenges that are inextricably linked to consumption levels in markets such as the UK, US and almost certainly most of Europe.

This presents a dilemma, in that if consumer spending makes up 60% of GDP, consumer spending in itself is the key engine in driving economic growth. Coming out of the deep recession as we write this, it is impossible to avoid the political rally cries for consumer confidence to return. Whilst there are some extremely vocal and influential voices that argue vehemently against a return to out and out consumption as a means to restore some sense of prosperity in our societies,[24] it still feels as if this is a one-horse race, with that horse called 'quantitative growth'. So in this situation, is it hardly surprising that corporates back this horse through their brands?

This rally cry for consumption-driven growth can be traced back to the provocative and often-quoted words of US economist Victor Lebow. In his highly controversial paper 'Price Competition in 1955', Lebow detailed the absolute reliance of the US economy on the power – and persistence – of the US consumer. Often referenced in connection with the need to keep US productivity running at high speed after the end of the war effort, his critics are divided over whether his words were prescriptive or descriptive. In many ways the impact is equal in terms of capturing the mentality and ambition of the era. It's a long and frequently referenced quote, but we feel it's worth sharing again:

'Our enormously productive economy demands that we make consumption our way of life, that we convert the buying and use of goods into rituals, that we seek our spiritual satisfactions, our ego satisfactions, in consumption. The measure of social status, of social acceptance, of prestige, is now to be found in our consumptive patterns. The very meaning and significance of our lives today expressed in consumptive terms. The greater the pressures upon the individual to conform to safe and accepted social standards, the more does he tend to express his aspirations and his individuality in terms of what he wears, drives, eats, his home, his car, his pattern of food serving, his hobbies.

These commodities and services must be offered to the consumer with a special urgency. We require not only "forced draft" consumption, but "expensive" consumption as well. We need things consumed, burned up, worn out, replaced, and discarded at an ever increasing pace. We need to have people eat, drink, dress, ride, live, with ever more complicated and, therefore, constantly more expensive consumption.'[25]

Consumption, GDP and economic growth seem inseparable. The challenge is that GDP is a quantitative and pretty unassailable (at present) metric when it comes to productivity and economic – and by association, social – health. So any process or event that is going to stimulate an upward move in GDP is going to have to drive an increase in aggregate activity. It is this unswerving 'quantitativeness' of GDP that makes it so attractive to economists and, at the same time, so inappropriate in so many ways as a meaningful metric. To quote Robert Kennedy from his seminal 1968 campaign speech:

'Too much and for too long, we seemed to have surrendered personal excellence and community values in the mere accumulation of material things. Our gross national product, now, is over $800 billion dollars a year, but that gross national product . . . counts air pollution and cigarette advertising, and ambulances to clear our highways of carnage. It counts special locks for our doors and the jails for the people who break them. It counts the destruction of the redwood and the loss of our natural wonder in chaotic sprawl. It counts napalm and counts nuclear warheads and armored cars for the police to fight the riots in our cities and the television programs which glorify violence in order to sell toys to our children.

Yet the gross national product does not allow for the health of our children, the quality of their education or the joy of their play. It does not include the beauty of our poetry or the strength of our marriages, the intelligence of our public debate or the integrity of our public officials. It measures neither our wit nor our courage, neither our wisdom nor our learning, neither our compassion nor our devotion to our country, it measures everything in short, except that which makes life worthwhile.'[26]

However, GDP remains our overriding metric to capture prosperity in our society, and with such a clear chunk of GDP produced by consumer activity, the argument that firms and their brands have any opportunity to pursue an alternative strategy appears naive. But this is not attempting to ignore the inevitable tension that is forming between brands leveraging their capabilities in order to meet the expectations of the market, and the expectations of consumers who are increasingly qualitatively focused. It is unfortunate that brands, built ostensibly on soft, qualitative qualities from the consumer perspective, are increasingly finding themselves in the cross fire between an industrial era mentality from business (which is slavishly devoted to production output as a driver of GDP), and this emerging consumer sentiment within what we call the Era of Social Capital Rising. As we'll discuss in the next chapter, firms and their brands that do not recognise and capitalise on the Era of Social Capital Rising run the real risk of redundancy – and in the not-too-distant future.

But what institution is directly at fault here? Brands, for their support of consumption, or GDP as an overriding measure that demands this consumption?

Without absolving brands of absolute responsibility, we would argue the latter. There are alternatives to GDP currently floating around the system: Bhutan with its Gross National Happiness metric is one, and the recent output from the Stiglitz Commission[27] also stressed the inappropriateness of a purely quantitative measure of economic and social wellbeing. This link between GDP and wellbeing has been explored over decades, with advocates for change in national statistics drawing attention to the fact that countries with higher levels of GDP do not automatically produce happier, or more

Percent above neutral on life satisfaction

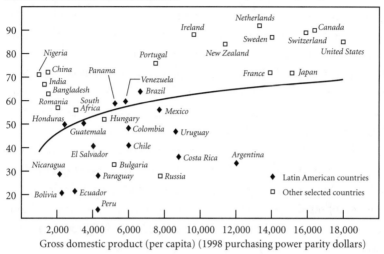

Figure 3: Happiness and wealth. Reproduced by permission of Brookings Institution Press.

satisfied, people. The first person to find this provocative paradox was Richard Easterlin in the mid-1970s,[28] giving rise to the Easterlin Paradox.

Carol Graham and Stefano Pettinato[29] explored this paradox with more recent data across a wider array of countries, and they found it to hold: at the end of the day, higher GDP per capita simply does not translate into happier people (see Figure 3).

Within countries, a similar paradox is apparent. The UK's new economics foundation (nef)[30] produced evidence of how, here in the UK, income affects life satisfaction. Plotting income (Low, Low–Medium, Medium, High–Medium and High) against life satisfaction scores, the data show that whilst higher income did improve life satisfaction, there was a clear case of diminishing returns. This is, in itself, an interesting observation. But when they then overlaid 'social connectedness' over those income brackets, a very interesting insight came to light. Dividing social connectedness into three brackets (strong, average and poor), they found that those people who were on low incomes but had high social connectedness were reporting higher satisfaction scores than those at the other end of the income scale on high incomes but with poor social connectedness.

The implications of this are significant. Firstly, income is a poor gauge of happiness. Second, it seems earning somewhere in the middle is the optimal amount. And third – and most striking to us – it seems earning more money literally gets in the way of having stronger social connectedness. This chimes with the point we made in the first chapter and that we'll investigate in the second part of the book, that consumption – especially consumption to meet hedonic wants – is a time-consuming process, taking us away from being normal social creatures.

So it seems GDP and income are terrible measures of overall prosperity, but still we persist with this quantitative route to measuring our progress. Could it be that part of the issue is that we've made such a structural, cognitive and emotional investment in these measures that the notion of doubling back and accepting anything new or improved is simply too unpalatable to policymakers?

With this in mind, a UK think tank[31] has issued a report that is the combined thinking of accountants, biologists and ecologists around quantitative and qualitative growth. Quite an unusual collection of authors, but the results are striking. In the report, they put forward the argument that in nature itself there is always a period of sustained quantitative growth before the organism or system stabilises into a prolonged period of qualitative growth (or development). A good example is us humans: we grow physically – or quantitatively – for the first eighteen years or so of our lives, and then move into what is primarily a qualitative growth period for the remainder (through receiving education, amassing wisdom, etc.). The reason we mention this paper here is that it may provide a sense of legitimacy for businesses and their brands to look forward and transition into being engines of qualitative growth without a sense of backtracking or admitting failure. It's just the natural evolution of things, and if Mother Nature does it that way, then why can't we in business?

We are acutely aware that this chapter is supposed to offer up a verdict as to whether we feel brands are responsible for what we've labelled the Era of Social Capital Waning. In getting to that opinion, we're trying to lay out a number of arguments or viewpoints that hopefully create enough vivid context that should our answer not be valid, then at least you can come to your own with hopefully more conviction. As such, we'd like to return for a moment to the concept of consumption and revisit some references made earlier.

We've recognised consumption's centrality to driving GDP, and we have discussed the evolution in consumption of meeting utilitarian needs and hedonic wants. In fact we've argued that the latter, through references to Solomon and Scitovsky, are also needs since consumers experience increasing levels of discomfort the more they repetitively consume the same hedonic goods. We talked before about adaptation and how we as creatures become accustomed to and tolerant of our environment unlike any other creature, giving us what Graham calls our 'miserable millionaires'. But Solomon's work suggests this is more than adaptation at work. The misery of the millionaire is created not by ambivalence towards their environment, but possibly the pain from repeated consumption. This isn't adaptation. This is addiction.

This idea that consumption, as a social practice, results in an addiction that could be called consumerism, is not our idea, although we like it very much, not least because it helps explain why consumers are so hard to predict: they're addicts, constantly looking for their next fix. Barry Schwartz[32] describes it well when he talks about how our incessant desire to remove the pain of Solomon's negative after-effect has us lurching from one hedonic experience to another. Our expectations are constantly being ratcheted up as we move from consumption experience to consumption experience. We demand novelty and delight at every turn, and are furious when those items that have long since failed to deliver these qualities let us down. As Schwartz says, '. . . because of this process, the pursuit of pleasure from material things becomes the pursuit of ever new and different things'.[33]

Describing this process as an addiction is not a throw-away line. We feel it captures some of the challenges we face in finding demand-side solutions to many of the problems we face. Consumption, we'd argue, is a 'practice' that takes place within society. By 'practice' we mean a sense-making, repeatable and repeating action by many. This is what sociologists call 'Practice Theory', with practices being 'linked and implicit ways of understanding, saying and doing things'.[34] Consumerism, on the other hand, is the broader social model that accommodates and encourages consumption as a dominant practice. As such, when people talk about tackling consumption issues, we'd argue the focus is in the wrong place. It's not the practice we need to tackle first, but the culture that encourages the practice to flourish. We need to tackle consumerism rather than consumption.

Linking this back to the earlier conversation regarding GDP, the arguments above at least seem to support the logic that consumption has to continue to drive GDP. As detailed above, our persistent desire to assuage the negative emotions associated with a lack of novelty around hedonic goods suggest we'll consume more and more to recover our 'hit' (addicts that we all are).

So there would appear to be a virtuous circle as far as GDP-obsessed economists are concerned: as GDP rises, so income rises and so consumers look more and more to meet hedonic wants, resulting in this desire to consume more escalating further. It's the hedonic treadmill. But this circle of increasing consumption raises the final issue we'd like to explore before giving our final verdict on the responsibility of brands in this Era of Social Capital Waning.

Are brands responsible for driving up overall consumption levels? Do brands create new demand?

Which came first – brands or demand?

This debate about the role of brands and their influence on overall levels of demand has gone back and forth quite a bit in the last sixty years or so. Aldous Huxley jumped in to the debate in the 1950s, arguing that brands, through their advertising, were forcing us to regress to 'emotional creatures'.[35] He claimed advertising even represented a genuine threat to democracy, since it managed to bypass our conscious, rational processes. Brands and their pernicious advertising practices were responsible for a lot, it seemed.

Many of Huxley's comments were very possibly inspired by those arguments laid out in a text that hit the shelves in 1957, and has now become almost legendary in its assault on advertising: Vance Packard's *The Hidden Persuaders*. In it, Packard repeatedly argues that the constant hidden probing and prodding by brands and their advertising catches us unawares and manipulates us into consumers.[36] These views were shared by British historian

Arnold J. Toynbee, who was extremely critical of advertising in the early 1960s:

> 'Advertising deliberately stimulates our desires, whereas experience, embodied in the teachings of the religions, tells us that we cannot be good or happy, unless we limit our desires and keep them in check . . . Advertising is an instrument of moral, as well as intellectual, mis-education. Insofar that it succeeds in influencing people's minds, it conditions them not to think for themselves, and not to choose for themselves. It is intentionally hypnotic in its effect. It makes people suggestible and docile. In fact, it prepares them for submitting to a totalitarian regime.'[37]

Toynbee, it seems, was against not just advertising and branding, but even the satisfaction of these hedonic wants and needs.

More recently, Naomi Klein, in *No Logo*,[38] argues that brands and advertising are direct drivers of what she calls 'overconsumption' in the West. She goes on to argue that this overconsumption is having horrific effects on labour in emerging markets, since the guardians of these Western brands continue to exploit these communities in order to meet this insatiable appetite. As a side note, we'd argue that this is not an issue of brand behaviour per se, but rather brand behaviour that extols the virtues of intoxicating exclusivity with consumers at the expense of all else: too much of one form of fake social capital, and not enough of the more natural, balancing types.

Klein goes on to argue that branding and advertising are divisive since they encourage people to consume products or services that they ordinarily would not have had access to, or knowledge of. She argues that brands and their communications amount to some form of emotional entrapment: if they weren't there, then there would not be the demand. In other words, the existence of brands and advertising directly increases demand. Much as marketers and agency people would love this to be the case, the evidence, however, suggests otherwise.

Tim Broadbent[39] argues that Klein has made a fatal error in her analysis, confusing correlation with causality. He argues that rather than brand advertising spending increasing the size of the market (so creating additional demand), the spending increases in response to increases in the size of the market. Broadbent goes on to argue that brands and their advertising are not responsible (could not be, even if they wanted to be) for creating new wants or desires, but are simply responding more accurately to those wants or needs that have been there since day one. He cites the example of Apple's iPod and the general MP3 music revolution. Is this a case of Apple manufacturing demand? Broadbent argues not – Apple was simply responding to a want that has existed since music itself. People like to listen to music whenever and wherever they can, and Apple's product met that need more effectively.

More generally, other research has shown repeatedly that rather than attempting to grow demand in the market, branding and advertising is essentially there to *channel* demand in the market. In other words, steal from competitors. If we think back to some of the earliest campaigns that came out from the likes of P&G, this desire to hold on to, or increase, market share is clear in the copy of the advertisements: P&G for Ivory Soap implored women only to buy the brand and to be aware of counterfeits, ignoring any efforts of the shopkeepers to offer alternatives.

As such, brands, and their highly visual and evocative advertising, appear to be focused primarily on protecting the interests of the firm, rather than growing the market. And in cases where it appears the market did grow as a direct result of advertising from the brand, we should be careful to ensure we know how to define the market in question. What we call the market and what the consumer considers the market are very probably different. Consumers assess products and services and make judgement calls on the likely value from consumption, comparing to others that fall within their own defined competitor set. As an example, Apple may consider all other music devices as competitors for the iPod, but for the consumer, other forms of mobile entertainment may constitute competition: so a paperback novel or indeed a strawberry ice-cream may suddenly appear in the consumer's informal and transient competitor set.

This is important to factor in, because where market analysis may suggest the overall market has grown (for digital music players), we have to view this from the consumer's perspective, since it is with them that demand resides. And in this case, what may look like an increase in a market from one perspective, will probably almost certainly be purely the substitution effect at work in the relevant market.

Viewed in this way, the argument seems pretty strong that branding and advertising do not create demand, but rather channel it. Brands and advertising work after the consumer has made a commitment to consume, and attempt to turn the consumer toward the brand in question. Certainly brands can be instrumental in building loyalty and repeat purchasing, but in almost all cases, their ability to stimulate what we could call 'net new demand' seems highly questionable and optimistic at best. It's easy to confuse correlation for causality, especially when there's an axe to grind. Probably one of the most compelling arguments that brands are indeed beholden to pre-existing needs and wants is the sheer number of brand launches that simply fail. With enormous marketing budgets behind many of them, if demand really could be stoked by brands and their advertising, surely these failure rates would be lower?

So if brands are unable to build aggregate consumption and its potentially pernicious effects in terms of materialism, individualism and sheer time spent 'being a consumer', is it then fair to say that brands have ostensibly been innocent bystanders in the transition to this Era of Social Capital Waning?

To answer this question, we need to go back and look at consumption *and* consumerism.

GDP needs consumption. Consumption is the quantitative part of consumerism – it's the practice that results in more stuff being made and sold. And changes in absolute consumption appear to lie beyond the control of brands and their advertising. But as we have argued, the wider context – the dominant social logic – that allows consumption to exist as a dominant practice is consumerism. Consumerism encourages consumption: more than that, consumerism is *defined* by a focus on consumption. And whilst brands appear unable to influence consumption, they can, en masse, influence the pervasiveness of consumerism. How? By presenting a faux social capital type that serves to reduce or eliminate the 'provenance costs' associated with mass migration, mass production and mass consumption, and that recognises consumerism as our defining social currency. Which leads us to our final analysis with respect to whether brands are bystanders or protagonists in the Era of Social Capital Waning.

We think they are both.

We know. That sounds like a healthy bit of fence-sitting from those who, on the one hand want to credibly challenge the role of brands, yet on the other, work for a company that makes its living by building brands for clients. But it isn't like that. Our genuine conclusion is that brands are both.

Brands are bystanders in the sense we believe their efforts to offer up plastic capital was a simple reaction to the fact that people no longer had high stocks of natural capital around them. If anything, brands were filling a void left by mass migration. To say they were instrumental in creating this void is wrong. Brands were an inevitable *response* to these broader social changes that were driven by increasing levels and scope of production and consumption. In this respect, brands were bystanders that reacted to events unfolding before them.

However, offering up a plastic capital fillip did cause problems, even if brands were not aware of this. As we'll explain in Part II, for social capital to allow society to operate effectively and efficiently, it needs a multitude of flavours in abundance: not just the thick, homogenous, 'glue' type favoured by brands. Social capital, as we will show, actually fights against itself in certain situations, and this antagonism, needed for healthy society, can only happen when there is this balance and abundance. So, with brands pumping in quantities of artificial capital, they exacerbated the situation, creating and inadvertently masking an imbalance in capital types, so accelerating the onset of the Social Capital Waning Era by removing natural checks and balances. So, neither bystander nor protagonist there – more a case of opportunist.

But these summary comments so far have been mainly focused on brands operating at the individual level, with consumption as a consequence. And as we have seen, increases in aggregate consumption lie beyond the reach of brands. But for consumption to thrive as a practice, consumerism as the overarching, dominant social logic has to encourage it. And, in turn, something has to support and encourage society to maintain this dominant social logic. It is here, in this support of consumerism, that we find brands guilty en masse of being protagonists in this move towards the Era of Social Capital Waning.

Individually, brand communications and advertising may be attempting to protect specific market share and the interests of their owners and stakeholders, but overall, the 3000–5000 messages that we are exposed to every day underwrite the dominant logic that consumerism is acceptable, constructive and defining. Brands support the conceit that consumption, as a practice, shapes our identity. That to opt out would represent opting out of society itself.

Brand advertising – rightly or wrongly – relies on repetition to get the message across; after repetition, we begin to associate the message or cue with another idea or thought. This is the Theory of Association of Ideas. In this sense, all brand communications represent repetition of the underlying idea that consumerism is the dominant social logic. This may be an inadvertent side effect of their more pressing and practical needs to protect their share of market from competition, but in aggregate, brands are sending a clear signal to all of us: consumption is a societal norm. On this last count, we believe brands collectively are guilty of accelerating the Era of Social Capital Waning.

This is our opinion, arrived at after a narrative that has been stitched together from a number of sources, arguments and other opinions. But when all's said and done, it doesn't really matter what we think. It's the perception of the consumer that counts for everything. As we've said before, understanding this consumer position is key in shaping how a brand can respond to these challenges; how a brand can move away from being perceived as a contributor to these issues and towards becoming a progressive force for restocking levels of social capital. A new breed of brand that we call a Social Equity Brand.

The choppy waters of consumer sentiment and perception are the focus of our next chapter, and set the scene for how brands are, and should be, operating in this emerging Era of Social Capital Rising.

Chapter 3

As is the case with any emerging and dynamic phenomenon that's going to have a lasting impact on consumer and brand behaviour, solid evidence-based insights are vital in order to really understand what's going on and offer genuinely useful advice. At Havas, we've recognised sustainability as such a phenomenon, and as a result have created a firm-wide initiative called Sustainable Futures. Working with the research company, GlobeScan, the initiative is focused on understanding sustainability in the broadest sense; in the context of firms and their brands; and – very importantly – from the consumer's perspective.

As part of this initiative, we have a conversation with more than 25 000 active consumers in nine markets each year to explore and understand their views, fears and hopes on a range of issues linked to the wider sustainability debate, as well as drilling down on how they perceive their most trusted brands when it comes to sustainability; and how those perceptions impact on brand equity. The research includes a number of proprietary components, such as a conceptual model for how businesses engage in sustainability at all levels, and a blended-variable output that allows a ranking to take place of any company across any sector, to explore which sectors and firms are leading from the consumer perspective.

We'll discuss many of these elements and their outputs in later chapters, as they offer valuable insights into the importance of social capital and its relationship with sustainability. In this chapter, however, we'd like to explore some of the insights we gleaned in the most recent outing of the research, relating to how consumers feel in general about these issues, and specifically how they see business as a part of either the solution or the problem when it comes to sustainability.

Whatever you do, don't panic . . .

Before even talking to respondents about businesses and their performance, the first thing that struck us from the results was the breadth and depth of consumer concern with the state of the world.

Overall, consumers are worried about almost everything, it seems.

From a list of about twenty different pressing social and economic issues, a staggeringly large proportion of those we interviewed told us they were 'very concerned' about a large number of them, where 'very concerned' was the far end of the response scale we presented. As is to be expected in a period of economic and financial instability (2009), the issues that attracted the highest number of respondents recording maximum concern were unemployment and economic uncertainty, with 43% and 42% respectively. Just to clarify, this is 43% of all those we spoke to on a global scale expressing the highest level of concern with respect to unemployment.

But hard on the heels of these economic issues are a range of concerns firmly within the sustainability sphere: 41% expressing maximum concern over crime and violence; 38% over poverty and inequality; 35% over environmental pollution; 32% over healthcare provision; 30% over the depletion of natural resources; 30% of water shortages; and 29% over waste and excess rubbish. To put these in perspective, the threat of terrorism registered at this level with the same number of people as waste and excess rubbish (see Figure 4).

If there's one conclusion we draw from these results, it is this: even in the glare of a financial and economic crisis, consumers are not losing sight of a number of other underlying issues. A short-termist view, it seems, is not something consumers necessarily suffer from (unlike many businesses in this climate). We'd like to put forward a hypothesis as to why consumers have hung on to these deeper issues: whilst sustainability may be very hard to quantify and observe, the events of 2008 and 2009 made 'unsustainability' all too clear and tangible. Going into 2010, we see these same concerns remaining at the top of mind for consumers.

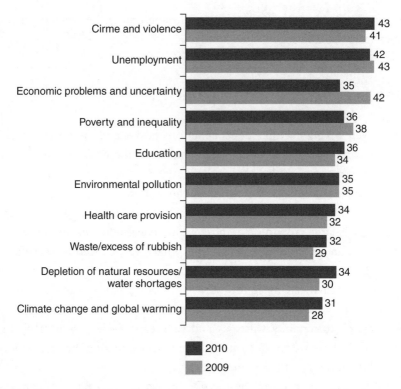

Figure 4: Consumer levels of concern. Sustainable Futures 2009/2010.

When asking about the role of business in tackling the issues we face, 83% of respondents in the most recent wave of the initiative (2010) told us that companies should be active in finding solutions. Interestingly, this is not some passive expectation of business to find solutions – only 28% of those polled felt environmental pollution was such a big issue that there was little they could do. This sense of consumer activism is reflected in another response, where 57% of consumers felt they had the power to influence a company to act more responsibly (although this number is a little down on the previous year, at 63%). And compared to the very high numbers agreeing that business should be active in finding solutions, only 24% felt these issues were the responsibility of government. A marked increase in the polarisation of results on the 2009 figures means that, like it or not, the mandate is clearly being given to business (see Figure 5), and increasingly so, year on year, it seems.

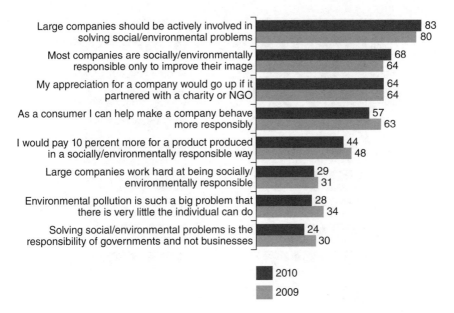

Figure 5: The role of business (and brands). Sustainable Futures 2009/2010.

A couple of red flags also go up in this chart. Firstly, when we look at the proportion of respondents who feel business is actually working hard at finding solutions to these issues, only 29% agree with the sentiment. The expectation and (perceived) action gap is significant. In addition, when asked if companies are engaged in socially and environmentally responsible activities purely for image gains, 68% of all those polled worldwide said 'yes' (up from 64% in 2009). In this one response, we think we've glimpsed a possible explanation for the continuing, yawning attitude–behaviour gap when it comes to the consumer and sustainable consumption. It's possible that it is not a case of consumers being fickle when it comes to consumption, but consumers simply being untrusting of, or disappointed with, firms' motives. Maybe we are underestimating the desire from consumers to see firms operate with a more determined intrinsic value set, rather than a historically appropriate suite of extrinsic motivations. Again, this is just a hypothesis, but if true, it could illustrate how a brand being seen and credited as an engine of social capital could produce incredible loyalty from its consumers. However, the upwards creep from 2009 to 2010 in the proportion of consumers who

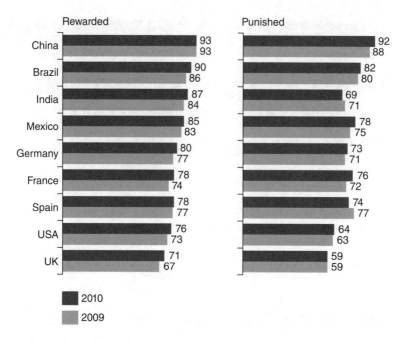

Figure 6: Consumer propensity to reward and boycott. Sustainable Futures 2009/2010.

see firms operating in this area for extrinsic gains suggests we're going in the wrong direction. Brands need to change direction and step up to the plate. Quickly.

This opportunity for loyalty is demonstrated further when our respondents are asked to report if and how often they either boycott or reward brands, based on their perceptions of firms' behaviour (see Figure 6). Two details of this response jumped out at us. First, the sheer number who told us they do one or the other regularly: the average across all markets was 80% for rewarding companies and 72% for punishing or boycotting companies. And the second detail: that in none of the nine markets researched was the propensity to punish higher than the propensity to reward. In other words, consumers are looking for opportunities to reward firms and their brands, with loyalty, for what they see as constructive behaviour.

So the data are painting a vivid and rosy picture for brands to engage on these issues, albeit with a raft of 'intrinsic' caveats attached. But one question that remains unanswered is whether sustainability as a context is perceived by consumers as a positive or constructive arena in which to engage. After all, considerable amounts of editorial and messaging focus on stopping this, reducing that and eliminating the other, and as we've already argued, sustainability can be seen as restrictive and dull. If this were the case, it could very much bias not only brands' willingness to engage consumers on these topics, but consumers' interests in engaging, especially on hedonic needs and wants (where a 'sobering' sustainability message could really take the edge off the brand experience – more on this in the next part).

So we put the question to all those consumers who were sufficiently familiar with the term: what associations do they have with the term? From a long list of positive, negative and neutral attributes or associations, the answer came back loud and clear: sustainability is something positive and aspirational. 83% likened it to the future; 75% to balance; 72% to health; 68% to community; 66% to integrity; and 66% to opportunity. At the other end of the scale, only 40% associated it with high price; 28% associated it with the past; and 25% with guilt (see Figure 7).

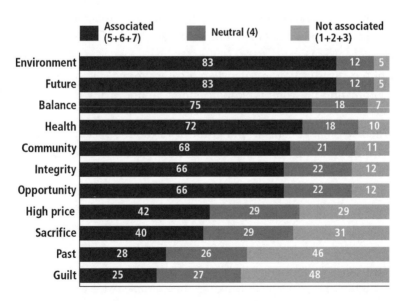

Figure 7: Consumer associations with sustainability. Sustainable Futures 2009/2010.

The good guys and the bad guys

Before asking our respondents to comment forensically on brands they're familiar with, we ask them to make some more general comments about certain sectors and industries, in terms of the damage they perceive they cause to both the environment and society more broadly, as well as their perceived efforts to make amends for these impacts.

As one would expect, when it comes to the environmental impact scores, the oil and petroleum industries take a heavy hit: they're considered the most damaging and the least willing to make amends. The second most damaging industry is automotive (again, not surprisingly), although it is also considered to be working the hardest of all the industries we review to compensate for those impacts. The third most damaging industry, according to our polls is a little surprising, however: personal care and beauty products. We can only assume this has made it into the 'top three' by association with chemicals and packaging. It's worth noting also that consumers consider these industries as being average in terms of efforts to address these issues. The industries considered to be applying the least effort to address their impacts are banking and telecoms (which also have the smallest impact, so arguably the response is in proportion to the perceived damage), and those considered to be working the hardest are retailers and food companies. With both of these, their impacts are also considered relatively low, so these industries really are the progressive stars of our investigation to date when it comes to the environment (they're also dominating the communication efforts around many of the issues, it seems).

When we look at damage and effort in relation to society, we see some interesting developments, in that each of these industries barely moves from their position regarding the environment. In other words, oil and petroleum are considered to be causing as much damage to society as they are to the environment (and doing as little to make amends), as is beauty, as is food, as is automotive, as is retail, and as are banking and telecoms. In other words, consumers at this moment in time are not really differentiating between these two distinct areas, and are not yet recognising the indirect impacts of the various industries. If we take banking, for example, whilst most recognise that the direct social impact may be minimal (branches in towns, online banking – how can these be disruptive?), their indirect social impact, as a result of their investment strategies for example, could be significant.

There is a reason for us flagging this point here. The similarity of perceptions across these two aspects of the debate suggests to us a continuing failure (or imbalance) in social capital. Dialogue and thought (two key components of social capital) are clearly not working effectively, otherwise more informed perceptions would be in place. We've no doubt this process is happening slowly but our point is this: brands need to be seen as engines of improvement in these areas. It is not simply a case that benefits will flow to those firms that are credited with advancing the debate through higher social capital, but think for a second what happens when consumers cotton on to the fact that where they thought impacts were only direct, a few and low, they are now known to be indirect, many and high. The risk of a sense of betrayal, and the subsequent loss of faith and loyalty, is considerable. Unless those firms take control of the issue and lead the debate, their corporate communications crash packs had better be within easy reach.

Devotees, Hostages and Critics

So our Sustainable Futures initiative is starting to paint a vivid, if slightly counter-intuitive, picture. On the one hand, we have consumers showing incredibly high levels of concern for a wealth of issues linked to the sustainability debate and a clear expectation of business to step into the breach. But on the other hand, a picture is emerging that consumers are not able (or willing?) to understand where industries are at present, in terms of their impacts and efforts.

In short, it seems consumers are possibly engaged with the issues, but not with brands.

To explore this further, we'd like to share another of the proprietary outcomes of our ongoing initiative. Starting in 2009, we produced a consumer segmentation that we hoped would shed light on these idiosyncrasies, since we were aware that existing segmentations were not really capturing a valid picture of consumer engagement on these issues. Our segmentation is different to many others that try to explore this dynamic, as it allowed us to test our hypothesis that engagement with the issues and engagement with the firm around these issues may not be the same thing. It was our experience that all other segmentations tended to make an assumption that consumer engagement was consistent across these contexts. The results are very revealing.

We segmented our 25 000 respondents across what we call 'activism' and 'enthusiasm' characteristics. By activism, we refer to the degree to which the consumer is factoring some aspect of sustainability into their reported purchasing behaviour, i.e. an active consumer is one who is already running a range of sustainability criteria through the process before making a decision. By enthusiasm, we're describing the degree to which consumers are prepared to inform themselves about the salient aspects of the firm and its brands. In other words, investigating the claims of the brand, sifting through what is relevant and not for that category, etc.

The result of the segmentation is that, counter-intuitively, activism and enthusiasm often do not move hand in hand. And, as a result of these findings, we are able to identify five distinct consumer types when it comes to these activism and enthusiasm variables; types we believe offer key insights into the relationship between the consumer, the issues and their trusted brands. As can be seen in Figure 8, there are three segments of particular interest that show varying degrees of enthusiasm, but similar – and above average – levels of activism.

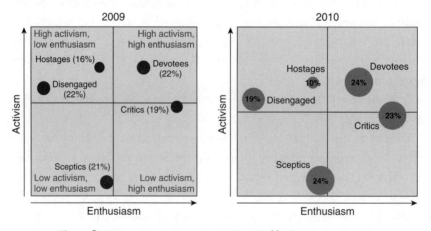

Figure 8: New consumer segments. Sustainable Futures 2009/2010.

Devotees

Devotees are the out and out success stories from the brand's perspective. These are consumers who are engaged in the debate and enthusiastic about brands being in the driving seat of finding solutions. Devotees are a great target for brand communication around sustainability because they want to hear what is going on and improve their understanding of the issues. Devotees are also more likely to be more affluent, better educated and female. There's been a modest (2%) increase in this segment across all markets between 2009 and 2010.

Hostages

Showing similar levels of activism, but lower than average levels of enthusiasm, Hostages – as the name suggests – feel imprisoned by the multitude of issues that confront them. These consumers are extremely engaged – too engaged if that's possible – in the issues and literally feel trapped from taking action. Recognising the possible benefits from taking action in one direction immediately raises a conflict or ambiguity with making the right decision in another direction. The consumers perceive themselves to be snagged on a whole range of issues, and are unsure of how, who, when or what could help them make better decisions. Despite the will, Hostages are blocked from being more enthusiastic in terms of their engagement with firms and their brands, by the simple fact they are 'too busy' being preoccupied by everything else. There's been a considerable (6%) drop in this segment between 2009 and 2010, lending weight to the argument that we are witnessing rises in ambient stocks of social capital.

Disengaged

Whilst showing activism levels a little lower than our Hostages and Devotees, the Disengaged still show levels significantly higher than the average. In other words, these consumers, despite their name, are aware of the issues sufficiently to consider them as influences in their reported behaviour. The Disengaged do, however, show the lowest levels of enthusiasm – by far. It appears that these consumers have almost no interest in exploring the issues further, or indeed understanding the motivations or actions of companies when it comes to these issues. The Disengaged appear simply not to care enough to find out – yet they are sufficiently aware to factor in their perceptions of the issues. This is a complex and important segment – not least because it represents more than one consumer in five. Without further qualitative research to explore their attitudes in more detail, we can only speculate as to why this paradox exists. It could well be a manifestation of the image concern we discussed earlier in the chapter – that these consumers willingly disengage from the firm and its brands, since they perceive most, if not all, of the communication efforts to be essentially about building image, rather than anything more intrinsic and authentic. It could also be as a result of these consumers having established an opinion – about both the issue and the brand's position on it – and there simply being nothing in place to challenge or augment that opinion. Either way, it does not paint a positive picture, either from the brand's perspective or the perspective of social capital. The Disengaged represent a sizable global contingent of active consumers who are willingly cut off from the debate, yet are still using it as a selective criterion in their stated behaviour. The Disengaged have dropped by 3% from 2009 to 2010.

Critics and Sceptics

Critics and Sceptics are our last two segments. Critics, as the name clearly suggests, are very doubting of brand and firm behaviour, yet they appear to be more focused on being critical than on actually acting on their opinions. As such, Critics are influencers – and their ability to influence is made all the stronger thanks to their very high levels of enthusiasm for the area and brands' roles within it. Representing almost one consumer in five (2009), this is a sizable and problematic segment that really needs to be brought onside from the brand's perspective. If ever the expression 'do as I say, and not as I do' was pertinent, it would be to describe these educated, vocal and influential consumers. Critics are up 4% in 2010.

Sceptics, in contrast, are so doubting of the role or benefit of the firm and its brands in this arena that they are almost ignoring any influence in their stated decision-making process. These issues are simply not on their radar, despite the fact that they show not inconsiderable levels of enthusiasm for the debate. Sceptics are up 3% in 2010.

At first glance, this segmentation supports a key argument for our social capital focus; that for nearly 40% of consumers polled in 2009 (29% in 2010), the problem is not one of engagement with the issues, but of understanding or caring what it means *in the context of the firm and its brands*. In other words, Hostages and the Disengaged are suffering as a result of low social capital. And it's not just these consumers who are suffering – their trusted brands are too. Swathes of consumers may be making poor judgements on issues that they clearly feel passionate about. By improving social capital stocks with these consumers, their levels of enthusiasm would naturally rise, and they'd be making smarter, more informed choices when it comes to which brands to build relationships with. Further, these freshly engaged consumers would also be more likely to display greater loyalty towards those brands that were perceived to be instrumental in this process.

And if brands are to remain close to consumers, and reflect their attitudes and ambitions, then this is even more important in this emerging Era of Social Capital Rising. Consumers want to be authentically enabled – not just as consumers but as citizens – and progressive brands are beginning to recognise the importance and opportunity in credibly and genuinely contributing to this process.

If we look at the changes in size for these segments from 2009 to 2010, this unstoppable transition is further demonstrated. In all nine markets of Sustainable Futures, we are witnessing an increase in the proportion of consumers who are Devotees, and significant drops in the numbers who are Disengaged or Hostages. The Era of Social Capital Rising is certainly upon us, helping to further evangelise the Devotees, release those held as Hostages and engage the Disengaged.

The questions now are how instrumental are brands in driving through these changes? And what's in it for them to try harder?

This first slug of the book has attempted to offer a broad, quick spin around a series of issues, histories and phenomena that we think combine to be important in this debate – important in understanding what brands can, and should, do in this increasingly connected and pro-social world.

Specifically, we've tried to capture the origins of brands and branding, and in the context of social capital, how they were initially profoundly useful for both the emerging consumer, as they travelled great distances to benefit from rapid industrialisation, and the firms that were offering these opportunities. Brands, we've argued, instinctively understood the importance of trying to replicate certain forms of social capital in order to maintain trust and appease the sense of 'provenance costs' for the new consumer. Social capital, then, was already emerging as a powerful force in allowing business to sustain itself, with brands aware of the fact that without any form of social capital, they could not exist. Social capital was – and is – oxygen for brands.

However, the combination of rational scientific approaches to consumer behaviour and brand communications, together with emerging hedonic needs as a result of new-found wealth amongst these new consumers, quickly led to consumers being overly taxed and tested in trying to make increasingly complex decisions by these arguably inappropriate criteria.

At the same time, as choice (or competition) exploded, so brands started to use more emotional levers and associations to reach the consumer. Dynamic hedonic wants (and needs) were combining with ever-more evocative messaging in the context of this intoxicating synthetic social capital environment.

Brand-built social capital was lacking a crucial element: the proximity of moderators and mediators found in the natural environment of balanced capital – people and processes that temper and balance the relationship between what we want for us and what we should give to others. In this artificial environment, it was just the consumer and the brand, with no-one in between. Consequently, materialism and individualism started to flourish. There were not seen as bad things but quite the opposite: they were further confirmation of the advancement of economic progress, rational expression and personal identification and development. As firms became increasingly powerful agents of economic, social and political influence, so the provenance of brands themselves started to become unassailable.

Brands were supplying society with what we would call low quality social debt. And society seemed happy to accept it.

Even though they were not explicitly aware of it, brands were emerging as opportunistic social hedge funds, looking to profit from this Era of Social Capital Waning. Brands were shorting social capital, and in doing so, furthering the development of consumerism as a social norm. Whilst driving consumption as a dominant social practice lay beyond the abilities of brands, supporting and nurturing the accommodating structure of consumerism lay firmly within them.

Consumers, for their part, seem less sure of this verdict and it is, at the end of the day, their vote that counts. Whilst levels of concern for a broad range of issues seem to run consistently high across markets today, equally large numbers of consumers seem ready to welcome business and its brands as our saviours in finding solutions. But caveats are clearly emerging – authenticity and a desire to see intrinsic motivation at work, most noticeably. To honour those caveats, brands will have to significantly re-evaluate their role in building social capital.

It's important to make clear that many of the ideas and themes developed in this first section pre-date our writing of this book. Be they academic theories or practitioner opinions and anecdotes, much of what you are reading here has existed and been shared before. But we believe combining these elements into a narrative around social capital, and how brands and social capital have had a symbiotic relationship since day one, is a unique and novel way to not only reflect on the past, but also look ahead to the future. It is the main argument of this whole exercise – that brands, to be genuinely construc-tive, must look beyond sustainability as their subject matter, and see social capital as both the message and the medium. And it seems the timing could not be better. Fresh updates on our consumer segmentation model show us that enthusiasm for the issues, and business's involvement, is rising.

It is, as we say, the unstoppable Era of Social Capital Rising.

But we should not assume this will be a painless transition and without casualties. For brands to benefit from, and lead, this transition, fundamental change is required – a level of change that not all brands will be able or willing to embrace. For them, we genuinely believe the Era of Social Capital Rising will witness their demise.

In the next part, we'll explore in more detail how brands today are operat-ing in this emerging Era of Social Capital Rising. We'll argue that despite brands being reliant on social capital for their very existence, it seems very few are aware of how to operate in order to create value in this new era, much to their, and society's, cost.

This investigation is key in order to understand what is required of a progressive brand in this emerging era; a brand that recognises the need to support society with stable investments for the long term, rather than short-term efforts for immediate gain; a brand that recognises that its health and vitality depend on the health and vitality of those around and amongst it; a brand that is valued.

Part II

The 'Unsustainability' of Sustainability and Our Need to Understand the Era of Social Capital Rising

So far, we've gone back to the beginning of brands and, recognising the shifts in society going on at that time, have attempted a quick and vivid sketch of how brands and social capital have been joined at the hip since day one. Brands need social capital in order to breathe, and society and all its actors, it seems, need social capital too. We've also argued that a mixture of unfortunate and deliberate actions set us all on the path to what we have called the Era of Social Capital Waning.

But things are certainly changing.

We're far from being the first to say this, but there seems to be a renewed spirit on the part of civil society to reconnect, engage and operate in a more balanced and harmonious way. We only have to scan the papers, blogs and websites to see anecdotal evidence of this emerging trend: parents wanting to take control of their local schools, communities trying to revitalise communal areas, consumer groups placing pressure on businesses – these are all examples of this rediscovered sense of 'togetherness'.

Undoubtedly technology has played a major part in this – social media have allowed communities to connect, share and learn in unprecedented ways. The same technology and media have also reduced snaking supply chains and complex distribution networks to short and visible operations, destroying the tried and tested corporate defence of 'we didn't know what our suppliers' suppliers were doing in that region'. The ability to glean, share and modify knowledge via these tools and platforms has had the twin effects of amassing everyone to 'now' and truncating all business to 'here'. It represents an emerging era of what British author Philip Pullman calls 'wakefulness'.[40] We call it the Era of Social Capital Rising.

The political economist Karl Polanyi[41] talked about dramatic pendulum swings in socioeconomic systems (Polanyian movements) as dominant models veer towards the unstable margins, causing the pendulum to move the other way. After such prolonged economic growth, trade liberalisation and globalisation, we could argue that we are now in the second Polanyian movement, back towards more governance (and maybe even protectionism) in markets. In other words, a renewed focus on what's better for most of us, rather than a few of us; and for the long term, rather than the short term. In the first Polanyian swing (towards liberalised trade and globalisation), a reduction in social capital was inevitable. That first swing was dependent on less governance, which in turn was arrived at by new social movements less interested in balanced and enduring social capital, and more interested in intense levels of tailored social capital designed specifically to encourage and abet trade.

In the early decades of the twentieth century, brands were adroit at spotting this swing and what it represented, supplying society with the appropriate fillip as these new social movements became hardwired into formal practices.

But can it be said that brands are as nimble today? Are they ready and able to reflect, anticipate and promote this return swing of the pendulum towards richer and more balanced social capital?

Chapter 4

There can be no doubt that brands are hurling themselves at sustainability as if it is the answer to everything. Not a day goes by, it feels, without more announcements that brands are championing environmental and social issues on our behalf: the trade press is full of the increasingly shrill chatter of their efforts. The US environmental marketing agency, Terrachoice, claims that in the US alone, 'green' products in store doubled between 2007 and 2008[42] and green advertising almost tripled between 2006 and 2008. Sustainability is big business for brands, it seems.

However, talking is one thing, and talking coherently and accurately is quite another. As part of their 'Seven Sins of Greenwashing' report,[43] Terrachoice go on to detail that in the US between November 2008 and January 2009, more than 2200 products found in mainstream US retail stores were making almost 5000 green claims between them. But on closer inspection, more than 98% of the products were guilty of some form of greenwashing. To be clear, greenwashing is the term given to any marketing or brand claim around environmental or social issues that is either false, misleading or exaggerated. That's a staggering amount.

Despite the risks of greenwashing, these issues and themes are becoming ever-more central in brand communications. Here in the UK, major brands such as Tesco, Marks and Spencer, E.ON, EDF, Coca-Cola and McDonalds are all keen to be seen for their efforts in these areas. In a 2008 study by The Climate Group[44] the pattern is clear – the big advertisers are advertising big when it comes to green and sustainability. In the US, it's the same story, with

GE, Toyota and Honda topping the league tables when it comes to ad spend around these issues.[45]

That said, it would appear these efforts are not resonating with consumers in the way they would like – the shadow of ROI is long and dark when it comes to brand efforts and sustainability. In our Sustainable Futures initiative, we always ask respondents to name brands they feel are doing great work in this area, as well as brands that they consider to be laggards. What is striking is that consistently across markets, people either struggle to name any company in either category, or the same company and brand ends up on the top of both lists (this is especially true of large retailers for some reason). This illustrates the dilemma faced by brands that often dominate their sectors: even where their efforts may be laudable, if the sector as a whole is considered weak or slow, their perceived performance can suffer as a result. It also reinforces the point that this movement is evolving, ambiguous and can cause contrary responses.

There also appears to be another interesting development from these commercial powerhouses. Many of them, through their brands, appear to be communicating what are essentially their CSR credentials. This raises an interesting question: is it efficient or even appropriate that a brand acts as this mouthpiece for corporate endeavour? Or should the relationship between the brand and its corporate guardian be different?

To explore this further, we've tried to visually represent what many firms currently appear to do when it comes to using brand communications in this area (Figure 9). In this instance, we are distinguishing between what the firm sees as its identity, and the various images the firm chooses to project to various audiences or stakeholders. Further, we're distinguishing between the target image (that which the firm wants the audience to receive) and the received image (that which is actually received). In many texts, this latter difference is called an identity–image gap, although we prefer the image terminology, since we feel identity is genuine and relatively stable over time, whereas images (targeted and received) are far more selective, contextual and dynamic over time. The main point here is this: many firms are currently using the brand as an extension of other images used, to engage with stakeholders in what is essentially a historical, accountable and reactive fashion.

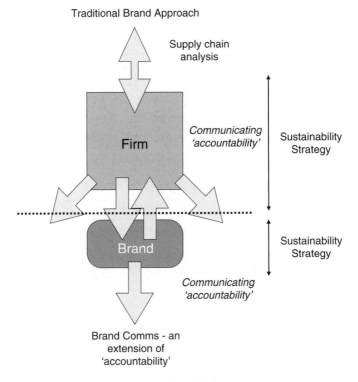

Traditional Brand Approach

Figure 9: Traditional brand behaviour

We feel this is wrong; that instead the brand should be considered a distinct selection of identity traits and motivations that can uniquely engage specific stakeholder groups (consumers and employees) in a forward-focused, proactive way. In other words, brands are separated from the other corporate images in their view and role. We've tried to depict this in Figure 10.

As to why firms are using brands in this way when it comes to sustainability, a couple of theories come to mind.

As we've touched on in Part I, at their birth, brands were keen to support the scientific rational approach to business – that was, after all, the business of business. One of the legacies of this keenness to comply is a persistence in marketing today to still hang on to this rational consumer approach – not necessarily because marketing thinks it effective or superior, but because it allows the marketing function to remain aligned with more 'serious' organisational departments or functions, such as operations, finance and strategy.

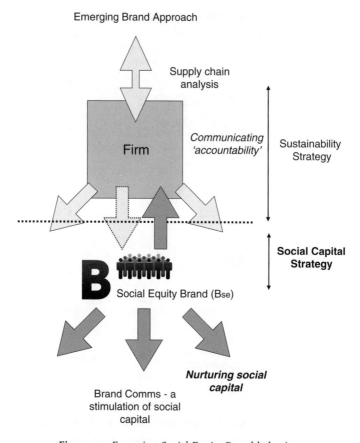

Emerging Brand Approach

Supply chain
analysis

Firm

*Communicating
'accountability'*

Sustainability
Strategy

Social Capital
Strategy

B Social Equity Brand (Bse)

***Nurturing social
capital***

Brand Comms - a
stimulation of social
capital

Figure 10: Emerging Social Equity Brand behaviour

We're not saying this is necessarily a conscious choice on the part of market-ing, but we're sure the function wants 'to belong' in this corporate culture. When it comes to sustainability, we then find ourselves in the realm of very serious stakeholder engagement indeed. Understandably these are serious matters, where reputations and market value are on the line. As such, when brands are then brought into this exchange with stakeholders, it is hardly surprising that those brand managers default even further to formal presenta-tions that mimic those made by other corporate images to their audiences. In these contexts, brands need to be seen as responsible stewards of the firm, and savvy brand managers and CMOs see the opportunity to gain further legitimacy for their work and expertise.

There's a second reason we think brands tend to operate in this way around these subjects. Again, in line with the rational consumer and the information processing model of advertising, brands have become very used to delivering short, sharp, pithy soundbites that attempt to resolve the consumer's conflict and confusion in their decision process. This is demonstrated no more vividly than with the notion of a Unique Selling Proposition (USP). Everyone likes to distil the messy process down to one underlying immutable aspect. The trouble is, all the issues that fall under the umbrella of sustainability tend not to conform to that approach. Not only is the raft of issues enormous and complex, but many are in permanent conflict with each other. New Zealand Lamb versus Welsh Lamb in terms of farming and transportation; roses grown in Kent versus Kenya in terms of fair trade and transportation. The more you dig into these issues, the more these conflicts and ambiguities arise. Brands tend not to like ambiguity and conflict in their messaging, so appear to go out of their way much of the time to avoid these hotspots.

This is an area we'll return to when we discuss the dominant traits of these emerging Social Equity Brands, but it suggests that brands are failing to engage consumers effectively on these issues, not necessarily because their efforts are too light or flimsy, but rather that they are too sterile, serious and apologetic. In short, brands are not doing what brands are really good at.

This issue is manifesting itself in what appears to be a strong division in the way brands are choosing to attempt to engage with their audiences. There appears to be a continuum emerging as to how brands communicate on these issues, with the really vocal brands marking out their territory either right down one end, or the other.

Once upon a time, everything happened

We originally created this continuum in order to plot the various brand-led efforts in this area, thinking we'd see a range of initiatives across the spectrum (see Figure 11). At one end, we marked 'narrative'. By narrative, we refer to framed stories, where language, style, metaphor, genre and other qualities combine to give the whole thing 'meaning' for an audience. At the other end, we marked 'transparency'. This is our way of describing those brand-led

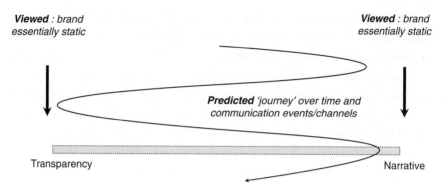

Viewed : brand
essentially static

Viewed : brand
essentially static

Predicted 'journey' over time and
communication events/channels

Transparency

Narrative

Figure 11: Narrative–transparency continuum

efforts that are predicated on hard data and fact – and plenty of it. It's important to say that we deliberately made it a continuum as we were sure we'd see brands sliding along it, communication from communication. We certainly didn't feel the two extremes were in any way mutually exclusive. But in the short period of time we've been comparing efforts to this scale, it certainly appears to us that brands *consider* these options mutually exclusive. Brands appear to be choosing to either pursue one approach or the other and remaining faithful to that approach. To reiterate, we're not talking about the sum of all communications from the firm on these issues, but specifically the efforts from the brand, considering the brand a highly distinctive image of the firm's identity (as per Figure 10).

A vivid example of a transparency-led brand approach is Walmart. Before saying anything else, it is undeniable that Walmart is moving to codify this emerging global social movement around sustainability, faster than any piece of legislation could. In 2009, the company announced its ambitious plans to create a comprehensive sustainability index across all of its products,[46] with the aim of giving consumers detailed information on the sustainability credentials of whatever it is they're after in the store. If we stop and think for a second, this is a Herculean undertaking, not least because of the number and breadth of products you'll find in your average Walmart store. That is a long, long list of suppliers to get on side and to present detailed and consistent information. And then there's the challenge of how to compare across categories. If Walmart's ambition is to present consumers with a single index (early indications are that it will be a spectrum from red to green, with a needle indicating where on that spectrum that particular product sits), how on earth will they make sure they are comparing apples with (organic) apples? To reiterate, it's a mammoth undertaking and one that is warmly received by interest groups worldwide.

But we cannot help thinking it is once again deferring to consumers as rational, iterative decision makers, who respond to a distilled single criterion. As we've said before, we don't subscribe to this view of the consumer, nor do we think the debate can be boiled down in this way, no matter how convenient it would be.

We'll talk in more detail about why we feel these are shortcomings, not only in dealing with the issue but in recognising important shifts in social capital, in the following two chapters. But for now, the question we ask ourselves is this: is this approach really recognising this Era of Social Capital Rising?

Put another way, do data encourage the development of higher social capital?

In the spirit of impartiality, let's also look at an example that would arguably sit at the other end of the continuum. Pepsi is another monolithic, extremely well-established and eminently valuable US global brand. In no small way, the brand is, thanks to considerable brand-building advertising budgets, frequently associated with other US institutions and events. But in 2009, in a break with tradition, the company decided to pull its entire Superbowl campaign and plough the equivalent dollar value ($25 million) into a novel experiment. The Pepsi Refresh project[47] saw the brand supporting a range of grass root social endeavours by making a commitment to pledge this colossal sum of money to whichever social initiatives were presented and supported online. Here was a brand-led encounter that was not about what the company was doing with respect to its social and environmental impacts, but was instead about what its *consumers* (and their communities) could do. In many ways, it represents the ultimate narrative, in that the brand is clearly enabling its audience to write whatever narrative it wants, full of jeopardy and conflict. All Pepsi is doing is ensuring there is a happy ending for those deemed most engaging and relevant by an unbiased audience of millions. The Pepsi Refresh project may not have given consumers concrete answers on what the firm is doing around many of the issues it considers pertinent and pressing, but it has given consumers the option to voice their own concerns and ambitions about what they consider to be the most pressing issues, start to find solutions on their own terms and then enable them to action these solutions.

As is pretty clear from these examples, both have their merits, and both their downsides. How can Walmart attempt to index Pepsi against Coke, when the former is running the Refresh project – surely this puts an additional tick against the brand? And how can Pepsi square-off championing local environmental causes when its own refrigeration efforts may be less efficient than they could be? It's this ambiguity and 'messiness' that brands are going to have to learn to love; that these emerging Social Equity Brands recognise as their new environment.

The wisdom of crowds

We've already introduced our Sustainable Futures initiative, which has, as its beating heart, a yearly, 25 000 consumer strong piece of primary research, looking at consumer sentiment and perception towards trusted brands in the context of sustainability. We understand it's the most comprehensive, focused and multi-market study of its kind.

Within our dialogue with respondents, we ask them to gauge the performances of a number of trusted brands. In order to keep the process robust, we created a conceptual framework within which we felt businesses – all businesses – operate when it comes to sustainability. Building on established models of how firms interact with value-creating assets,[48] we accepted that businesses could draw down on a maximum of five different types of capital in order to create value (to any and all of their stakeholders). The question then becomes: are they drawing down on these sources of capital in a sustainable way? The five capitals in question are: natural capital; financial capital; asset capital; human capital and social capital.

Starting with the most obvious, natural capital refers to the raw resources needed to produce anything – raw materials, fuel for energy, etc. This represents the 'operand' resources we introduced in Part I. Not surprisingly, natural capital has attracted the most attention over the last decade or so, since the unsustainable use of this capital (not just in terms of resources, but also natural sinks, for example) is very visible and tangible, with global issues such as climate change and deforestation high on the agenda.

Another capital high on the agenda (now) is financial capital. Up until the summer of 2008, we genuinely felt this source of capital, whilst vitally important to those in business, was pretty much superfluous and beyond interest for most other audiences. But then the sub-prime mortgage crisis hit, credit dried up and established and supposedly secure banks began to fail. Suddenly the unsustainable use of this source of capital became all too apparent and painful for many.

When we talk about asset capital, we're describing all of the assets of the firm that are used to produce value (through goods and services) but that are not for sale themselves. So this would include plant machinery, vehicles, offices, etc.

Human capital is used to describe everyone who works for the firm, or its suppliers – everyone who is, in some way, a part of the supply chain for the firm. Traditionally this would represent an 'internal' capital source, but increasingly we could argue that consumers are a part of this type of capital, considering the value they can create in the use of products and services. Pepsi's Refresh project is a clear example of this, where 'external' human capital is being used to add value to the experience and the brand.

Which leads us to the last capital type – social capital. In some ways, we need to add a word of warning here, in that when we talk about this social capital, we are not strictly talking about the same social capital that crops up in the rest of this book. In this context, social capital captures a source of value for the firm since it represents the myriad ways it can, most likely through its brands, extract value from the interactions, experiences and exchanges between individuals and groups. Whereas human capital is about the intellect or imagination of individuals, social capital here is about how those intellects and imaginations interact within either structured or informal networks that in some way are influenced by or impinge upon the firm.

To put it another way, human capital describes the potential value locked up *within* each of us, whereas social capital describes the potential value locked up *amongst* all of us.

The reason it's important to separate the scope of the definition in the model from the definition we are using for the main thrust of this book is this:

we argue that in the context of brands and their audiences, all other forms of capital are beholden to social capital. In the context of our research within Sustainable Futures, we are asking those familiar with the brands for their *perceptions* of how the firm is operating with respect to these various forms of capital. In other words, a respondent's view on the firm's use of human capital is going to be entirely shaped by social capital, since it is the latter that informs and enables them to have an opinion or perception on the former. As such, being able to have an in-depth view of how those familiar with a brand view the use of these capitals is as much a route to insight on the stocks of social capital around that brand as it is a view of the use of capitals.

Breaking down these five sources of capital into their component parts, we end up with a long list of what we call 'sustainability attributes' – attributes or qualities of the business that have an impact on its overall sustainability performance.

However, very aware of the slightly abstract nature of the 'capitals' model when discussing an already complex issue with consumers, using Exploratory Factor Analysis, we rearranged the list of attributes (25 in total) into a number of clusters that we thought would be more intuitive to consumers: marketplace, workplace, environment, community, economy, and governance and ethics. So, in marketplace for example, there were questions about issues such as responsible marketing and clear labelling. In environment, questions focused on the use of energy, packaging, delivery fleet, etc. And so it goes on, with what we believe is a pretty comprehensive list of characteristics – all linked to one capital source or another – that combine to shape an overall opinion or perception for the consumer of that brand.

With these perceptions recorded, we are then able to correlate them with broad brand equity measures, to understand how important these individual attributes are to what we call 'brand health'. We're using brand health in this instance to describe the aggregated effects of loyalty and advocacy. We felt these appropriate to use across multiple sectors due to their general applicability to any brand. When looking at the relationships, we concluded that the stronger the relationship between movements in the attribute and movements in our brand equity measures, the more important that attribute to the health of the brand. We think this is a more sophisticated way to ascertain the importance to the brand of the attribute in question, rather than simply asking the consumer outright, for the simple reason we can get to the answer without *having* to ask, and so potentially alerting the consumer to the sort of relationship or insight we're trying to uncover. Of course there may be an issue of causality in this approach – we are looking at correlation not direction – but after a lot of head scratching, we and our research partners at GlobeScan are confident it is a valid and safe assumption that the direction of the relationship is as we believe.

To make this more digestible, we've plotted some examples in the figures below. In each case, we're using a 2 × 2 matrix (which, as you know, is obligatory in any text on brands and sustainability . . .), with all of the sustainability attributes plotted on the axes of performance (perceived) and brand importance (derived). Attributes that find themselves in each quadrant tell a different story. Those of high importance and high performance are the success stories for the brand to date – in other words, attributes that relate to hot issues for consumers and are considered to be being dealt with effectively by the brand. Those attributes that appear bottom left, in comparison, are neither being addressed by the brand nor are considered materially relevant (yet). Whilst the business may not be lavishing resources on these areas (so leading to poor performance), these are areas to watch, as they could suddenly move to become far more salient to the brand for the consumer.

Those attributes that end up in the bottom right quadrant are those where performance is considered to be good, but at this moment in time, the value to the brand is still in question. Maybe these attributes simply represent part of the argument or debate that consumers cannot map on to the brand at this time. But this is not to say these attributes are not important, and with a strong performance already recorded, they represent an opportunity for the brand to educate its audiences and *make* these attributes salient and relevant.

Finally, those attributes that appear in the top left quadrant are the real problem areas. Here there are attributes that are considered vital to the health of the brand, but where perceived performance is low. Whereas the bottom right attributes represent an opportunity for the brand to create an expectation from the audiences, those that appear in the top left are a red flag representing an unmet consumer need or demand when it comes to the debate. And this unmet need is having a detrimental effect on the brand health. Interestingly, across all categories and all markets, the one cluster of attributes that seems to be lodged in this problem quadrant is governance and ethics. In other words, there are virtually no brands in our study that can demonstrate what consumers consider to be acceptable levels of performance when it comes to these broad, ill-defined but elemental areas (this suggests an underlying, foundational issue with trust, and is something we will return to when we look more closely at what this means in the context of a brand).

Back to the quadrants within the matrix; if firms and their brands are doing well in terms of respondent-perceived uses of capital (so high social capital around these issues) then we would hope to see plenty of attributes jostling in the top right quadrant, and some in the bottom left (after all, not every issue is going to be perceived as pertinent to every brand). More importantly, what we don't want to see are attributes scattered across the two 'problem quadrants'. As such, the optimal graphic is a strong trend line running at 45° from the bottom left to the top right of the matrix.

In some cases, there are clear success stories. Figure 12 shows this analysis for a leading FMCG (dairy) brand. Immediately you can see the strong trend line across the 'healthy quadrants'. But closer inspection suggests weak-

Figure 12: Drivers analysis #1. FMCG brand. Sustainable Futures.

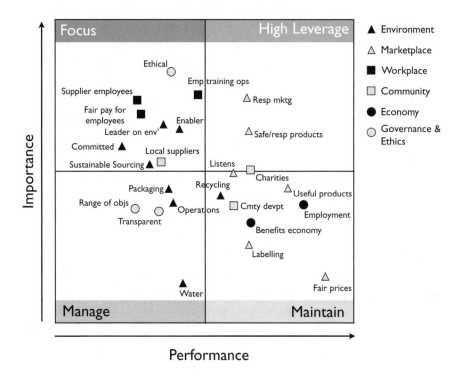

Figure 13: Drivers analysis #2. Retailer brand. Sustainable Futures.

nesses in their communication of environmental issues, with all of these attributes remaining clustered around the centre and the bottom left quadrant. Considering this firm is working hard on environmental performance, this lack of clarity and resonance with consumers has to be seen as a disappointment.

But not all brands enjoy such a constructive outing. Figure 13 shows a large retailer which, despite significant efforts to move forward in this area and take a leadership position, seems to be caught with some entrenched opinions and perceptions. In particular, employee and supplier relations seem to be sour with our respondents. Of course, this may be far from the truth, but as we've pointed out, perception rules the day in this context.

These analytical tools help us recognise that in many – if not most – cases, brands are not engaging their relevant audiences effectively around these issues. That is to say, social capital is not as high or as balanced as it should be.

We can explore these dilemmas further, with a more detailed analytical view of the brands in question using more complex forms of analysis such as structural equation modelling (SEM). In a (large-ish) nutshell, this analysis allows us to explore the effect and causality of relationships between a number of variables, including perceived sustainability performances, our brand health proxies and, in this case, repurchase intent (as a more tangible consequence of stronger advocacy and impression). It's of particular use in this context, since it allows us to see whether sustainability is perceived as a holistic effort from the brand in question, how different aspects are perceived to relate and just how constructive these perceptions are for this idea of brand health. Just to add some additional context, we've also included some more emotional personality trait variables to see how they interact with the more rational sustainability attribute clusters.

Again, we're starting with the same FMCG brand (Figure 14). What we need to check for first is the relationship between our measure of brand health and repurchase intent – if you like, the all-important connection between attitude and behaviour in this case. In this instance – shown by the path coefficients – it's pretty strong, meaning a substantive proportion of the variance in repurchase intent is controlled by our equity proxies. In other words, our proxies are holding up. Working back from this relationship and exploring what drives the proxy measures, we start to see a more vivid picture that supports the glimpses we had in the 2 × 2 matrix – this brand enjoys a pretty healthy patchwork of perceptions that criss-cross most of the sustainability clusters, many of which are driving our health proxies. The interconnectedness of these attribute clusters suggests that where consumers are aware and appreciative of efforts or performance in one area, this appreciation flows over into other areas. In other words, trust is underpinning 'safe assumptions' being made by consumers in many cases. We can also see that the more emotional qualities of the brand are significant drivers of perception in these areas – again, this suggests deep stocks of trust towards the brand to be 'doing the right thing'. At first sight, this seems an excellent state to be in – and it certainly is – although we'd voice one word of caution. With so much perception possibly being driven by trust-driven assumptions, there is a small risk of these perceptions running away from the brand, and should it ever materialise – through more information or greater understanding – that actual performance

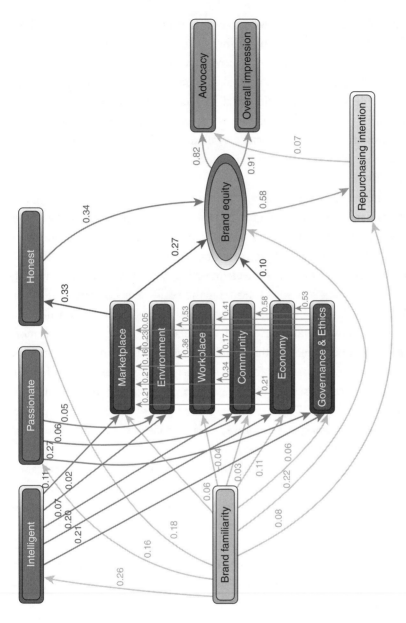

Figure 14: Path analysis #1. Sustainable Futures.

or ambition falls short of these runaway perceptions, the sense of betrayal could be significant and painful for the brand, despite its innocence.

And whilst this schematic is positive and constructive (the best we saw in our research of 2009, as it happens), the other gaping opportunity for this brand is to derive greater – and direct – brand health from the other sustainability attribute clusters, not just from the marketplace and economy clusters. In other words, create more social capital around these areas, especially community and environment, considering how increasingly important these areas are becoming.

Let's now turn to the retailer we introduced a little earlier (Figure 13), and look at its path analysis (see Figure 15). Using exactly the same technique, we can see that brand health as we define it has a strong effect on repurchase intent. So far, so good. But from this point on, the story is very different. There is no evidence of interconnectedness between the various sustainability clusters, suggesting very siloed thinking and really no social capital at play at all. The other interesting aspect is the statistically significant and negative relationship between familiarity and workplace. In other words, the more familiar consumers are with the brand, the less they consider the workplace practices of the firm sustainable. This is a terrible result, but looking further, we can also see that a second negative relationship exists, between workplace and repurchase intent. This second negative link implies that where perceptions around the workplace improve, so the propensity to repurchase from this brand decreases.

This is an odd outcome, to say the least. But the most likely explanation is this: the brand value proposition is low prices, every day, and where consumers perceive more sustainable workplace practices in play, they assume this will mean higher overheads (health insurance, better wages, training, etc.) for the business, and as a result higher prices. And it's the last step in this assumption that causes consumers to be less likely to engage with the brand, as there's a perception that sustainability is directly at odds with the core brand proposition.

This is just our opinion of course (albeit based on the evidence within the analysis) and there may be other explanations if and when in dialogue with the brand in question. But regardless of the explanation, this level of analysis allows us to uncover not only ambient stocks of social capital around the brand

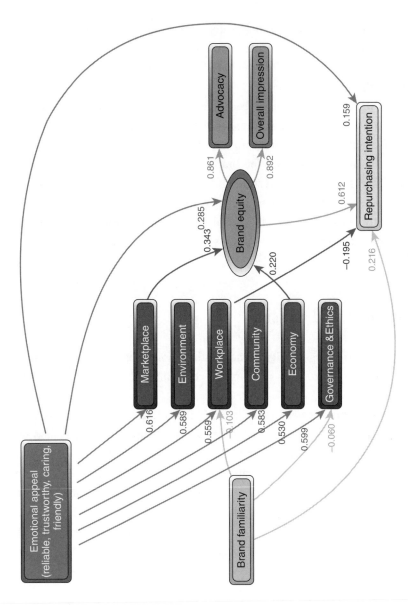

Figure 15: Path analysis #2. Sustainable Futures.

in this context, but structural holes, disconnects and – as in the case above – even negative relationships. All of these are vital tools in helping to pin down, diagnose and formulate ways to systematically and accountably increase levels of balanced social capital.

These different forms of analysis allow us to explore at a forensic level how brands and their audiences are interacting and engaging around these issues. Remember, the entire output of these models is dependent on the levels of social capital around the brand and amongst its audiences. Where social capital is high, then perception is likely to be close to reality. And where social capital is low, the chances of perception being close to reality drop significantly. As such, low social capital introduces a wealth of risk, volatility and hard work when it comes to brands wanting to engage audiences around these issues.

Symptoms and causes

This inability to engage audiences across the whole debate is, we feel, a direct result of brands – probably all brands – confusing what is a symptom with the cause.

We believe brands need to understand that the root cause of these problems lies in the collapse and reduction of social capital. As we've laid out elsewhere: where social capital is low, bad practices – including externalisation of costs and the marginalisation of voices – start to happen. It is an inevitable, immutable side effect of low social capital. We saw it starting to appear in Part I, where consumers became fixated on their intimate relationships with brands, without the natural modifiers and mediators that should be in place in genuine, balanced social capital environments to temper tendencies and outcomes. The result is a 'tragedy of the commons', where in this case, the common is our collective social fabric.

As a result, it is key that brands recognise that the most effective and efficient way to approach addressing these issues is to start to rebuild social capital. It may sound like semantics, but thinking in terms of social capital rather than sustainability has the potential to unlock considerable expertise and ambition currently locked up within brands in this context. Social capital is a unique, enabling lens through which brands should view these challenges, their responses and their opportunities. Social capital presents a wealth of opportunities for competitive advantage – opportunities of the best kind, since they are causally ambiguous and near-impossible to mimic by others.

Placing brands in the driving seat of the firm's endeavours will stimulate activity that knocks out unsustainable practices at source. It will become less about 'end of tail pipe' solutions, and more about 'are we even sure we need a tail pipe' innovations.

Think back to the matrices and charts for the FMCG brand. Yes, the results are impressive, but still levels of engagement around the environmental issues are low and ill-formed. How much more effective would it be if the brand engaged those audiences in processes of collaboration and co-creation in a bid to not only make these issues valid and pertinent to their consumers, but couched in language that, whilst not shying away from the conflict and jeopardy involved, pointed firmly towards innovative solutions?

Probably the most concise way to describe the potential is to quote a young mother of two who recently took part in a focus group for us on many of these issues. Half-way through proceedings, she suddenly asked, 'When I throw something away, where is away . . . ?' It stopped the conversation dead in the room, with everyone trying to think of an appropriate answer. But of course there isn't one. Because really, there is no 'away'. Well, certainly not when there is high social capital of all flavours. And in that one question, that young mother managed to increase the stock of social capital considerably within the focus group.

We cannot overstate the importance of this continued confusion by brands. It continues to render most of what brands do as window dressing at best, and destructive at worst. As any doctor will tell you, to really get better you have to look beyond the symptoms, no matter how grave and unpleasant, and get to the cause. The added danger here for brands is that everyone else seems to be cottoning on to this. We've already talked about this sense of a pendulum swing, of new social movements and 'wakefulness'. If brands fail to adapt and read this, they risk being left behind and becoming mute in what is undoubtedly set to become one of the most important conversations of our time. Brands need to re-orient themselves rapidly, and deploy their considerable arsenal of abilities to immediate, better use. Once again, we call for brands to prepare to build their own Social Capital Strategies in order to emerge as relevant, valued and durable Social Equity Brands.

We started this chapter by recognising that brands are charging at sustainability as if it's some magic bullet cure for all of their ills. There's no doubt brands (and agencies) are experiencing their own sustainability crisis in that their potency appears to be under attack. This is having considerable impact on brand-building marketing budgets as well as agency fee models. This is, of course, no coincidence: brands spring up in response to changes in our social fabric. Brands are, in their traditional DNA, reactive and opportunistic (and extremely agile). So the very fact that today's brands – and the agencies that create and service them – are feeling excluded or even a little redundant is not surprising if we accept the hypothesis that we are indeed in this Era of Social Capital Rising. Brands are out of step with this emerging social movement.

Recognising this apparent disconnect, in their race to leverage sustainability hastily for their own rewards, brands are increasingly being seen as thin, false and dry. This, we argue, goes a long way to explaining the persistent gap between attitude and behaviour, and deflects the attention away from what many see as inherently inconsistent or fickle consumer behaviour, and instead towards a lack of intrinsic motivation from the firms that present these brands to their audiences. As we'll return to in following chapters, this historic assumption held by brands that consumers are only really interested in the direct bilateral relationship is now very much out of date.

This increasing consumer complexity is reflected in our Sustainable Futures analysis, showing a lack of holistic communication around these issues, resulting in disjointed, ambiguous consumer perception and, worse still, a fundamental lack of engagement. It's important to stress again, people are not struggling to engage with the issues, but they are struggling to engage *with brands* around these issues. And in their panic to address this issue, brands continue, it seems, to churn out what many or most see as rhetoric that is hollow, exhaustive and misdirected. A forensic analysis of symptoms is not what you go to your (trusted) local doctor for. You go for a succinct diagnosis of the underlying problem, and the confidence that you are then embarking on the right journey to be rid of the issue.

So it should be pretty clear – we are not fans of the current efforts from most brands, and believe these efforts are neither helping the wider cause nor building value for the brands themselves.

In the next two chapters, we'd like to explore decision making, and the processes that lead into it, in a little more detail – from both the brand perspective and the consumer perspective. What will become painfully obvious is a need for brands to change the way *they* operate, as we realise the truth about why and how *we* operate the way we do. Many of the behaviour traits and assumptions now hardwired into managing brands need to be reviewed, challenged and updated. Brand managers need to become genetic scientists, comfortable and expert at re-engineering their brand's DNA. In doing so, not only will we find creative and engaging solutions to many of the challenges we currently face, but brands will also become engines of economic value for their firms. It will make sustainability sustainable and reinvigorate the marketing and brand management function within organisations and agencies.

It will, in short, break us out of what is probably the most unsustainable way for brands to approach sustainability.

Chapter 5

We opened this book by talking about how brands initially attempted to help consumers slash search costs as a result of the disappearance of what had been the established methods to ensure 'provenance' of the goods and services chosen. The mass migration and the creation of vast armies of specialist workers, operating in highly mechanised industries had given rise to what we have called 'provenance costs', and brands stepped in as a powerful fillip, offering up a plastic social capital in an attempt to assuage these costs.

But is it the case that brands actually 'help' us choose? We introduced the idea in Part I that in the transition from utilitarian needs to hedonic wants (and, in turn, hedonic needs), suddenly brands – still slavishly devoted to manifestations of scientific management – became less useful in the decision-making process.

Or, possibly, became less useful in what was becoming a *different* decision-making process.

And today? Are brands really that good at guiding us to make the right decisions? It all depends, of course, on what we mean by the right decisions. When it comes to decisions about which brands to interact with, is the right decision simply the right decision or does it need to be the *very best decision*?

Again, this may sound like semantics, but to us it is an important distinction. As we've already touched on, consumption is one quantifiable and measurable thing, but consumerism is altogether different. And whilst consumption may entertain making simply the right choices at the time, it is our belief that consumerism encourages us to make the *very best* choices. In other words, we're encouraged to strive to make the best possible decision from the increasingly daunting choice in front of us. Our social identity depends on it.

Maximisers and satisficers

When it comes to deciding what and how to consume, we're encouraged by brands to become what psychologists call 'maximisers'. Maximisers – as the name suggests – are those people who attempt to make the best possible decision when it comes to choosing what to consume. This suggests near-exhaustive searching, assessing and filtering. Maximisers, of course, cannot actually make the very best decisions, but they can *aspire* to make such decisions. This is an important distinction to make, since it suggests that, with the odds stacked against them, maximisers are setting themselves up to be disappointed before they've even made a commitment to consume, as they will not be able to meet their own expectations.

The alternative to maximising is what US psychologist Herbert Simon[49] called 'satisficing'. Satisficing is the behaviour characteristic where we 'simply' opt for what feels like a good enough decision at the time. So it's not about 'perfect', but rather 'good enough'. Simon argued that, since it is practically impossible to search exhaustively and make a balanced, filtered rational decision from this exhaustive list, when you consider and factor in the breadth and depth of search and processing costs, satisficing is, in fact, a maximising strategy.

But despite this 'rational' argument for satisficing, it seems huge swathes of us are keen to keep on going with the less efficient and possibly destructive alternative. Maximising is big business. Why this aspiration persists is a little bit of a mystery, especially when we consider the rise of a post-materialistic stance in many developed markets, together with the burgeoning push-back against consumption for consumption's sake. Some research suggests these emerging movements are being over-reported, and post-materialism is not as established as predicted.[50]

Frederick Hirsch, the US economist, discussed one possible explanation almost thirty years ago, in his book *Social Limits to Growth*.[51] Hirsch argues that no matter how affluent society becomes as a whole, there will always be goods that are only available to the very richest or most successful. For example, rising prosperity across the board may allow everyone to own a car, but there will always be those people who belong to the elite club of owners of Bentleys. Maybe rising prosperity across the board will allow everyone to own their own house at some point, but there will always be those people who want to have great views or privacy. Maybe rising prosperity will allow everyone's children to attend university, but there will always be a limit on the number that can get in to Cambridge or Harvard. The point is, there will always be scarce products regardless of overall prosperity, and these scarce products are extremely valuable to certain people exactly because of this scarcity. Ownership of these scarce products bestows status on the owners. Hirsch argues that the more prosperous a society becomes, so the more utilitarian needs are met, and the subsequent hedonic wants and needs cluster around these emotional aspects such as prestige and status, delivered by increasingly scarce experiences. In other words, maximisers have plenty to focus on.

As such, increasing prosperity itself may be the cause of this increase in maximising behaviour. We know that brands attempt to meet these hedonic needs and wants, and it seems brands are instrumental in pushing us toward being maximisers. Their communications are predicated on the creation of some perfect, intimate connection; some exclusive bilateral relationship in which very little outside of it matters. Implicit in brand communication is the desire to congratulate us for making the right – perfect – choice with that brand. Just think of any brochure or literature you've received with a purchase – its opening comment is almost always thanking you for choosing the brand, and *congratulating* you for having made the perfect choice. Our entire relationship with a brand is built upon the conceit that it only exists because it is perfect – and we are too (albeit momentarily) for having chosen it.

Why would a brand choose to do this? The answer is pretty simple: competition.

Possible buyers of any brand now have at their fingertips access to a panoply of alternatives. The consumer-defined competitive set is not only huge but almost impossible for those who create the brands to control or understand. As we introduced in Part I, markets – and competitive sets – are not defined by firms and their brands, but by those who experience and consume the brands. As such, brands need to convince us that our burgeoning relationship is indeed special; unique in fact. There is no way we'd be able to replicate this experience with any other. Brands attempt to instil in us a desire to maximise our decisions – to their benefit – by implying there are no credible substitutions available, and if there were, the switching costs would be crippling.

So whilst encouraging swathes of consumers to become maximisers may be momentarily good for brands, is it good for us?

Surely the answer is yes. After all, having more choice has to be a good thing, and we're always being told that better decisions involve detailed investigation, level-headed analysis and filtering and a resultant rational decision. Choice, and striving to make the perfect choice, seem to support and defend our desire to be autonomous and in control of our destiny. Not for us this reliance on emotion and gut feeling, it seems (although we will investigate this further in the following chapter).

Unfortunately it seems this is far from the case. Research[52] clearly shows a link between maximiser tendencies and lower levels of happiness and well-being. Maximising is even linked with higher levels of depression.[53] If we just think about the logistical and mechanical process of being a maximiser for a second, it's fairly easy to see how it could give rise to these traits. Think about the mental anguish of trying to amass exhaustive options, then trying to analyse this list rationally. Think about the pain of trying to assign values to disparate qualities, and hoping those subjective values remain stable long enough to make a decision. And think about the sheer number of sacrifices you would have to make, just to have the *time* to do all of this. You would end up being consumed by the act of consumption. It feels – at least to us – that it would be very hard work indeed being a maximiser. It also comes as no surprise to us to read that maximisers are more likely to enjoy their positive experiences less, and suffer more when the experience is not what they expected.

This, of course, is not a bad thing for brands. We've already described how hedonic wants can arguably migrate into being hedonic needs, in the same way that an addiction develops. Couple this with the brand attempting to foster maximising behaviour that may then result in diminished enjoyment or satisfaction during and after consumption, and it is easy to see where the hedonic treadmill argument finds a foothold. We race ever faster through products in an attempt to extract the expected type and level of value from this plastic capital relationship, with products increasingly being what Chilean economist Max-Neef[54] calls 'pseudo satisfiers'. Suddenly, maximising sounds not only like an inefficient way of approaching relationships with brands, but actually quite destructive for those involved.

Of course, people are not maximisers across the board in every decision they make. Instead, the maximising tendency rises and falls depending on the category. I would never consider myself a maximiser although I do recognise the trait in myself when I am shopping for something like a camera or a new laptop. Maybe I am an electronic gadget maximiser. This raises an interesting question: am I more aligned to a maximiser profile with these types of products because there is not only so much choice, but it is so easy to initially filter and review options? In other words, have Canon, Nikon, Apple and others, as pervasive and persuasive brands, managed to turn me into a maximiser when it comes to their products? We're not aware of any science to support this, but our gut feeling is that this proliferation of choice, and ease with which we can browse that choice, is indeed stoking the maximiser tendencies in all of us. If that is true, then our current trajectory is not a good one, and the onus falls heavily on brands to break this vicious circle.

We can't have it all

One of the most divisive aspects of a maximising mentality is that it forces a forensic investigation of many rival options, creating higher levels of what psychologists call 'buyer's regret'. Buyer's regret describes the pain you feel when you suddenly think, feel or realise you've made a bad choice. We've all had that feeling from time to time. But maximisers have it far more frequently. It's an inevitable outcome of going through the process a maximiser goes through in their ambition to make the best possible choice. Buyer's regret is really a shorthand way of capturing the subjective opportunity costs of any purchase decision. Notice we say subjective rather than objective.

Nobel Prize-winning psychologists Daniel Kahneman and Amos Tversky[55] studied the interplay between 'subjective' value and 'objective' value (via gains and losses) in forming their highly influential Prospect Theory. Objective value describes the utility derived from an exchange that is recognised by any player in the market regardless of their position: so objective utility increases linearly with units gained, and decreases with units lost. Subjective value, however, is the value to the person actually acquiring the good or service. Subjective value or utility does not increase linearly with units acquired. For example, the first chocolate out of a box tastes exquisite; the second tastes pretty good too, and maybe even the third. But the subjective utility (value) is certainly diminishing, until the point that the following chocolate delivers no value whatsoever. This – at least at this point – is in line with the traditional economic argument that there is diminishing marginal utility gained from repeated purchases of the same thing. But in this context, subjective value is linked to the notions and processes that we have explored already, namely novelty and adaptation.

Figure 16 shows the familiar 'S' function graph at the centre of Kahneman and Tversky's Prospect Theory. To really understand why this is relevant to the way brands operate – and indeed the way we operate – it is worth spending some time exploring its make-up.

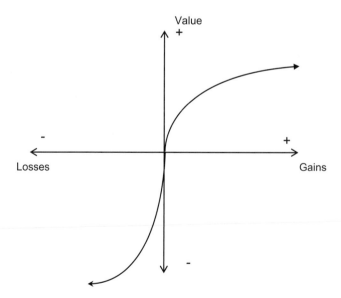

Figure 16: Prospect Theory. Reproduced by permission of The Econometric Society.

Focusing on the top right-hand side of the graph (which represents the value that results from the purchase or gain of a product or some other utility-providing process), the curve illustrates the diminishing returns argument we have already touched on. This is in part a graphical representation of the 'miserable millionaire' paradox from Carol Graham's[56] work that we referenced in Part I.

It also represents an interesting characteristic in us, in that we are what Kahneman and Tversky called 'risk averse' when it comes to seeking gains or additions. A simple way to depict this (and the authors use a similar device in their experiment design), is to ask whether you would like to be given £1000 right now, no questions asked, or 'risk' a toss of a coin, where you'd have £2000 it if came up heads, or nothing if it came up tails. In the cold rational light of day, this looks like a straightforward 'double or nothing' decision. When asked, we are far more likely to opt for the guaranteed £1000. Why? Because the value of £2000 to us is not quite double the value of £1000 – the first £1000 is more valuable. This is shown in the slope of the curve in that top right-hand quadrant and the fact that it is concave. So, in fact, why would we take a risk to gain an additional £1000 when it may 'cost' us the original £1000, which is 'worth' more to us?

This tendency to be risk averse is not the case, though, when we look at losses – the left-hand side of the graph. On this side of the graph, it suggests that the 'cost of loss' is greater with the early losses.

Imagine you now have that £1000 and you are offered two options. One, you hand back £500 no questions asked. Or two, the coin is tossed, and if it comes up heads you get to keep the whole lot, or if it comes up tails, you have to hand back the full £1000. What the graph depicts is our natural tendency to go for the gamble in this context of a potential loss. In this situation, we are what Kahneman and Tversky call 'risk seeking'. The reason for this apparent interest in now accepting the risk is that we would feel the pain of losing the first £500 more than losing the second £500 and as such, are prepared to gamble the second loss in order to avoid the first. This is why the curve is convex here. So there's a resounding asymmetry when it comes to our perceived value from gains and losses – even of the same thing.

One explanation of this increased sense of discomfort when it comes to loss is what psychologists call the 'endowment effect'.[57] As the name suggests, it describes the sense of ownership we have of something – anything in fact – once it passes to us, and the subsequent discomfort of then letting it go. In other words, when it's ours, it's worth more. There are plenty of experiments that amusingly demonstrate the endowment effect at work,[58] and it goes someway to explaining the confidence brands exhibit in offering money-back guarantees – they know that once you've got your hands on it, the chances of taking it back are typically pretty slim.

Prospect Theory is important in the context of brands and social capital for a number of reasons. For instance, we can see here how the diminishing experience of subjective value would prompt people to pursue alternative consumption options, in order to derive the maximum, novelty-influenced utility in each case. This could lead to increased consumption, as consumers widen their net to capture more and more hedonic novelty.

There are two other key aspects to this theory that are also very relevant to this discussion. The first is the rate of change in the function curve on the left and right sides of the graph. The rate of change is far greater on the left than on the right. What does this mean? Well, for each successive unit of loss, the subjective loss of value is more severe – certainly for the first couple of rounds. In other words, from a psychological perspective, unit for unit, we seem to feel the pain of a loss more than we feel the hit of a gain.

This has serious repercussions for our investigation into how brands operate, and how they interact with our consumption patterns. If brands are offering up such detailed information and engaging us in relationships that encourage maximising tendencies, then the outcome is that we are more able and willing to evaluate the opportunity costs of choosing one option over another. We'll talk more about these costs and the effects of perceived trade-offs in the next section, but the key issue is the possible emergence of what psychologists call 'counterfactual thinking'.[59] Counterfactual thinking describes the process whereby we imagine a better outcome than the one we experience. It describes the classic '. . . if only I'd not sent that email but called instead . . . ' sensation. The reason this is important is that maximising behaviour, coupled with the plastic intimacy offered up by brands, makes it all too easy to imagine alternative outcomes that seem more attractive than the one that *we may not have even actioned yet.*

In other words, this is not buyer's remorse, but *'speculator's remorse'*. And the fact that the curve slopes so sharply on the left-hand side of the Prospect Theory graph suggests that these anticipated pains of ignoring those choices may even outweigh the benefits of the 'right choice' from the start. It implies a painful sense of limbo for consumers, where brands are instrumental in contriving this vivid potential anguish of choice. Suddenly we're caught in consumption purgatory. Who said maximising behaviour was good for us?

We'll return to these experiences of trade-offs and opportunity costs in a moment, but before we leave Kahneman and Tversky's Prospect Theory, there is one more key characteristic of the graph we'd like to linger on – a characteristic that has significance for how brands respond to their audiences when it comes to sustainable consumption choices. It's the centre point; the point where subjective and objective losses turn into subjective and objective gains. Importantly, this can be determined in the consumer's mind by the wording or language used by the brand.

Frames

Presenting information in a certain way in an attempt to steer the recipient of that information in one direction or the other is called framing. And aware of it or not, we all do it and respond to it. Frames can be established with hard edges thanks to the selection of certain topics or points of view over others, or they can be created more subtly with the use of metaphors. News channels and newspapers are experts in framing, and many headlines that we initially would consider 'neutral' are, in fact, frames. Think about business headlines that talk about 'plunging' share prices and 'crashing' indices. These metaphors create powerful frames, which in these cases serve the media well to capture attention and, in many cases, engender a sense of concern and reliance on these sources to follow the issues.

This agility from the media has given rise to a thriving industry of corporate communication specialists that attempts to defuse potentially explosive situations through reframing the issues faced by many firms in moments of crisis. In 2010 British Petroleum (BP) battled the off-shore drilling crisis in the Gulf of Mexico on two fronts – physically in terms of trying to cap the spill, and reputationally, as the US and global media depicted the company as uncaring and sanguine about what it considers an inevitable occupational risk. No doubt many specialists tried to reframe the debate to present the company as diligent and decent, a victim of an unfortunate malfunction whilst trying to deliver important resources for us all to continue with our lifestyles.

But it is not only corporate communications that can take advantage of framing; brands can and do too. If we look back at the Prospect Theory graph, we can project a hypothetical context on to it, and see how different language could determine where consumers set their own centre point, which in turn determines whether they see gains or losses associated with the choice. Imagine you are a retailer selling organic cotton T-shirts, where workers are paid a decent wage, alongside regular cotton T-shirts. The former are priced at £20 each and the latter at £15, to reflect the higher costs to you. You have two marketing approaches in mind: one positions the regular T-shirts at a 25% discount, and the other positions the organic option at a 33% premium. The strategy – the frame – you choose will influence the consumer with respect to where they place their mental centre point. Seeing regular T-shirts at a discount may represent a gain in utility for them (greater value as a result of the same benefit but at a lower cost), or may present greater value for the organic option, as utility from value around better and more sustainable production is delivered at the 'regular' price. Conversely, positioning the normal price at £15 with a premium for the organic option may incentivise people to pay the premium in recognition of the 'extra good' the T-shirt represents, or indeed push them towards buying the normal T-shirt at the normal price.

It's difficult to ascertain which way consumers would move, but it is clear that how the brand positions the products can have a dramatic effect on how the consumer views their gain against the opportunity costs involved, as gains, losses and costs are asymmetrical as well as dependent on the centre point. Effective framing is a key component of our Social Capital Strategy process.

So how do consumers weigh up the perceived opportunity costs of making a decision one way or another? How do they reconcile the inevitable trade-offs that take place? If maximising behaviour is everywhere and encouraged – partly because of our increasingly hedonic motivations and partly because brands want us to approach the engagement process that way – aren't the consequences of these more informed choices making the decision-making process harder and harder? More specifically, what is the impact on our ability to make the right choices when it comes to more sustainable consumption?

Are brands making it easy for us to make these choices?

Opportunity costs and trade-offs

Opportunity cost is a term that gets bandied about a lot, but in the true, traditional economic context, it refers to the costs that should be considered in making any decision based on the fact that that decision will eliminate the opportunity to make an alternative decision. As such, if we say 'value' is a product of benefits and costs, then opportunity cost has a fundamental impact on perceived value from the outcome of the decision made.

In this case, we are using the term value to represent a qualitative measure of the net benefits that are experienced. Value is not the same thing as benefit, as the latter is only concerned with the positives generated as a result of the exchange and does not consider the costs involved.

Benefits can be either tangible or intangible. Tangible benefits are those derived directly from the product or service. For example, the new Mercedes you buy has the tangible benefits of getting you from A to B in incredible comfort, with full AC and a smooth drive experience. Intangible benefits are those that arise from aspects associated with the product or service. So these could include the sense of social status you gain as a result of getting into and out of such a prestigious make of car. Benefits can be exploded even further with functional, social, emotional, epistemic and conditional dimensions,[60] reflecting their utilitarian, hedonic, contextual, personal and temporal nature. The point we want to make here is two-fold. Firstly, benefits are multifaceted and often mutually exclusive. And second, considering we are made aware of potential benefits so vividly, by advertising and other brand communication strategies, these alternative benefits can coalesce to represent a considerable perceived opportunity cost for a consumer.

The traditional economists amongst us would argue that these opportunity costs could not mount up this way, since we should only consider the costs associated with the next best alternative. But this is predicated on both the decision maker being rational and able to ignore a wider selection of alternatives, and this wider selection not being made fully available to the decision maker.

But as we've already shown, this wider selection *is* available. More than available, in fact – unavoidably central to the decision-making process. What's more, our maximising tendencies will encourage us to assemble as complete a set of alternatives as possible, with brand-driven communications constantly striving for attention. As such, any decision we undertake risks having considerable opportunity costs attached to it – costs associated with alternatives that may not be genuinely viable, but have some sparkling redeeming feature that lifts them to the top of the alternative pile albeit momentarily. More than this, many of these alternatives may combine (in the process of 'counterfactual thinking' as we've already discussed) to form some 'hybrid' best alternative, with a whole range of wonderful – but in reality mutually exclusive – benefits.

The end result is that the opportunity costs associated with any decision can suddenly mount up to be a considerable dampener on the chosen outcome. And we should not forget the Prospect Theory insight, that subjectively, costs pain us greater than gains, 'unit for unit'.

Opportunity costs, then, are a real challenge in our modern consumption practices, forcing us to make a range of trade-offs with what may amount to hypothetical, unrealistic alternatives. No wonder buying stuff has become so stressful.

Trade-offs, it seems, cause us extreme pain during the decision-making process and when given the chance, we'd prefer to walk away and make no decision at all, rather than one laden with compromise.

And it appears it is not just consumers that suffer from this pain and a desire to flee a trade-off ridden decision. In an experiment[61] with General Practitioner doctors, one group was presented with a fictitious history where the patient was suffering from osteoarthritis and asked to recommend either a new medication or refer the patient to a specialist. 75% recommended the new treatment. But the second group was given the choice of two new medications, or the option to refer. With this second group, only 50% recommended a treatment. In other words, when the number of choices increased, even professional decision makers in this critical context found the trade-off too complex or uncomfortable, and so backed away from making a decision, which in this case involved referring the fictitious patient to a specialist.

So it seems trade-offs, as a natural by-product of greater choice, actually encourage us not to commit to a choice, as we strive to remove that discomfort from the decision-making process. This has serious repercussions for the way brands communicate complex issues riddled with ambiguity and inherent trade-offs; issues such as sustainability.

Barry Schwartz[62] makes an additional important argument around this expanding choice, our pressure to maximise and our overall wellbeing. As choice increases, so a bad decision becomes increasingly our fault, for which we must take the blame. In other words, we cannot pin the failure on a pitiful choice or limited information.

The terrible consequence here is that, with mounting choice and a supposed responsibility to make the right choice, consistently failing to deliver value to you in your decisions can have a serious long-term effect on your wellbeing and self-confidence. If the modern world is all about choice and control of destiny, and brands are so expert in presenting these choices 3000 times a day in pithy, ballistic form, what does it say about you when you consistently fail to make what you feel is the right choice?

Why encouraging satisficing would be so much better – for everyone

This is an awful vicious circle that we seem to have got ourselves into: consumerism relies upon consumption as the practice that maintains the culture; brands offer us an intoxicating and convenient – but plastic and asymmetrical – form of social capital that stimulates this consumption; we are increasingly striving to be maximisers in the decisions we make in these brand contexts or environments; and the trade-offs and sense of personal failure we feel in being apparently unable to capitalise on this level of choice nudge us towards lower self-confidence and even depression. Where many of us then head out of the front door to buy something new to feel better.

It's a process that adds to the sense of society spinning faster and faster, as we try to assimilate more and more information to make better and better choices and decisions. This centripetal force is hurling us to the edges of the drum; pinning us to an ever-widening boundary where we are travelling with greater and greater velocity, with fewer and fewer people around us.

Wouldn't it be so much better for us to be satisficers instead? We think so.

Satisficing would slow the 'societal centrifuge', no doubt. Satisficing would remove the angst from the forensic attention given to choices and trade-offs, and would release us from the logistical and emotional burden of trying to maximise every decision. Suddenly we'd have time to reconnect with family, friends and colleagues, and find pastimes and hobbies to fill the yawning gaps left by the removal of maximising behaviour. We'd peel ourselves off the edges of an accelerating drum and recongregate in the centre.

Of course, many people are satisficers already. But here's the problem. These people tend not to develop brand loyalties. If anything, they shun brands. And we could argue that brands are only really useful when maximising tendencies are at play – maximising, materialism and economic prosperity are all interlinked and show strong correlations across developed markets – and the latter two are the natural homes for any self-respecting brand, it would seem.

But we would argue this is the world of old-school, industrial brands – brands that grew up in the Era of Social Capital Waning, initially providing our plastic capital fillip, and continuing to contribute low-grade social debt to the funding of society and its levels of social capital. These are the brands that are currently engaged in what we genuinely believe is the most unsustainable approach to sustainability.

With its myriad themes, complexities and conflicts, and by trying to 'out sustain' their competitors with new claims, new endorsements and new revelations about their supply chain-driven guardians, these industrial era brands are using the broad sustainability debate to prompt consumers into trying to maximise their consumption choices around supposed sustainability criteria. The result is a raft of supposed 'best choices' being tossed about on a sea of irreconcilable trade-offs and opportunity costs. And we've already seen in other contexts what happens when we have too much choice, are striving to make the best decision and then realise we haven't. Or more accurately, couldn't.

Certainly this sense of buyer's remorse, with respect to sustainable consumption choices, is rising – just look at the flow of data that show consumers
find the whole experience stressful and complex. But the system is in a
process of recalibration as part of this Era of Social Capital Rising. And if
brands want to be instrumental in this transition, and avoid being shunted
to the margins of relevance, something has to change.

The challenge rests with finding a way brands can remain relevant and
credible in a transition to satisficing tendencies.

Old-school industrial brands have built into their DNA the concept that
value is embedded in the product or service that they represent. As such,
loyalty is seeded in this moment of purchase, since without purchase the value
cannot be accessed. Our emerging Social Equity Brands, however, recognise
that loyalty is built not through the product or service, but through the value
derived from the experience afforded (Figure 17).

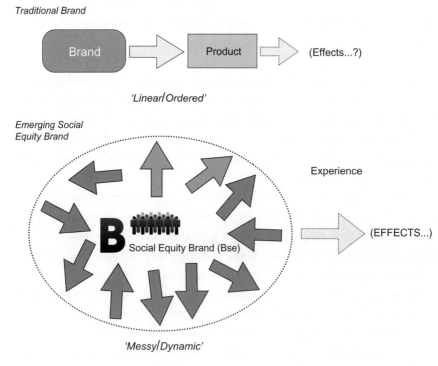

Figure 17: Product versus experience focus

This experience may be delivered with the product or service, may precede the product or service or indeed extend beyond the product or service. The point is, value is not embedded in the product at the moment of consumption, but is released throughout the entire direct or vicarious experience with the brand. This draws on current marketing research investigating value propositions around value-in-use and value-in-context,[63] but the application to the way brands must function is a key tenet of our Social Equity Brand and Social Capital Strategy concepts.

By focusing on the experience, Social Equity Brands can afford to reduce the actual product or service choice to a satisficing exercise, for the simple reason that the consumer is *more focused* on the value distributed throughout the experience. In other words, it becomes less about making the absolute right choice at the moment of purchase and consumption, and more about realising the potential value throughout the experience; value that is crucially not bound by an intoxicating bilateral relationship between the brand and the consumer.

This approach chimes with our earlier discussion around the logistical and emotional burden of trying to exercise maximising behaviour in consumption choices. In that situation it was implicit that value was determined by the choice of product or service, not the ability to create value subsequently. In addition, the intense focus on trying to make the right choice precluded the decision maker from being able to engage in other social behaviour that is important.

A Social Equity Brand recognises these burdens and lightens them by firstly shifting the notion of value being 'bottlenecked' in the moment of purchase and consumption, to being wherever you want to find it within the experience. And second, by allowing the decision maker to restore many of these social behaviours that have been historically marginalised. The very act of being able to restore these social behaviours represents, in itself, a key part of the value creation for the consumer – the experience is giving back in whatever way the consumer determines is most valuable.

Certainly this involves the break-up of the exclusive bilateral relationship between the brand as product and the consumer, but it also represents the most striking opportunity to embed the brand as an enduring value provider within this Era of Social Capital Rising. Social Equity Brands will be defined by removing the angst and discomfort being felt by consumers still caught in the plastic capital – maximising – product-led world.

This chapter has rattled through a fair chunk of brand theory and practice, in an attempt to show how this is, in itself, fundamentally unsustainable and chronically unsuitable in the context of sustainable consumption behaviour. It has tried to outline current dominant practices that have to change if brands are to be considered useful and valuable in this emerging Era of Social Capital Rising. It has also attempted to introduce why these practices can cause so much discomfort for those involved, and what this discomfort can lead to.

Questions still remain, however, over how and why this approach to decision making, foisted upon us by brands and their marketers, causes us to make poor decisions, and the impact this can have on relationships in general and specifically with brands. The answers – or certainly the beginnings of answers – lie in picking through not just what brands do, but how we respond both cognitively and emotionally. The latter is crucial, we believe. The next chapter attempts to build this argument further, and in doing so finishes our groundwork for what we believe this new breed of brands needs to do and become.

Chapter 6

In the closing moments of British film director Guy Ritchie's breakout hit
Lock, Stock and Two Smoking Barrels, ex-professional-footballer-turned-actor
Vinnie Jones turns to the ensemble cast of misfits and delivers what became
the tagline for the film's marketing efforts, '. . . thanks boys, it's been emotional'. It was a great way to sum up the experience of watching the film – a
raucous, brash but unashamedly good-fun, modern-day Ealing comedy. But
if we are to believe most traditional and still dominant marketing and advertising texts, this would not be the best or most effective way to get us to
experience and remember the film. It seems the school of rational thought
still has a firm grip on how brands are encouraged to connect with their audiences: engage on rational, cognitive grounds for best results.

An exploration of this continuing grip and emerging alternatives is important, as it throws more light on how brands do and should interact with their
audiences, and further shapes the recommendations we can make in terms
of how brands transition to being Social Equity Brands.

Back in Part I we touched on how 'scientific advertising'[64] emerged as
a consequence of the broader school of scientific management. Both
approaches subscribed to the argument that our 'higher' calling was to master
our apparently inefficient emotional side, and emerge rational, efficient decision makers, giving rise to what are still the dominant consumer behaviour
models, built around the cognitive (awareness and consideration), the affective (preference) and the behavioural (purchase and consumption). These
three distinct phases continue to be seen by many as a linear process,

applicable to consumers in whatever market and whichever category. Measurement techniques to capture communication effectiveness and efficiency, in turn, continue to rely on the 'hard' outputs of this cognitive-dominant model, namely recall.

Only recently have viable alternatives to this model started to surface,[65] recognising the nonlinear, iterative and more fluid nature of consumer decision journeys. In addition, research has started to look at the mediating and moderating effects value systems and goal theory have on how consumers navigate the decision-making process and subsequent engagement with a brand.[66] In other words, it's not as cut and dried as many would like to think.

Indeed, many now argue that this formulaic and mechanised view is a simplistic – possibly outright incorrect – approach to understanding how we absorb, use and react to advertising and messaging.[67] There's mounting evidence that where recall-based metrics such as awareness are low, the effectiveness of the advertising is not necessarily low as well. In other words, we do not need to be committed slavishly to brand communication and in 'full cognitive mode' in order for the advertisement or communication to have good effect. This is part of the progressive Low Attention Processing (LAP) Model,[68] which is a firm supporter of the argument that emotional involvement is far more effective than rational involvement.

In a recent report from the IPA looking at effectiveness in advertising, the authors also conclude that, '. . . communication models that use emotional appeal (emotional involvement, fame and more complex models) are more likely to yield strong business results than rationally based models (information and persuasion)'.[69]

Emotion, it seems then, is a key component to us engaging with content or messaging, despite our fixation on rational approaches.

This relationship between our rational and emotional sides has received incredible levels of attention, especially over the last few years, in line with the 'rediscovery' of behavioural economics. US psychologist Jonathan Haidt[70] describes the monumental struggle that rages between these two processes, and likens it to a rider on an elephant, where the rider is our rational, cognitive self, and the elephant our emotional self. The rider may like to think he's in control and steering the beast beneath him, but in reality that elephant's going to go wherever it wants to go. Haidt goes on to argue that we cope with this apparent dissonance by rapidly post-rationalising any event to maintain the illusion of rational dominance.

Remembering our earlier representation of value (as an outcome of costs and benefits), we can chart the rising importance of emotion as part of the overall value equation for consumers.[71]

Overall value (or utility) for a consumer as he passes through the relationship with a brand consists of a predicted, or anticipated, utility phase, a consumption – or, increasingly, experienced – utility phase, and finally a remembered utility phase. We'll look at the second two phases a little later, but let's start with the predicted or anticipated utility component – a vital component in that it shapes expectations and determines whether the consumer commits attitudinally and behaviourally to the brand.

Originally, brand management theory viewed the predicted utility phase as being a product of anticipated value derived from benefits (intangible, tangible, epistemic, conditional, etc.) *plus* anticipated value derived from price (if low, then value would be higher). Some beta factor is attached to each of these variables to reflect how they apply to each individual. (1) In its simplest form, this is a slight reworking of our established value equation, considering benefits and costs. Importantly, emotion is nowhere to be seen, as it was thought to play no part in the creation of predicted utility.

When emotion initially entered the equation, it did so as a distinct variable alongside value from benefits and value from price. Weighted again, overall anticipated value was then considered a product of value from emotional associations *plus* value from price (so, in effect, cost) *plus* value from benefits. (2) Even though emotion was now in the equation, it was still an 'optional extra' – in other words, it could be used as an additional driver for anticipated value, but was not in any way a prerequisite.

But an emerging and increasingly influential school of thought[72] places emotion far more at the centre of the predicted utility equation. In this emerging school, emotion is a multiplier of the combined value anticipated from benefits and price. (3) The striking implication of this is where emotion is zero, the overall anticipated value is zero.

1. Predicted Utility $= f(\beta Vb + \beta Vc)$
2. Predicted Utility $= f(\beta E + \beta Vb + \beta Vc)$
3. Predicted Utility $= f(\beta E * (\beta Vb + \beta Vc))$

This would imply, then, that some emotional involvement is crucial in order to assign value to a proposed course of action. Or, to put it another way, with no emotion involved in the decision process, the likelihood of feeling satisfied or delighted with the subsequent decision is severely hampered.

We really cannot afford to underestimate either the importance of the emotional component to our decision-making ability, or the complexity of its relationship with the rational component of the process.

US neuroscientist Paul Maclean's[73] model of the 'triune' brain is a striking illustration of how it seems we have chronically misread this importance and complexity. Maclean proposed that our brain has three distinct areas, each one originating from a different group of our ancestors. Specifically, Maclean claimed that our 'emotional brain' (the Limbic brain) far outdates our much more recent 'rational brain' (the Neocortex), with the two elements in constant conflict. The rational brain tries to temper, channel and control the outputs from the emotional brain, and the emotional brain attempts to steer, motivate and energise the rational brain.

Researcher Joseph LeDoux[74] has explored the relationship between these disparate processes, and proposes that emotion can influence behaviour both directly (such as the fight or flight reaction) and indirectly via cognitive inter-pretation. As such, regardless of the direct or indirect nature of routing between the emotional and rational elements, the evidence seems to suggest the emotional component is highly influential towards the subsequent rational interpretation, and the behaviour that results.

Baba Shiv[75] from Stanford's Graduate School of Business expands on the importance of the emotional element in decision making, introducing the idea that people are either 'Emotionals' (more sensitive) or 'Vulcans' (cold, rational and muted). He goes on to argue that despite most of us being conditioned to try and make calculated, balanced decisions whenever and wherever possible, in actual fact Vulcans are far more likely to vacillate, and invariably end up being less committed to the decisions they do make.

This seems very counter-intuitive. Aren't we always told not to let our emotions get in the way of making the right decision?

It turns out that emotion really should get in the way, as it's key in resolv-ing one of the divisive aspects of decision making we introduced and discussed in the last chapter. Emotion is a vital ally to us in resolving complex and painful trade-off and opportunity cost dilemmas.

More specifically, emotion allows us to develop a handy short-cut in what would otherwise be a painful forensic iterative decision-making process. What our cognitive, rational side would like us to do (and in line with the way we're taught to make 'good decisions') when confronted with the choice of shampoo A and shampoo B, is to sit down, diligently amass information on each and then review each, back and forth, on new refined data until a natural winner emerges. But we've already seen what happens when the cognitive element has free reign of decision making – we burrow ourselves in detail, getting further and further from an overall decision, and all the more anxious in the process. Instead, what the brain prefers to do – driven by the Ventromedial Prefrontal Cortex (VMPC) – is to recognise some sort of emotional bias in the options available. And in many cases, it identifies this emotional bias at the very beginning of the choice process.

As a consequence, the iterative review process is drastically reduced, as there is now what psychologists call a 'pre-decisional distortion' in the decision-making process. The whole thing becomes essentially a charade for the brain to justify the emotional bias it has introduced. This emotional bias is terribly important, since it skews or distorts the genuine costs of the trade-offs involved in the decision, and so removes swathes of angst that would otherwise undermine the decision.

So if emotion can reduce the impact of opportunity costs and resolve trade-off conflicts, surely it has to be central to brands that want consumers to make better choices around sustainability? But again, this is not what seems to be happening.

Instead brands pursue maximising strategies when it comes to sustainability, the result being a continued obsession on choices and subsequent (rational) analysis, all of which continues to marginalise and relegate the very aspect – emotional involvement – that could lead to a better, more committed decision – a decision that we *feel* better about.

Not only are brands approaching sustainability from the most unsustainable – maximising – angle that accentuates the inconsistencies and ambiguities in the debate, but when it comes to our own decision-making processes and preferences, it seems we are not much better.

Wanting versus liking

Let's return to the consumer journey we've already sketched out, where predicted or anticipated utility or value then leads to consumption, or experienced utility, and then ultimately remembered utility. What we're interested in looking at now is the relationship between anticipation and consumption or experience utility. Again, if a Social Equity Brand is defined by providing valuable and meaningful experiences to its audiences, then it is extremely valuable to find insights that point to how to heighten the experienced utility from engaging with a brand.

High predicted or anticipated utility often translates into high experience, or consumption, utility. In other words, the anticipation actively, positively influences the experience.

The emerging academic thinking[76] on this focuses on another part of our brain, called the Striatum. This is the 'wanting department' of our brain, and until very recently was considered to be the reward centre. As such, it was believed it released dopamine – one of our pleasure hormones – as a reward for certain behaviour, and in doing so, made us feel good. However, new thinking is now leading psychologists to believe that rather than being the reward centre, in actual fact the Striatum is the reward *prediction* centre of the brain. In other words, the greater the reward prediction, the greater the release of dopamine into other parts of the brain, giving the resultant good feeling.

This has significant implications for brands and their ability to build meaningful relationships through value-creating experiences. If the brand – an emerging Social Equity Brand – wants to engage its audience to derive a plethora of value from the experience, then that audience has to be motivated and enthused to create this value. And it seems one of the most important ways to ramp up this enthusiasm is to build a suitably powerful sense of anticipation that, in turn, releases higher levels of dopamine which act as a 'fuel' for this level of engagement.

Of course, ramping anticipated or predicted utility alone will not deliver higher experience or consumption utility levels – the product or service has to 'deliver' after all the hype and fanfare. But it does not necessarily have to meet a specific target, but rather must deliver an acceptable level of consumption or experience utility. In other words, there's a range of acceptability.

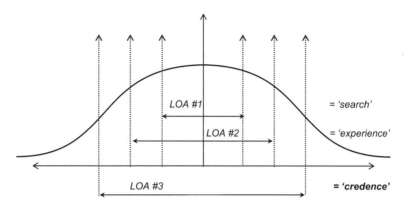

Figure 18: Latitudes of Acceptance

These 'Latitudes of Acceptance' (LOA)[77] represent boundaries for the experience, outside of which the actual experienced utility is considered a let down based on the predicted utility (Figure 18).

What is interesting to see here is that LOA boundaries move, depending on the attributes that are contributing to the experience. As we move from search to experience to credence attributes, so the LOA widen.

Product or service attributes are considered to come in these three flavours regardless of the product or service.[78] Search attributes, as the name suggests, are those attributes that are discernible in the search process. So if you're looking to buy a new shirt, search attributes may include a certain collar shape, long sleeves and the colour blue. Experience attributes, in comparison, are attributes that can only be ascertained in the act of consumption or experience. So with the shirt, if it's cotton you're after, the feeling of cotton on your skin is only possible once the shirt has been bought and put on. The third attribute type – credence – is beyond direct tangible experience. Credence attributes are those attributes for which there is no direct confirmation or effect. In other words, we just have to believe and have faith in whatever is communicating this credence attribute. Back to the shirt purchase, a credence attribute could be some form of Fairtrade or labour agreement in its production. Does it change the colour or cut of the shirt? No. Does it change the feeling of the shirt when worn? No. But is it important as a value-creating attribute? Certainly. And we can see that when it comes to credence attributes, the likelihood of brands 'failing' in their audiences' eyes is far smaller.

Credence attributes would seem, then, to be a great way to garner higher levels of anticipated or predicted utility with 'minimal' risk. Which is good news, considering how much of the sustainability debate lends itself to credence attributes, brought alive through richer social capital.

But if credence attributes afford the brand such wide latitudes of acceptance, how ready are we consumers to embrace such qualities? Are we prepared to have our brand relationships increasingly defined by such aspects? It appears the transition from the Waning to the Rising Era is not as clean and swift as we'd like to believe.

Where have we ended up?

Work by US psychologist Martin Seligman[79] details a variety of ways in which we deal with what appear to be failures in decision-making situations. Seligman argues that we recognise six different causes, and will settle on one irrespective of whether it is the most accurate. In other words, the cause of failure is considered to be perceptual rather than factual. The causes split into three categories: global versus specific; chronic versus transient; and personal versus universal. As the names suggest, a tendency to identify global, chronic and personal causes for failure can have a serious impact on our mental state, in the long term, both due to the notion of helplessness and the resulting inevitability of any choice (as we have discussed earlier in this part), and the inescapable sensation that *we* are the ones screwing up the decisions. Where global, chronic and personal causes are repeatedly recognised as the causes of failure – or in this case, bad choices – we are more prone to suffer from depression. And depression, counter-intuitively, is very much on the rise in Western, developed societies. Barry Schwartz, in *The Paradox of Choice*, presents some horrendous statistics on this inexorable rise, citing that as many as 7.5% of Americans have had an episode of clinical depression by the time they reach *fourteen*. This is double the incidence rate for this age group just ten years earlier. Suicide rates amongst US college students have trebled since the 1970s, and this is now the second highest cause of death amongst this group (after accidents).[80] What are US college students doing any differently? Well, for one thing, their aspirations are changing. Between 1970 and 2000, the proportion of college students who focused primarily on financial success almost doubled, from about 40% to nearly 80%. In the same period, the proportion prioritising the development of a 'meaningful philosophy of life' more than halved, from over 80% to 40%.[81]

Is this an indicator of the continuing desire to maximise all decisions for personal gain?

But surely autonomy and control over one's decisions should be an empowering and positive experience, and quite the opposite of the sense of Seligman's 'learned helplessness'? In theory, very possibly, but this sense of empowerment can only emerge if we feel the option to choose delivers a superior outcome. What happens if every decision we feel in control of is incapable of delivering such a result? What if we are destined to be continually disappointed with whatever result we labour over?

This is what happens when we adopt a maximising, rational mindset in response to the burgeoning choice we face in even the most mundane decisions we make as consumers. We are condemning ourselves to some exhaustive iterative selection process, where all else is marginalised, only for the outcome to render us disappointed with the product, and questioning of our own abilities to make good judgement calls.

This link between maximising behaviour, consumerism and its consumption contribution to GDP on the one hand, and general wellbeing on the other, is well illustrated in Figure 19.[82] Across OECD nations, it plots growth rates in GDP per capita over a 45-year spell, with scores on the nef (new economics foundation) proprietary wellbeing scale (called the Happy Planet Index – HPI). As can be seen, from the early 1970s onwards, there is clearly a strong negative relationship between wellbeing and GDP growth. In other words, pursuing GDP – and let's not forget that more than 60% of GDP is consumer spending driven – seems to be bad for us.

This graph does nothing to explore underlying drivers of either variable, nor does it address questions over causality. But added to the mix of other research we've touched on, which persistently nudges at unhealthy outcomes of consumption, consumerism, materialism and maximising behaviour, it seems another vote in favour of a change in the way we go about engaging with business and brands – and the way they engage with us.

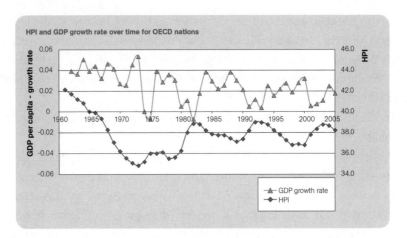

Figure 19: Wellbeing vs GDP. Reproduced by permission of the new economics foundation (nef).

After forty pages of bleak but compelling evidence that we're chasing the wrong dream in GDP, at the end of its Happy Planet Index 2.0 report, the UK's nef turns to slightly more optimistic thoughts. They highlight a series of initiatives that point to what they call 'a happier planet'. These include a community in Scotland that has come together to part own a wind farm in conjunction with the developers; The Big Lunch, which is a UK-wide initiative to get neighbours to sit down and eat together in a string of street parties for one day over the summer; and a council estate in Luton (UK) that has partnered with tea-growers in Southern India to go beyond fair trade for those workers.[83]

These are all wonderful examples of members of communities taking the initiative to reach out and challenge the status quo, and all for more positive, virtuous outcomes. This is not individualism at play, but some rediscovered sense of awareness. And that's not to say that brands cannot be instrumental in this change. Approached in the right way, and with the appropriate motives, brands can drive through this transition. As it happens, The Big Lunch is an initiative only made possible with the might and creativity of some of the UK's most prominent brands.

Looking more closely at the examples given above, one common theme runs through all of them. They are all driven by rising stocks in social capital. Whether it's a combination of bonding and linking capital in the case of the

Scottish wind farm project, bonding capital in the case of The Big Lunch, or bridging and linking capital in the case of the Southern Indian tea-growers, social capital, it seems, is central and crucial to us finding more durable, innovative and outright enjoyable ways to be sustainable (even restorative).

All of these examples support the argument that underneath all of our current problems lies the denudation of social capital; that the replenishment and nourishment of social capital will lead us towards more sustainable outcomes. What's more, these examples represent to us just some of the many green shoots we're seeing of the arrival of the Era of Social Capital Rising. The question, though, is how can brands be more instrumental, more central, in this inexorable process of change?

Where the first part of this book rattled through the briefest history of brands in an attempt to highlight how social capital and these alleviators of 'provenance costs' were inextricably linked from the off, this second part has attempted to focus on how that heritage is still in play today, shaping how brands interact with the audiences and how they attempt to 'guide' us in the myriad purchasing decisions we seem to face every day.

In the context of sustainability, we've argued that brands seem, in the main at least, hell-bent on reaching out to their constituents with a message predicated on transparency and data: that accountability is everything and the brand needs to step up to this responsible role, as faithful interpreter of its guardian's endeavours.

The result is a sea of conflicting, ambiguous and often unfathomable information, which fills us with dread and concern at the mountain of trade-offs and opportunity costs that loom with what will undoubtedly be the wrong decision made. This current approach from brands is cracking open the scale and complexity of the issues to the point that we consumers literally *cannot* make the right choice.

And as we have shown, when faced with these sorts of dilemmas, we prefer to walk away, making our choices on more palatable, simpler and emotional criteria. It seems there could be almost no more ineffective a way for brands to be trying to engage us around these issues. We've built the most perfectly unsustainable model possible for communication around sustainability.

The rationale for brands behaving in this way is not so hard to fathom: brands and marketing have always suffered from a slight inferiority complex when it comes to the other, more established (and defined) corporate functions, so the opportunity to be needed is simply too great to pass up, even if it does mean becoming what we believe many see as thin, brittle and even false messengers.

Brands may also be reluctant to engage in this debate in any other way for the simple fact that it is just too complex to do anything other than narrowly focus on the incremental, operations-led advances from the firm. As we discussed in the first part, brand communications need to be pithy and ballistic in order to get any sort of cut-through, and if there's one topic that doesn't lend itself to such a process, it has to be this thing we're wrapping up as sustainability.

But we are adamant that brands need to break this 'transparency habit' and invest instead in sense-making narratives. Narratives that allow audiences to filter, sort and bias alternatives, removing many of the trade-offs and opportunity costs that swirl around us in our decision-making milieu; narratives that are shaped and told by audiences, often away from the brand.

As well as helping us all to make better decisions, this also has to be the most effective route to more lasting cut-through. It's tricky enough as it is, but in the context of sustainability, the propensity to be paralysed with trade-offs and then held hostage with buyer's remorse from near-endless 'what ifs' and opportunity costs increases exponentially. Brands have to make the process simpler and more attractive.

To achieve this, brands need fundamentally to re-evaluate not only the way they tend to behave, in terms of leaning on data and transparency in this area, but also the way they encourage *us* to behave. The constant preoccupation on expanding choice, and making best decision from that choice, is not only unworkable in this context, but is continuing the denudation of our social capital. We are spending more and more time disconnected from more balanced social exchange, instead focused on more and more complex purchase decisions, of which we're encouraged to take greater and greater control.

Many of the behaviours of brands, and the behaviours they provoke amongst consumers, are fundamentally bad for balanced and healthy stocks of social capital. And this is only exacerbated when we get into the sustainability debate, with its flaws, inconsistencies and myriad trade-offs. Now is not a time to be cosying up to the more traditional functions within the business (who have had a pretty torrid time of it lately too, it has to be said), but instead it is a time for marketing and branding to step out and play the role we need them to play. As we've tried to argue, maximising needs to give way to satisficing, consumers need to give way to citizens (who consume) and brands need to engage genuinely in collaboration with their audiences. In short, brands have to understand that their role is to create value *in a fundamentally new way*. Value that is discovered, nurtured and sustained in networks often away from the brand's corporate guardian; value that emerges from, and gives rise to, new networks with stronger dialogue, shared thinking and trust; value that can only come from being genuinely valued.

Whilst this sense of dispersion and loss of control will fill many with dread, for those with foresight and vision it will seem an obvious evolutionary step. Brands will remain a symbol of the trust one has in a promise to deliver value. But that value is now more complex, temporal, contextual and subtle.

To meet these emerging value needs and wants, emotion has never been more important, engaging us with the issues in the most enduring way and removing a reliance on analytical trade-off analysis, thanks to potent and trusted emotional biases. Pulling this off will credit brands with an unassailable role in rebalancing our lives, so relieving many of the chronic symptoms we face as social capital starts to rise and rebalance.

It is these criteria that this new breed of brands will meet, and they will do so through a well-planned and executed Social Capital Strategy. Social Equity Brands will understand the unwavering importance of building a balanced and healthy long-term stock of social capital, since it is this social capital that will provide the most effective context within which we can all make sense of the challenges we face, and within which we will be able to find more dynamic, imaginative and enduring solutions.

In short, it is within that deeper, broader stock that these brands will uncover new opportunities to create value (to their and society's mutual benefit). As Rowan Williams, Archbishop of Canterbury here in the UK, says, we need to go beyond the relationships and exchanges that only take place within defined and structured markets, and instead '. . . we need to focus on all of the "unproductive activity" – it is these extra things that make us human'.[84]

Social capital is a barometer and celebration of these 'extra things'. And we need more of them.

Which leads us to the next part of our narrative.

We've already introduced certain elements of it, and highlighted how its rise, fall and lop-sidedness can affect us all. We've argued that it represents the very machinery and function of our societies – the 'engine bolts' holding the right parts together, and the 'engine oil' allowing the right parts to move without friction or damage. We've argued that it is the very thing without which brands – and we – cannot survive.

But what exactly is social capital?

Where does it come from, how is it maintained, nourished and destroyed? And why is it really that important to us all? These are the questions we will attempt to answer next. The answers are important for three reasons. Firstly, an understanding and appreciation of social capital helps us see beyond reactive and piecemeal sustainability efforts, by focusing on the root cause of our current problems. Second, through focusing on social capital, brands have the opportunity to become more than just shrill cheerleaders of sustainability endeavours, and instead genuine engines of value creation within society. And third, brands have neglected social capital to our, and ultimately their, disadvantage – because without social capital, brands simply fail. It is their oxygen, their sunlight, their host. In their haste to establish overpowering relationships with consumers for the short term, it seems this key aspect has been marginalised.

As such, getting to grips with social capital from the perspective of the brand is probably the most important and strategic market analysis any forward-thinking brand can undertake.

Part III

The Elixir of Life – Literally. Why We Depend on Social Capital

This whole book is about the importance of social capital – its importance for *our* general successful functioning and, more specifically, in the very near future for the successful functioning of brands.

We've argued that the myriad problems we currently face – problems that are lumped together under the catch-all of sustainability – are as a direct result of a prolonged period of low social capital. This is the period we've labelled the Era of Social Capital Waning. We've tried to build the argument that 'unsustainability' is a symptom – albeit chronic – of a deeper malaise, and that the denudation of social capital lies at the root of the problem.

The sustainability debate has, pretty much up until this point, focused on communicating the technicalities of the issues to consumers and nonspecialist audiences. These technicalities may be about the actual science of climate change, such as apocalyptic messages around ppm of CO_2, frozen methane in Siberia or the loss of biodiversity, or numbingly dull (to most) accounts around issues such as waste and recycling challenges and the minutiae of what the business is actually doing to address these issues.

So the debate is focused on either impending apocalypse on such a grand scale as to be almost too large to comprehend, or on the little detail, so fine and fiddly as to be almost too granular to make a meaningful difference.

To us, both routes are flawed in terms of delivering to consumers or employees what would be most useful in helping them make sense of the debate. If we look back at the major milestones in consumers encouraging or challenging business to adopt more sustainable practices, it has never been as a direct result of either apocalyptic vision or forensic analysis. It has been because of a groundswell of social capital: a groundswell that not only allowed the information to be shared, but for it to be understood and contextualised.

And this is our argument: that whilst some communication delivers information to audiences, where there is also high social capital that information is *meaningful*. In its right form, and in the right context, it becomes the catalyst for action.

Rising social capital helps audiences sift and filter data and information in order to find what is appropriate to them and the issues at hand. Rising social capital is, then, an incredible tool for, and by-product of, the democratisation of information and knowledge. Rising social capital allows for a re-evaluation as to what costs or audiences can be credibly and fairly externalised or marginalised in the exchanges and understanding that take place.

In actual fact, when we talk about the Era of Social Capital Waning, we should really call it the Era of Social Capital Waning and Lop-sidedness. Not only has social capital generally diminished over the last sixty-odd years (but with significant changes starting way before then, as a result of the Industrial Revolution), but it has also bent itself out of shape. As we proposed back in Chapter 1, brands – in their attempt to fill an emerging void created by mass industrialisation, migration and specialisation – offered up a form of plastic social capital, as a fillip to assuage the rise in what we called 'provenance costs' as a result of these dramatic and seismic changes unfolding across society.

The result was a distortion of social capital, with natural checks and measures removed. From this intense and exclusive relationship that grew rapidly between brand and consumer, we've argued the seeds were sewn for greater levels of maximising behaviour within that relationship. This 'lack of balance' in the machinery and process of social capital supports the argument that it is a complex, dynamic and multifaceted phenomenon, and contributes to an additional argument that it is one that is not always harmonious and constructive – an argument that we will look at in more detail in this part of the book.

Whilst social capital has emerged as a hot topic in policy language, its relevance or contribution to commercial life – and specifically its impact on brands and branding – appears to be relatively undiscovered. Considering its central role in both what we see as the fundamental cause of our current state *and* the rejuvenation and reinvention of brands and branding, we recognise the need to explore it further. As such, we believe we're in new, uncharted but exciting territory.

In this section, we'll look more closely at what are recognised as the different forms of social capital – bonding, bridging and linking – and how their relationship and interaction, whilst not always harmonious, are essential for a healthy society and business environment. We will also explore the different strands to each type of social capital – structural, cognitive and relational – and explore how these different elements do not necessarily present themselves in equal measure in different situations, nor necessarily follow on from each other.

Finally, we explore why social capital is even worth focusing on. We'll look at the arguments around what it potentially delivers to host societies, as well as empirical evidence that suggests it shapes economic as well as social vibrancy and health. We'll then apply those arguments to the world of business and brands, and in doing so start to look at what architectural considerations need to be acknowledged, at the firm and brand level, to ensure the sustainable generation of social capital within the business environment.

Social capital, it seems, is at the very centre of the myriad challenges, crises and transformations that are playing out around us. Its demise has created a panoply of issues, and its re-emergence as a phenomenon of intense scrutiny and anticipation is in danger of promising a panacea to cure all societal ills. As we've started to show, social capital is not just a fancy piece of jargon for policymakers the world over, but represents a crucial lens through which brands can glimpse the opportunities that lie ahead. But its apparent boundless ability to cure all ills hints at the danger of blindly relying on it without thought and caution. A deeper understanding of objectives, and a coherent and relevant strategy to reach those objectives, is vital.

As business and brands now find themselves at such a crucial crossroads in terms of validity, legitimacy and durability, we would argue that whichever route they choose to take into these uncharted territories, their destination, ultimately, has to be one of high social capital.

Chapter 7

Social capital, despite its popularity in sociology and policy circles, is not a new concept. In various forms, and with various labels, commentators and researchers have looked on with curiosity for hundreds, if not thousands, of years. The University of Toronto's Barry Wellman describes our long (but not always smooth) love affair with the topic:

> 'It is likely pundits have worried about the impact of social change on communities ever since human beings ventured beyond their caves. In the last two centuries many leading social commentators have been gainfully employed suggesting various ways in which large scale social changes associated with the Industrial Revolution may have affected the structure and operation of communities . . .'[85]

One of the most famous advocates of the study of social capital was Alexis de Toqueville, the young French sociologist who studied societal make-up in various countries at the start of the nineteenth century. Having toured southern Italy, he recorded such high levels of duplicity and 'moral degradation' that '. . . murder was considered a right'.[86] Whilst this may have been construed as a failure of social capital to banish these destructive practices (and there really is nothing more destructive than murder, we suppose), we could easily argue that these practices flourished as a result of *too much* of one type of social capital. To use the analogy we introduced earlier, where social capital can act as the 'engine bolts' to hold society together (as opposed to the 'engine oil' that reduces friction when elements need to combine), in these cases, the bolts were way too tight. The continued presence of Cosa Nostra in

Sicily is a timely reminder of what happens when the bolts refuse to be loosened.

A few years after his damning report of Italy, de Toqueville travelled to the US, where he had a wholly different experience. Here he noticed how a profound commitment to self-interest led to an unswerving desire to cooperate, in order to better satisfy that self-interest:

> 'Americans enjoy explaining almost every act of their lives on the principle of self-interest properly understood . . . it gives them great pleasure to point out how an enlightened self-love continually leads them to help one another and disposes them freely to give part of their time and wealth for the good of the state.'[87]

A quick search online of academic papers listing social capital as a key word pretty well illustrates its rising popularity over the last twenty years. Up until 1981 the total number of journal articles referencing the term totalled 20; between 1991 and 1995 the number rose to 109; and between 1996 and 1999 the number had climbed to more than 1000.[88] More than this, in the last ten years it has started to establish a strong foothold outside of these academic and professional circles, being embraced by mainstream media.

We're all for the wider recognition, exploration and understanding of social capital, and all its foibles, as this helps the vital transition to seeing it as an issue of importance and opportunity for business and its brands. But with the glaring sunlight of wider recognition come further challenges. The very term social capital seems so concise yet powerful, there's a real danger it'll be pulled and tugged in various directions to give meaning and justification to too broad a range of issues, hypotheses and action plans, stretching itself meaningfully thin in the process. Social capital is in danger of suffering the same fate of near immediate exhaustion as 'sustainability' in the communications context. Sustainability has been used to such an extent in brand communications that it has been rendered thread-bare before most audiences even got to feel the fabric in the first place. One of the leading contemporary academics, Michael Woolcock, expresses this concern, arguing, '. . . [social capital] risks trying to explain too much with too little and is being adopted indiscriminately, adapted uncritically, and applied imprecisely . . .'[89]

Social capital, then, is in danger of being packaged and promoted to a degree that ignores its complexities, ambiguities and dynamism. As such, the need to tightly conceptualise and define it is paramount.

Social capital defined

Despite its widespread use, a single definition of social capital proves elusive. What potentially makes a working definition harder is the fact that social capital has never actually been measured or studied over time. Instead, datasets originally designed for other purposes have ended up being re-sliced and re-diced in order to uncover and explore trends in social capital. As Robert Putnam[90] suggests, social capital researchers struggle with the same issues that face global warming scientists, in that no-one was focusing on creating consistent datasets all those years (millennia) ago. As a result, both sets of researchers have to 'triangulate' data in order to capture a sufficiently accurate and consistent picture in periods gone by.

Despite these challenges, it's fair to say that social capital is essentially a focus on relationships, reciprocity and networks. Putnam quotes L.J. Hanifan, a West Virginia state supervisor of rural schools in 1916, as providing a broad definition of social capital that in his opinion captures the clear majority of components:

> '(Social capital refers to) . . . those intangible substances that count for most in the daily lives of people: namely good will, fellowship, sympathy and social intercourse among the individuals and families who make up a social unit . . . The individual is helpless socially, if left to himself . . . If he comes into contact with his neighbour, and they with other neighbours, there will be an accumulation of social capital, which may immediately satisfy his social needs and which may bear a social potentiality sufficient to the substantial improvement of living conditions in the whole community. The community as a whole will benefit by the cooperation of all its parts, while the individual will find in his associations the advantages of the help, the sympathy, and the fellowship of his neighbours.'[91]

A key aspect captured in this emerging definition is the public and private benefits that are associated with social capital. In other words, social capital has positive externalities, being not only of benefit to the protagonist, but also the bystander. French social theorist, and co-responsible for bringing social capital to a more mainstream audience, Pierre Bourdieu offers up this definition:

'Social capital is the aggregate of actual or potential resources which are linked to possession of a durable network of more or less institutionalised relationships of mutual acquaintance and recognition.'[92]

So what is starting to emerge is a definition that focuses on value as a result of some action of aggregation. In other words, social capital – as a resource from which to derive value – resides not with the individual, *but with the network*.

Social capital can also take either formal or informal forms. Well-defined institutions such as professional associations can create considerable levels of social capital in a more formal environment, whereas the crowd you regularly meet for a drink on the way home on a Friday gives rise to social capital in an altogether more informal but equally important context.

At the more formal end of the scale, the World Bank and the OECD commit considerable resources to understanding, measuring and nourishing social capital, and in doing so have created their own working definitions. The World Bank believes social capital:

'. . . refers to the institutions, relationships and norms that shape the quality and quantity of a society's social interactions . . . Social capital is not just the sum of the institutions that underpin a society – it is the glue that holds them together.'[93]

The OECD, along similar lines, defines it as:

'. . . networks together with shared norms, values and understandings that facilitate co-operation within or among groups.'[94]

Two interesting insights emerge from these overlapping definitions. Firstly, they suggest the 'clubbiness' of social capital; the propensity to know other people's business and to spot immediately when something starts to operate out of an established order.

Second, the World Bank definition draws attention to one of the thorny issues with trying to measure social capital, in saying it is not 'just the sum of the institutions that underpin a society'. We've already established that social capital as a resource from which to derive value resides within the network and not at the hands of any particular agent, but this World Bank definition goes even further, in suggesting that even summing the component parts within society fails to capture accurately the qualitative value of the phenomenon.

Amongst these fragments of definition, we can glimpse the complexity of the concept. In each case, we find ourselves having to insert the caveat that the definition may be more appropriate for certain types of social capital. In an attempt to embrace this complexity, sociologist James Coleman suggests that:

> 'social capital is defined by its function. It is not a single entity, but a variety of different entities, having two characteristics in common: they consist of some aspect of a social structure, and they facilitate certain actions of individuals who are within the structure.'[95]

All of these definitions point to a multifaceted phenomenon – one that is immediately engaging and promising as some undergirding operating system for society, within which we can potentially rewrite small bits of code for extraordinary benefit. But at the same time, almost beyond reach of traditional research and analysis methods.

What is beyond question, however, is its importance to the smooth running, protection, growth and development of society. And this smooth running is reliant on a recognition of network, reciprocity and mutual norms; in other words, interconnectedness.

It's not that frequently we hear of businesses or their brands genuinely embracing interconnectedness. Just think of the rhetoric and metaphors in use – at the business level, stakeholders are there to be managed, and at the brand level, consumers are still, more often than not, there to be targeted. The sad truth is that brands and their corporate guardians are still not that great at genuine interconnectedness. Quite the opposite. But this new breed of brands is. They know they have to be.

Having grazed on a number of definitions of social capital, drawn from the fields of political science and sociology, we've worked to create our own definition as we feel it relates to businesses and their brands. From our perspective, social capital – in the context of brands – can be defined as:

> 'The quality, depth, breadth and frequency of brand-inspired dialogue, exchange and interaction that occurs within a community. It is the benefits – both private (to the brand) and public (to the community) – that are generated as a result. And it is the resultant collective ability to maintain and enhance these processes and benefits.'

What we believe brands should focus on in this definition are the four descriptors in the first line – quality, depth, breadth and frequency. Whilst many brands prioritise the last, we believe most neglect the first three. The result is arguably plenty of chatter, but not very much social capital.

The question now, though, is having arrived at a working definition of social capital as we feel it applies to brands and their messaging and communication, what makes up this social capital? We've alluded to the various forms earlier in the book, and that they have different strengths and weaknesses. But it is worth exploring in more detail the three principal types of social capital, what they are best suited to do and how their relationships are far from static or harmonious.

Forms of social capital

We've likened the different types of social capital to either the 'engine bolts' holding key parts of society together or the 'engine oil' allowing other parts to work alongside each other without too much wear and tear. Both of these functions are needed in society, and especially today's, as it spins around us faster and faster, pushing us further and further towards the edges of this societal centrifugal drum.

But engine bolts can sheer if overtightened, and lubricants can fail if left too long without a change. In other words, too much of the stuff or too little maintenance can cause a problem. And so it is, it seems, with social capital and the efficiency and smooth running of communities and society. We have talked already about the plastic capital fillip brands offered in response to increasing provenance costs for emerging consumers. Specifically it mim-

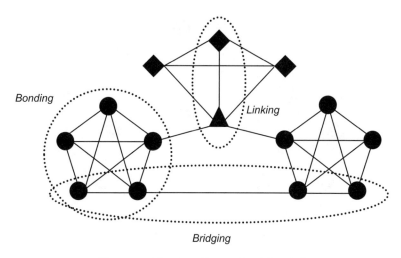

Figure 20: The three forms of social capital

icked what is labelled 'bonding social capital' and, as we'll explain, this is a very different creature to the other forms of social capital, namely 'bridging' and 'linking' (see Figure 20).

Bonding Social Capital

Bonding social capital is the tightest, and probably most easily identifiable, form of social capital. It's the 'engine bolt' variety we talk of. Bonding social capital is what exists between you and your family (hopefully), or you and others with whom you spend plenty of time, share plenty of routines, and trust. Your work environment may be a rich source of bonding social capital (if you're lucky), or your local football team or even your local pub quiz team. Bonding social capital can be either formal or informal. And bonding social capital has some characteristics that are unique compared to other forms of social capital. For a start, where there's often high bonding social capital, there is often a high degree of homogeneity amongst the members of the group.

Bonding social capital is extremely valuable, and something that we crave, based on the effectiveness of brands to mimic the relationships it gives rise to. But bonding social capital can also be damaging, or certainly unreliable, giving rise to moments when the 'engine bolts' are too tight. We mentioned Alexis de Toqueville's observations of life in Southern Italy and the culture

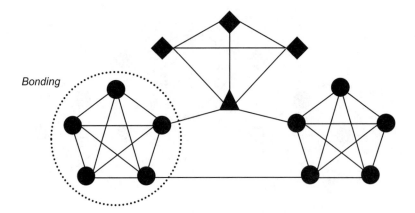

Figure 21: Bonding capital.

that condoned murder: it is extremely high levels of bonding social capital that allows the Cosa Nostra to continue to function, offering immense protection and privilege for those within it, but less wonderful benefits for those outside of it. When looked at through the social capital lens, the Mafia is a striking example of what happens when one aspect of social capital grows without check and to the detriment of other forms.

To reiterate, it has not been purely the waning of social capital that has given rise to so many problems, nor is a brute increase in social capital a guarantee of answers. Social capital has to be nourished and encouraged to grow in a coordinated, concerted way. Bonding capital – as a key part of this mix – is unique and intriguing.

Back in the 1980s I took three sociology courses as part of my first degree, and had the accidental good fortune to focus on the sociology of war – a course run by Dr Tony Ashworth.[96] As well as offering a timely antidote to the economics elsewhere, Tony Ashworth's work was interesting for his focus on the World War I truces that broke out amongst the front line trenches. Made famous by the Christmas truces of 1914, where soldiers would climb out of their trenches and play football, share a cigarette and swap stories, in reality the scale and frequency of the truces were even more impressive. In fact, they were happening with such frequency, high command on both sides of the war started to wonder how they could maintain the necessary levels of combat. In other words, how they could actually keep their soldiers fighting. Various methods were used, such as enforcing a number of rounds that had to be fired, but in each case the troops found novel work-arounds, such as always firing at the same time of day, and at the same target.

What these trench truces demonstrated was the power of bonding social capital. These troops, technically each other's enemy, but separated only by metres and sharing routines, not to mention discomfort and a general sense of 'we're all in this' (homogeneity), were quick to develop almost unshakeable bonds. In this instance, bonding social capital certainly did not behave the way their respective high commands wanted it to. Our desire to establish such bonding capital, and to enjoy its benefits, seems innate.

The way the generals finally broke what they saw as a collapse of authority and rise in anomie amongst the trenches also highlights a key quality of social capital – the belief in reciprocity. To destroy the climate of the truces, high command demanded blisteringly aggressive raids seemingly at random. The influence of what was seen as an intervention from an outside entity disrupted the established confidence of reciprocity, and quickly dismantled the bonds that existed between the trenches. It was the reassertion of another form of social capital – linking capital – over bonding capital. As we will discuss later, this conflict or competition that can arise between different forms of social capital is an important consideration when attempting to stimulate its overall development.

Bridging Social Capital

Bridging social capital is different to bonding social capital, since where the latter exists between members of homogenous groups, the former acts as a bridge between distinct groups. Whereas bonding capital reinforces shared practices, norms and general similarities, bridging capital can bring together distinct communities, where each community has its own set of norms, codes and practices. Bridging capital is very important, since it encourages under-standing and an appreciation of differing opinions. Bridging social capital is a part of what we've described as the 'engine oil' in society, in that it helps introduce moving parts in a way that reduces the amount of friction. A good example of the creation of bridging capital is the effects of a wedding and the subsequent marriage.[97] The union of the husband and wife brings together

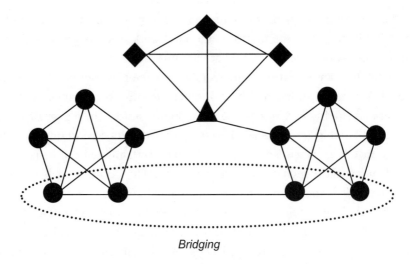

Bridging

Figure 22: Bridging capital.

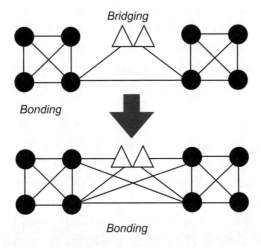

Figure 23: Bridging capital evolving to bonding capital

his personal community, rich in bonding capital (family, friends, colleagues, etc) with hers. And in time, as more and more members of each community recognise similarities in the other, so this bridging capital starts to morph into bonding capital, since the sense of homogeneity starts to widen (see Figure 23).

Bridging capital, then, is a crucial tool with which to lower barriers between distinct communities, regardless of how or why these communities are distinct. Considering the contextual and regional complexities and impacts of sustainability issues, it is immediately striking how constructive brands could be in building bridging capital between distinct audiences, providing engaging insight into similar or complementary norms, codes and practices.

Linking Social Capital

Linking social capital is really an extension of bridging capital, in that where bridging capital represents the connections between disparate, but what we could call 'horizontally equivalent', groups, linking capital is captured in the links between disparate groups that are in some way vertically – or hierarchically – separated. Examples of this would be between elements of civil society and governments, or local action groups and either national or trans-national bodies. Linking capital is the form of social capital that can exist most effectively over wider geographical and cultural distances and often works hand in hand with bridging capital.

With this particular capability in mind, it is easy to see how linking capital is a key pillar in sustainable development, if we consider that many of the sustainability issues have arisen from globalisation, and the subsequent marginalisation of audiences and externalisation of costs.

Linking capital, in its purest and theoretical form, allows two things to happen. Firstly, it allows remote communities to realise the full value of their local assets on the world stage – assets that may not be particularly highly valued locally. And second, linking capital allows distant audiences access to the practices occurring at the local level. So linking capital can play a significant part in alleviating poverty and raising standards at the same time.

An example of linking capital at work – and a company being the creator of the capital, as it happens – is described by Boutilier[98] in his work on stakeholder politics. Boutilier cites researchers who investigated the work carried out by an international firm to develop more effective cotton yields from farmers in West Africa. Through introducing new growing techniques, the firm worked through the local government officials (who were also the landowners, with tenanted farmers) to deliver these developments to farmers

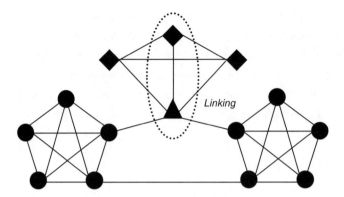

Figure 24: Linking capital

across the region. The result was higher organic cotton yields, resulting in better conditions and incomes for the tenant farmers, better returns for the landowners and a higher quality, more stable supply of cotton for the international firm. The international firm had managed to build linking capital between the farmers and their own business, releasing a lot of the latent value in growing and harvesting organic cotton effectively. But more than this, by working with the local government, the firm had also leveraged its stocks of bonding and bridging capital (across farms and communities) to generate greater results.

This example highlights the need for all three types of capital to be working in harmony, to really deliver results on alleviating the issues facing society. That said, research shows that linking capital is particularly good at unlocking the potential of closed rural communities for the creation of value.[99]

Bonding, bridging and linking capital, then, all have their own unique qualities and all act in different ways to deliver an overall level of social capital to communities and groups. Bonding capital is our 'engine bolt' capital and helps keep tight communities working well, with lower crime for example. Bridging capital, in comparison, is a form of 'engine oil' and contributes to the banishing of exclusion and prejudices. And finally, linking capital offers the vital connection that allows distinct communities to interact via governmental or international trading platforms. So it's not a simple need to bolster aggregated social capital to alleviate our problems and find innovative solutions at source: it's a need to nourish all distinct forms in a harmonised and coordinated way, allowing each 'flavour' of social capital to do what it does best.

The vital roles brands can play to increase these levels is becoming more and more apparent. To reiterate, brands' capabilities to create abundant stocks of bonding social capital have already been demonstrated, to the point of the bonding fillip becoming intoxicating to those involved.

But what they haven't done a good job at, to date, is building all three forms of capital in a coordinated and complementary way. Fanatically focusing on one form of capital for the short-term gain of those involved in the exclusive bilateral relationship is what we refer to as the low-grade social debt that brands have historically used to supposedly encourage social capital. What we need now is long-term, high-grade investments – equity investments – and these can only happen when brands recognise the multilateral nature of these relationships, made possible by developing and utilising all forms of social capital, for the long term.

This is the role of the Social Equity Brand. This is the *opportunity* spotted by the Social Equity Brand.

However, before leaping in to replenish levels of social capital – whether bonding, bridging or linking – we should poke around a little to understand in more detail what actually makes up each type of social capital. We've looked at the physiology of social capital in terms of the interplay between the various forms and what can happen when it all becomes a little lop-sided. But what about the anatomy of social capital?

Regardless of capital type, social capital has three main ingredients that combine to determine the quality of the capital, and these ingredients give rise to two immediate reactions. Firstly, each of them is wholly within the grasp of progressive brands to influence and stimulate. And second, each is a vital contributor to, and indicator of, the health of any brand.

Again, it seems social capital and brands are intertwined.

Strands of social capital

Despite the broad range of opinions on what constitutes social capital, where it comes from, what it can deliver and what happens when it starts to

Figure 25: Social capital development process

disappear, there seems to be more consensus on what it is fundamentally made up of. Leading researchers and academics Nahapiet and Ghoshal[100] set out what has to be one of the clearest breakdowns of social capital elements, with their three dimensions of social capital: structural, cognitive and relational.

As we've already touched on, the structural dimension relates to actual dialogue and exchange that takes place between individuals or actors. In many ways the structural element represents the initiation of social capital, whether that be bonding, bridging or linking, which is then amended and enhanced through the other dimensions. As such, we've chosen to depict Nahapiet and Ghoshal's classification as a process model, rather than as distinct or independent dimensions (see Figure 25). We're fully aware this may be a somewhat blasé interpretation of their theoretical framework, but we feel it a valuable exercise, since at a practical brand management level, embarking on this process helps ensure the adequate foundations are laid for the creation of high quality social capital by the brand.

The structural – or 'talking' – phase is naturally one that all brands focus on: it represents the output of marketing and communication efforts for the brand. Many agencies are still rewarded by the sheer amount of talking the brand is credited with. But of course, to really cut through the cacophony of competing messages, the sheer volume of speech is just one element. In addition, brands need to focus on how they say what they want to communicate. As Heath and Feldwick say, '. . . how you say it is more important than what you say'.[101] The emotional/rational discussion that persists in marketing circles takes on an additional importance in the context of social capital, since our process view of Nahapiet and Ghoshal's work shows how the outputs of the structural (talking) phase lead on to both cognitive (thinking) outcomes and relational (trust) outcomes.

To reiterate, we believe a hard reliance on the transparency approach is denying the brand the opportunity to develop far greater levels of social capital, and the benefits that flow from that social capital. Why? Well, it relates to the relationship between transparency and trust and the potential confusion or even disappointment that the former can generate in this context. In the simplest of terms, if you know everything there is to know about someone, is there then any *need* to trust them? Isn't trust a highly valued substitute for transparency – one that we often crave *in place* of transparency?

The point is this: the underpinning of the structural dialogue phase – the tenets upon which it is predicated – can have profound effects on the subsequent generation of the other key components of social capital. Think back to the Pepsi and Walmart examples earlier – the former with its Refresh campaign, and the latter with its Sustainability Index: which one – as a dialogue primer – is likely to lead to higher levels of the cognitive and relational dimensions within Nahapiet and Ghoshal's theoretical model? We'd wager the former.

We're convinced the structural dimension is the gateway for the development of social capital: without it, there are no foundations upon which the other elements that improve the quality of social capital can position themselves. But even where the structural dimension is well developed, it does not necessarily follow that there are rich stocks of well-developed social capital. In other words, a commitment to talking is no guarantee of thinking and trusting.

This may sound obvious, but when the structural dimension is shown graphically with the other two dimensions (see Figure 26), it is striking how many brands are stuck in this trap: where sheer volume of contact and communication is assumed to be a suitable proxy for quality of exchange. In this matrix, Boutilier[102] shows what he calls a 'conflicted relationship' when there's high contact and communication but low 'mutual trust and understanding'. Overlaying where we believe most brand conversations sit today, that's a pretty dismal way to describe the type of relationship most brands have with the bulk of their established consumers. Actually it's not a relationship – or certainly not one you'd value. Away from sustainability, looking at brands through the social capital lens can shine a light on what previously was assumed to be satisfactory, and illuminate it as a gaping inadequacy in the brand's communication and engagement strategy.

Two other interesting observations emerge from this graphical representation of the relationship between the structural, and the relational and

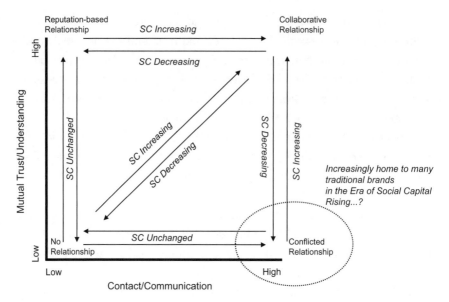

Figure 26: 'Relationship matrix'. Reproduced by permission of Greenleaf Publishing.

cognitive. Firstly, if brands genuinely want to collaborate with their audiences to ensure as much and as varied a supply of value is unlocked in the experience, then there is no alternative but to strive for high social capital relationships. It is only with high levels of all three dimensions that these 'collaborative relationships' can be sustained.

Second, there are two directions in which relationships can move within the graph that result in neither increases nor decreases in levels of social capital. From a high contact but conflicted relationship to one where the relationship collapses, there is no further loss of social capital – this reinforces the weak position of the conflicted relationship in the first place. And from no relationship to a 'reputation-based relationship', despite the rise in the relational and cognitive aspects, still there is no increase in social capital *within that relationship*. In other words, in the absence of brand-instigated communication and exchange, this reputation-based relationship is delivering nothing to the relationship between the brand and that specific audience. In fact, in this case, it is almost certain that social capital is rising in the relationship between that audience and the third party that is nurturing (or challenging) that reputation.

The consequence is this: even if brands are not considered to be instrumental in a particular issue or concern, the act of stimulating dialogue and exchange around this topic can lead to an increase in social capital between themselves and the audience. To put it bluntly: if you don't have anything to say, someone else almost certainly will.

Chapter 8

We started this book with a comment that the last thing anyone now needed was another book on sustainability and branding; that new titles seem to be coming out on this combination of topics with alarming frequency. But if there's one topic that seems to trump these in terms of corporate and management literature column inches, it has to be trust. That said, as was the case with combining sustainability and branding, we believe there are perspectives to the trust debate that deserve more attention. We hope we've still something to add to this part of the debate, especially considering the central importance of trust not only to social capital, but to brands themselves.

As we covered in the previous chapter, trust represents one of the three dimensions of social capital, and is the third stage in our process model of social capital development. Trust, we believe, develops and emerges as a result of the prolonged and consistent structural phase (dialogue) and the cognitive phase (thinking). Of course, each phase does not happen in isolation, and there are not clear breaks between each phase that mark the transition. But trust is essentially the end result of the previous two steps of the process, with the results then feeding back into the dialogue and thought phases (see Figure 27).

The concept of a brand is well known if not consistent, and definitions abound as to what exactly constitutes a brand. Amongst all of these viewpoints, one common element seems to surface consistently: that a brand encapsulates a promise, from the products or services that are bound by the brand, to those who are considering deriving value from them.

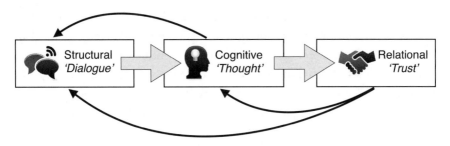

Figure 27: Social capital development process – feedback loops

Certainly a promise is a key part of what constitutes a brand – it is some form of assurance that what is physically representative of the brand has the qualities and advantages it says it has. We discussed in the earlier sections of the book how brands emerged as a short cut to appease what we labelled 'provenance costs' for consumers as a result of their being away from the trusted sources and environments that used to frame and contextualise their purchasing experiences; in these cases, the brand was certainly a promise or assurance.

But we would argue that a brand is more than a promise: that what makes a brand strong is not the promise it makes, but the faith we have in that promise.

Brands – strong brands with brand equity – are not the representation of a promise, but rather the representation of trust we have in that promise being kept.

Considering trust is so important to a brand, logic states then that brands are dependent on social capital, or certainly the processes at work within it. We believe this is the case – brands can only nurture trust amongst their audiences if they are instrumental in building suitably strong and valuable levels of dialogue and shared thinking. Historically that dialogue was primarily about the basic or utilitarian benefits that would flow to the user upon consumption or experience. It was a bilateral relationship, focused on the specific benefits of the product or service for the user in the context of very specific requirements. Again, we're circling the same argument that brands became proficient in building a certain form of social capital (bonding capital) on a certain kind of contained and controlled (bilateral and exclusive) relationship.

Today, however, that relationship is no longer bilateral or 'dyadic' (as we've discussed in the previous chapter) and is certainly no longer contained or controlled. What's more, the sources of value identified and sought by those who interact with the brand have exploded. Now consumers not only look for a wealth of hedonic outcomes at the moment of consumption or experience, but they apply some temporal filter to those wants and needs, meaning the brand has to embody different values at different times.

For example, let's take a cup of Starbucks Fairtrade certified coffee. As you walk up to the counter to buy the coffee on your way to work, your value-seeking antennae are far more sensitive and demanding now than they would have been just fifteen years ago in your search for a coffee on the way to the office. Back then, if the coffee was hot, with milk and sugar (if wanted) and in a fairly well-insulated cup, the job was done. But now, as you walk up to the counter, that cup of coffee has to meet a panoply of needs and wants. Yes, it still has to be hot, white, sweet and secure in an insulated (and very engineered) cup. But it also has to deliver on the value sought in terms of benefiting farmers and bean pickers in plantations on the other side of the world with better wages, training and education opportunities. In addition, it needs to assure you that the staff in that actual branch of Starbucks are being looked after; that any donations are going to the requisite local good causes; that the cup is as recyclable as possible; that the ground beans are recycled as nutrient-rich compost for the local urban garden project; and that Starbucks is operating in a wealth of other ways deemed to be important in being a model corporate citizen in a well-defined and constructive community. And that's before we've even touched on the music playing as we wait for it to be served, brought to us by Starbucks' own record label that ensures more of the revenues get back to the new musicians.

That's a whole lot of promise in just a cup of coffee – and one that will be finished by the time you reach the lobby of your office building.

But more than a blistering array of promises – not only about the experience you are going to have with the coffee, but that others have had in the long process to make that cup of coffee – it's a blistering array of conditions that have to be met with trust. For the Starbucks brand to deliver value to its corporate owner, it has to ensure you trust it to meet all those direct, vicarious and temporal value needs as you potter on, on your way to work. And all those strands of trust – that coalesce into an overall sense of trust towards the brand itself – need to be derived from a range of processes of dialogue and shared thinking: processes that will almost certainly be distinct, but that must also be complementary. The route to being valued is certainly complicated.

So whilst brands may have always been competent – excellent even – at building a certain form of dialogue (more often than not, a monologue) to meet certain types of needs and wants and a certain shared thinking (blunt brand loyalty in a bonding capital environment), what is required today is something altogether different.

The requirement for trust is as important as it's always been. But whereas in the (near) past, dialogue was needed to create trust in a very controlled and tight relationship – resulting in a narrow and giddy-making form of plastic social capital – now a whole different type of dialogue is needed, to provide trust across a range of criteria that combine to form a far more complete and stable social capital 'whole'. This is, after all, the Era of Social Capital Rising.

What, then, is trust?

The good news is that from where we stand, trust is the same today as it has always been. But that's not to say that it can be generated by recognising and meeting the same traditional criteria. In a hyper-connected and digitised world of empowered and mobile consumers and employees, everything a company does, whether at a corporate level or a brand level, says something to someone, who then repeats it to someone else, and on and on it goes. In short, everything communicates. As such, there needs to be consistency or at least reason behind that myriad of comments sloshing around about your brand. Without that, trust cannot develop and social capital around the brand cannot flourish.

In his influential book, *Trust – The Social Virtues and the Creation of Prosperity*, Francis Fukuyama defines trust as:

> '. . . the expectation that arises within a community of regular, honest and cooperative behaviour, based on commonly shared norms, on the part of other members of that community. Those norms . . . also

encompass secular norms like professional standards and codes of
behaviour.'[103]

There are two important aspects here. Firstly, there's the reference to
expectation. As we described in the context of a brand, this expectation is more
solid where trust is higher – an expected course of action moves from maybe,
through possibly and probably, to almost certainly, with correspondingly
higher levels of trust. So we can say that an antecedent of trust is anticipated
reciprocity. Trust is characterised by the expectation that certain behaviours
or interactions will be reciprocated in some way. If you go to your doctor, you
trust that your frankness, candour and willingness to listen to their expert
advice will be reciprocated with such expert advice. Similarly, in the context
of a relationship with a brand, you trust that your acceptance of the promise
being made by that brand is reciprocated with the delivery of those promised
benefits (and very possibly more on top). It is this trust in appropriate reciprocity that determines the ultimate goal of any brand and its management
team – brand equity. Brand equity amasses as the brand builds its reputation
to reciprocate consistently and appropriately in its relationships with those in
its audiences, be they consumers, employees or investors.

This leads us to the second interesting dimension of Fukuyama's definition, where he talks specifically about communities, and the expectation of
appropriate reciprocity in that environment. To put it another way, this definition focuses on the trust that develops from, and influences the behaviour of,
defined and homogenous groups. Where we've extrapolated his definition to
apply to the relationship between brands and their audiences, we are still
implying a tight, homogenous community; in other words, trust and its antecedents in a bonding capital environment.

But just as important is the creation of trust in far more fragmented
assemblies, such as community to community, or country to country. In these
cases reciprocity is still vital, in that trust still has the same anatomy. Rather
than being what social scientists call 'specific reciprocity', these more heterogeneous assemblies rely on 'general reciprocity'.[104] These variations in
reciprocity pretty much align with the parallel concepts of 'thin trust' and
'thick trust'.[105] The latter is the sort of trust that emerges from environments
where specific reciprocity is abundant – tight-knit homogenous communities,

including families. The former – thin trust, as a result of generalised reciprocity – is far harder to build and sustain, for the simple reasons that the same norms, codes and expectations find it harder to take root in those more fragmented and heterogeneous assemblies.

An example of generalised reciprocity and subsequent thin trust is when you step out on to a pedestrian crossing, even though there are two trucks steaming down the road towards you. Despite knowing you are no match for eighty tonnes of DAF engineering, your expectation is that they will stop to let you cross, based on a generalised rule that on the pedestrian crossing you have reasonable right of way, and your being on it will result in them reciprocating and recognising your rights. In other words, you trust the drivers of the trucks, albeit 'thinly'. Of course, we do not rely purely on this thin trust – the criminal consequences of mowing someone down (on a pedestrian crossing or not) – are significant. Laws are needed as a backstop in case codes, norms and expectations flex just a little too much.

The terms thick and thin trust are not ours, but are established terms in the social sciences, and can portray the wrong impression. Thin trust just doesn't sound as good or as meaningful as thick trust, but in actual fact it is arguably more important, not only because it is harder to establish and maintain, but because without it, we tend to remain in tight, homogenous units. If we go back to our engine analogy for social capital, without thin trust, we've no confidence to even try running the engine to see what interacts with what. A monopoly of thick trust would keep us solely focused on the engine bolts, ignoring the need for engine oil. Thin trust – and generalised reciprocity – is key to widening the horizons of society and giving us confidence to stride out and try new stuff with new people.

Of course, communities, companies and countries all interact – all have to interact – in our globalised world. But here's the interesting thing – where thin trust and generalised reciprocity are high, transaction costs reduce, allowing those relationships to function more efficiently. This idea of transaction costs in connection with trust, and more widely social capital, is one of the most compelling and well-documented arguments for attempting to build social capital. We'll return to this in far more detail in the next chapter, but many of the social and political scientists referenced thus far in this book[106] link higher levels of social capital to lower transaction costs and then to more productive societies. So a brand that is both capable of and credited with increasing levels of social capital could be a very valuable thing. To many people.

Companies, organisations, countries, any group in fact, has no choice but to interact today, so what happens when there isn't the appropriate rise in thin trust to accompany this increase in interaction and specifically expectation? Well, it's pretty easy to see. As an example, think back to the last time you boarded a train. Think about your experience at the station: buying a ticket; going through the barrier; waiting for the train; getting on the train; and then the train setting off. You probably bought the ticket from a kiosk where a sign said 'staff have the right to work without physical or verbal threats to their safety'; you put your ticket through the turnstile where maybe there were signs warning about travelling without a valid ticket; you stood on a platform with a yellow line painted eighteen inches from the platform edge, with the instruction not to stand beyond it, and walking on the tracks was, in fact, trespassing; you got on the train and had your ticket checked for the fare and date and were watched to make sure you didn't duck into the First Class carriage. And so it goes on.

All of these additional checks and measures are there to compensate for low thin trust and low generalised reciprocity. If the reciprocity and trust were higher, the fact that tickets were for sale should be enough for people to do the right thing and buy a ticket before boarding (and without threatening the person selling the ticket or insulting their mother). With high thin trust, there would be no need to stop people climbing on to the railway track as we'd respect others' property. And finally, with high levels of generalised reciprocity, the train company would not need to check your ticket or the carriage you're in, because they'd have confidence in you reciprocating their offer of travel with a ticket, by travelling in the right class.

Think about all the additional costs involved in this transaction between you and the train company. Certainly they are costs that they bear, because of their sense of low generalised reciprocity and thin trust, but ultimately their costs end up in your train fare. So no-one wins.

Actually, someone does win. Lawyers. Someone has to draw up all of those notices, formalise those penalties and then process them. If you're one of those people who has always secretly hated lawyers but couldn't quite pin down the reason why, well, this section's just for you. It looks like lawyers are the main beneficiaries of the reduction in generalised trust within the Era of Social Capital Waning.

We're not the first to spot the potential link between diminished generalised trust and a flourishing legal industry. In a paper for the World Bank, Robert Putnam[107] describes how he decided to see if there was a sufficiently strong (negative) correlation between numbers of lawyers and social capital in the US (assuming that thin trust and generalised reciprocity are antecedents to bridging and linking social capital). Putnam looked at the 'relative share of lawyering in the American economy', and in doing so established what he called 'Putnam's constant': that for the first 70 years of the twentieth century, there were 40 lawyers per 10 000 employees in the US (give or take one lawyer per year). The number was stable every year until the early 1970s, when it then started to climb. Today, that number has more than doubled to over 80 lawyers per 10 000 employees.

One immediate reaction to this statistic is to say that rather than being an illustration of the collapse of trust and social capital, it simply shows the rise in professional people over the latter half of the twentieth century, and as such should be applauded as a clear sign of the progression and prosperity within the US economy. Sadly, this is not the case. Putnam ran the same analysis for doctors and engineers, hoping to see, in the case of the former, some sense of parity in terms of doctors per lawyer over the years, and in the latter, even an increase, as society became more technologically advanced. But in both cases, the ratio dropped: the growth in lawyers has not been matched by growth in other professions. It really does seem lawyers are a good litmus test for the amount of trust, and consequently social capital, in our society.

The importance of trust in building social capital takes us back to the causality issue in our basic process model. On the one hand we are saying that trust is needed to stimulate social capital, since it encourages stronger, deeper dialogue and shared thinking. But on the other, we are saying that trust is the outcome of these processes. This circular relationship makes sense when we think about the practicalities of the real world: in environments where there are high levels of social capital, there are more opportunities to demonstrate trustworthiness. In those environments, because dialogue and shared thinking are more prevalent, so the chance to trust and be trusted goes

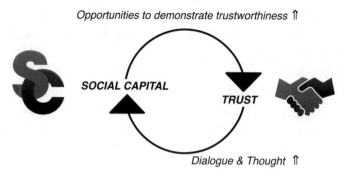

Figure 28: Social capital – trust virtuous circle

up. In this case, the trust–social capital relationship becomes a virtuous circle (see Figure 28). This is exactly what we see in various markets where the vicious circle of low trust and high transaction costs is 'cracked open' through some innovative action, often on the part of business.

In Kenya, the aptly-named Equity Bank[108] has done just this. When all other banks were leaving the region due to cripplingly high transaction costs and miserable margins, Equity Bank set out to find an alternative, effective business model. The bank's new management was driven by a desire to offer banking to all as a cornerstone of economic and social development. The resulting model saw the bank making loans to workers with the loan underwritten by neighbours and family. In other words, where there was no real financial collateral, the bank relied on social collateral. What was interesting was that as more and more micro-loans were made, so more businesses were started and so social capital stock levels started to rise – more dialogue, more shared thinking and more opportunities to demonstrate trustworthiness. So the bank managed to increase the overall supply of the very thing it was using to underwrite its loans. And it should be pointed out that this was not a semi-philanthropic endeavour from the bank – Equity Bank set out from day one to create a new business model that would allow the bank to make money. The result today is a bank opening more than 4000 new accounts a day, with more than 50% of the market share.[109] But the really startling statistic is its default rate: across the industry, the standard default rate on bank loans is close to 15%, but for Equity Bank it is only 3%.

This in a market considered to be too risky in which to operate by most other banks.

This 3% figure highlights the commercial benefits in terms of lower transaction costs, from nurturing higher levels of social capital and generalised trust. Equity Bank, it seems, is leveraging the renewed notion of 'credit' based on its original Latin origins, from the verb 'credere' – to believe.[110] This idea of belief – deep belief as a result of taking a genuine interest in those you interact with – represents a key component of a Social Capital Strategy.

The good news is that overall generalised trust in business seems to have inched a little higher in the last year or so. Edelman[111] data for 2010 show modest increases in the amount of trust people have in comments made by CEOs since the credit crunch and subsequent financial fall-out, although corporate communications and corporate or product advertising still bounce along the bottom, with only 17% of respondents considering them credible sources.[112]

We believe this somewhat sorry evaluation of trust in brands – both corporate and product – is a direct result of many of the issues we've already raised in this and previous chapters; that brands have been preoccupied with trying to nurture a bonding capital fillip, based on exclusivity, and largely ignorant of the majority of externalities. The result is a brittle, hollow relationship, utterly out of step with what internal and external audiences now want and expect.

Brands have to respond, and indeed have the power and ingenuity to embed confidence and expectation of reciprocity across a panoply of criteria in highly disparate communities. As we'll see in the next part of the book, this willingness and ability to build thin trust amongst a myriad of audiences, rather than just thick trust with its own audience, is one of the characteristics that makes a brand stand out as being a Social Equity Brand. Social Equity Brands are engines of thin trust.

But what about the majority of brands right now? Beyond the headline figures, how are the sustainability debate and the broader rise in social capital impacting on the trust consumers have in their most familiar brands? Do their communication efforts assuage consumer fears over sustainability, or are they leaving themselves open to criticism, laying bare awful gaps between image and action?

Brands and trust

Brands have to be trusted: if they're not, then the brand stands for nothing. It doesn't matter what sector or market the brand operates in, it has to engender trust in those who come into contact with it. As we've already tried to argue, considering trust is central to, and a product of, both what a brand stands for and the creation of social capital, it becomes pretty clear that brands are essentially in the business of creating social capital, with the virtuous relationship between capital and trust manifesting itself as brand equity, in measures such as advocacy and loyalty. In short, brand equity (which we believe resides only within the brand community) is derived from the various forms of trust that are salient for that community. This, then, supports our argument that the seemingly unshakeable foundation of bonding-led trust is now no longer a solid foundation for brands in this new era.

With the ambition of exploring this relationship between sustainability, social capital and brand equity further, as part of Havas's Sustainable Futures initiative,[113] the research investigates how consumers perceive the performance of their most recognised brands across a wide range of sustainability issues, and then maps these to measures of brand equity. As we've outlined earlier (see Chapter 4), these sustainability issues – 25 in total – are chosen to allow us to look at perceptions across a range of industries, to see how much these issues are impacting – positively or negatively – on 'brand health'.

The matrices shown in Figure 29 present a quick and easy visual as to how that particular brand is building social capital with its consumers around the myriad sustainability issues. Ideally, we would see a clear trend line running across the matrix, from bottom left to top right, reflecting the varying magnitude of issue importance being met with perceptions of strong performance where it counts, and a sensible saving of reserves where it is, as yet, not considered hugely material.

But whilst these matrices offer detail as to the social capital swirling around the brand when it comes to a variety of aspects that fall under the umbrella of sustainability, what they cannot capture is the amount of trust in play between respondents and the brand. To isolate that, we created what we

---

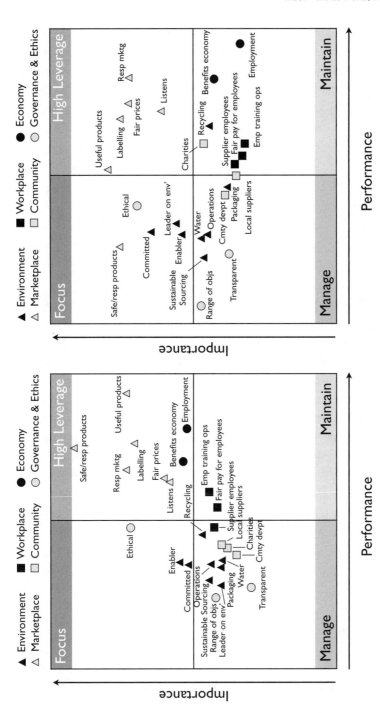

Figure 29: Drivers analysis #3. FMCG brand & FMCG (soft drinks) brand. Sustainable Futures.

call the Sustainable Futures Quotient – or SFQ for short – which blends the performance scores with a weighted contribution from the various attribute themes to brand equity. The second part of the quotient – the contribution to brand equity – is the crucial part that we believe captures the degree of trust in those consumers' perceptions, since it represents the degree to which those perceptions are influencing our brand equity proxies. Considering we're arguing that trust is essential to building brand equity, and we're showing that brand equity is being built by these perceptions around aspects of sustainability, then the conclusion is that only in the cases where these perceptions are driven by trust are they adding to brand equity.

The result is an overall score out of 100 for each brand that allows us to review brands quickly across sectors and markets, not just in terms of their performance, but more importantly in terms of *consumer trust* in their performance. We've included the Top 20 SFQ brands from the 2009 release of Sustainable Futures in Figure 30. What we'd expect to see over time is more of the SFQ being shaped by contributions to brand equity rather than performance, as brands become more adept at building social capital with their audiences. And this is already starting to be the case, with rises year on year for a number of progressive brands that we believe are emerging as Social Equity Brands. However, with many of these progressive brands, the sustainability area that consistently crops up as the most powerful current driver for brand equity is 'marketplace', which raises a small red flag in terms of the type of social capital these brands are still focused on nurturing. The specific type of trust and social capital that is still dominant appears to be the thick and bonding variety. For brands to truly emerge as Social Equity Brands, it's not just a case of nurturing social capital and trust, but nurturing the right blend and balance of the various forms.

Clearly, then, a strong performance from brands – perceived or actual – is not enough. Whilst brand audiences may believe the performance, what's needed is for them to believe *in* the performance.

This starts to touch on another major theme that will dominate the next part of the book, but is worth seeding here: the underlying motivations of the firm and its brands to engage in this area. Professor Bill Barnett of Stanford's Graduate School of Business describes how there are three fundamental motives for acting, which are as applicable to business as they

	Brand	Sustainable Futures Quotient (SFQ)
1	Danone	69.5
2	Nestlé	68.8
3	Unilever	67.5
4	Procter & Gamble	66.3
5	Walmart	66.0
6	Volkswagen	65.2
7	BMW	64.7
8	EDF	64.7
9	Carrefour	63.8
10	Toyota	63.7
11	L'Oréal	63.5
12	Reckitt Benckiser	63.4
13	Vodafone	63.0
14	Peugeot	61.2
15	Citroën	60.6
16	Santander	59.9
17	HSBC	59.6
18	BP	59.4
19	Telefónica	59.4
20	BBVA	57.8

Figure 30: SFQ 2009. Sustainable Futures 2009.

are to individuals.[114] Our actions can be considered *coercive* – where we act in compliance with a law or regulation; *reciprocal* – where we act because we're confident we'll get something back or in return; or *intrinsic* – where we act because we feel it is the appropriate and right thing to do (see Figure 31). It is our belief that most brand audiences today perceive the behaviour of brands as being either coercive or reciprocal in nature, which whilst most likely generating the same outcomes, creates a very different belief in that audience's mind. It's our view that the progressive brands that are deriving higher levels of brand equity from their endeavours today are those that are being seen as being far more intrinsically motivated. Why is this working? Because, in the Era of Social Capital Rising, brand audiences are no longer solely consumers,

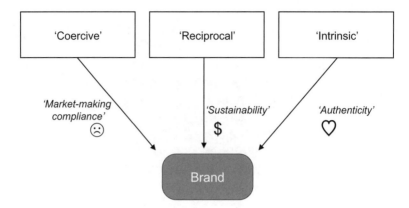

Figure 31: What motivates the brand?

but rather are citizens – more accurately citizens-who-consume – and, as such, the motives typical of market behaviour, namely coercion and reciprocity, just do not present themselves as authentic. The brand has to be comfortable above and beyond the traditional confines of the commercial market.

This persistence of coercive and reciprocal motives from companies and their brands manifests itself in a predictable way: the growing obsession of using transparency as the default start point for any communication when it comes to issues around sustainability.

We're not aiming to be critical of transparency in communications, but rather to recognise its limits. Of course there are many cases where brands on behalf of their sectors need to bare all in the name of resetting the needle in this hyper-connected world. But surely this is just the first step? What comes after the transparency? And what does transparency do to trust? Reports fly out of the doors of corporate PR firms, reputation firms and ad agencies, announcing the latest wave of criteria that firms and their brands need to meet in order to be trusted, and increasingly transparency is amongst them.

But to repeat one of our central questions: surely transparency is a substitute for trust? Where there isn't trust, and there's little hope for trust, then you demand transparency. But does transparency build trust? Well, it may assuage a sense of mistrust at the outset, but once this mistrust has been removed? Probably not.

Away from the world of marketing and branding, Onora O'Neill[115] makes an eloquent observation on the relationship between transparency and trust, where she argues that despite its frequent use to try and build trust, transparency is essentially about the removal of secrets. She goes on to say that secrets do not undermine trust; it is *deception* that destroys it. And the problem is that transparency can never remove the option or tendency to deceive.

We'd go as far as to say that beyond the very short term, brand audiences would actually prefer to trust, rather than be confronted with a blisteringly broad vista of transparency, especially when it comes to issues around sustainability and the wealth of ambiguities, trade-offs and compromises involved. We're back to our earlier chapters on consumer and brand behaviour, in that trust in a message immediately gives us that vital emotional biasing cue, which lifts so many of those painful opportunity cost issues away from us.

The implications of this argument are significant, when we consider how many progressive brands are predicating their communication efforts on transparency. The use of the corporate and product brands as faithful cheerleaders for the corporate endeavours is both a chronic waste of the potential of those brands and a chronic waste of the pent-up desire to believe in those brands on the part of their audiences. A double misfire.

So if not transparency, then what? The answer – our answer at least – is story. Stories are the most effective means by which to build trust and, for that matter, social capital. The role of stories will make up a sizeable chunk of the next part of the book, but suffice it to say, brands should feel comfortable adopting this role since, as we've already discussed, there's a considerable argument already in place that says brands are perfectly placed and excellently resourced to tell wonderful, timely, pertinent and enduring stories. The challenge, of course, is which story, when and to whom – not an easy task, considering the variety, complexity and general confusion around sustainability. But the fact remains – stories are powerful creators of social capital, can nurture high levels of trust and are cleanly in the middle of the sweetspot of brand capabilities. It seems a win-win, and we think it very much can be.

Stories – or sense-making narratives – are a vital tool for Social Equity Brands, and represent a key element in a Social Capital Strategy.

But just before we close the door on this part, there is one more question that remains to be explored in detail. Is social capital actually useful? Our assumption has been that social capital is a good thing, and that this emerging Era of Social Capital Rising is all positive. This certainly feels right, but do we know this? And even if social capital is useful at a societal level, can it really deliver anything at a business and brand level?

Our only brush up against an answer to this question has focused on the reduction of transaction costs – something considered valuable to both sociologists and economists. But what specifically are these transaction costs, and what, if any, are the other benefits of social capital? And are all forms of social capital beneficial, or is it the case that a dominant form over others can cause problems?

Chapter 9

Throughout this book we've tried to build an argument that brands and social capital are natural bedfellows, and that through leveraging their considerable abilities to grow social capital, brands could contribute far more effectively to the challenges presented within the sustainability debate. Rather than being shrill cheerleaders for their corporate guardians' endeavours, brands have the opportunity to lead the charge on finding durable, engaging and innovative solutions to sustainability issues. In short, sustainability that is sustainable.

And we've started to introduce the various qualities this new breed of brands will demonstrate, such as a commitment beyond image, an intrinsic motivation, a recognition of the citizen-who-consumes and an understanding of the importance of a deeper, more intelligent form of trust, built in part through a credible commitment to communicate through sense-making narratives rather than blanket transparency.

The one major reason we've presented so far for this refocusing on social capital, rather than sustainability specifically, is that we feel the current raft of challenges around sustainability has been caused by the slow collapse in social capital: that where social capital is low, so the tendencies and desires to marginalise audiences and externalise costs rise, and conversely, where social capital is higher, so these tendencies and desires tend to diminish. In short, we're saying that a focus on sustainability is a focus on a symptom, and if we're to find meaningful and durable solutions to these issues – solutions that work not only from the supply side but appeal wholesale to the mainstream demand side – then we need to focus on social capital; to focus on building social capital – and not in a brute and quantitative way, but in an intelligent, balanced and qualitative way.

This, in itself, should be a reason for investing in social capital – for turning brands into what we call Social Equity Brands that are focused on making long-term equity investments in the health of society, rather than injecting what is low quality, almost toxic short-term debt for their own immediate gains but at the expense of society. But this argument doesn't go nearly far enough in convincing those that manage brands that there are sufficient incentives to place their brands front and centre in this Era of Social Capital Rising, even if it is the case (and we think it is) that in this era of 'wakefulness' they do not really have a choice.

We need to present more arguments as to why social capital can be such a good thing, not just for society, but for those who are credited as being responsible for nurturing it.

Social capital, brands and society

Higher social capital allows society to operate more smoothly and efficiently. If we think back to the train journey example, we can immediately see how higher social capital and the subsequent norms, codes, trust and more collaborative thinking could remove many of the costly and rigid processes needed to compensate for its absence. It is not necessarily that higher social capital removes the need for 'infrastructure' within society, but rather it replaces a rigid and overbearing infrastructure with one that is leaner, more flexible and inherently more intuitive. And in a society that is developing – evolving – fast, this has to be a good thing. In easing these exchanges between disparate people or groups, this transaction cost perspective appears to be more focused on the benefits that flow from well-established linking and bridging capital – the 'engine oil' type of social capital, as we described in the opening chapters. In many cases, bridging capital – specifically the development of bridging capital – is marginalised, most probably because bonding capital naturally develops as we tend to coalesce into homogenous groups. In the very first chapters, we talked about how brands stepped in to offer a fillip for the apparent loss of this type of social capital. It's almost as if we're naturally addicted to bonding capital, yet need to be a part of bridging and linking capital as some counterbalance and for our own wellbeing. In other words, social capital is only really beneficial when all three forms are thriving in some form of harmony.

From an economic perspective, higher social capital levels appear to generate more prosperous societies. Many theories exist as to why this may be, and there are the constant issues of causality in trying to promote any one of them. But with an eye on the importance of being able to extrapolate these arguments into the realm of business and its brands, Mark Granovetter's[116] research from the 1970s determined that someone's career opportunities were more strongly influenced not by those you know well, but rather by casual acquaintances. His argument is elegantly simple, in that our close circle of friends is likely to be very much like us (homogenous and bonded), which means they are likely to only hear of the same career opportunities we do, and probably at the same time. Conversely, loose acquaintances are bonded to other groups, so are more likely to pick up information and opportunities within those groups, rather than yours. As such, strong levels of bridging social capital are likely to generate better opportunities for those within that society, and benefit society itself in very possibly finding the best people to take those opportunities.

If we look at this economic value from social capital through the lens of the firm, it's clear higher bridging social capital can offer incentives to employees to eke out new relationships within the company as such moves may improve their chances of promotion or diversification. Plus it encourages knowledge-sharing and innovation within the firm, which represent extremely valuable sources of highly ambiguous competitive advantage.

In short, from a purely economic perspective, a high social capital environment within a firm – and indeed between firms – can offer more opportunities for ambitious and motivated employees, with constructive consequences for those firms. Putnam[117] describes this advantage being used to excellent effect in the development of California's Silicon Valley. Created around the technology and engineering departments of some of the US's most prestigious and cutting-edge universities on the West Coast, Silicon Valley developed with an almost campus-like atmosphere, where incredibly valuable industry developments and market-defining breakthroughs were nurtured within a highly collaborative atmosphere. Regular 'extra-curricular' activities, such as inter-start-up baseball and evening beers, fostered an environment where swathes of new knowledge flowed freely amongst participants, somewhat counter-intuitively. Rather than destroying competitiveness, it seemed to sharpen those firms' capabilities, allowing the region to corner the technology market and become globally famous for technology development. And the frequent 'swapping' of staff between firms, or the creation of new start-ups seemingly overnight, only added to the culture rich in not just bonding capital within firms, but linking and bridging capital across firms. Recognising the uniqueness of this approach, when the culture started to stall in the early 1990s, a nonprofit entity was created, as a joint public–private initiative, with the sole aim of keeping this degree of collaboration, cross-fertilisation and fluidity alive in the region.

Away from innovation and employee engagement, the firm can also benefit economically from higher social capital simply through the reduction in controlling or monitoring processes required. A more engaged, social capital rich workforce simply needs less cajoling to work intelligently and efficiently. People are less likely to be away from work through illness. This, we believe, is a product of the positive effects of social capital both in terms of connectedness and openness and actual health levels, to which we turn in a moment.

And the positive economic effects of high social capital need not only be felt by the firm in terms of internal audiences. Externally, with consumers and even nonconsumers, high social capital can drive innovation. Where firms create high social capital amongst their external audiences, the opportunities for those audiences to interact, discuss, share and develop ideas increase. And these ideas can be extremely valuable for the firm. Lego, the children's brick-building toy brand, has been reinvigorated over the last few years, through recognising that a considerable amount of value in the toy resided not just in children playing with it, but with parents getting involved. The company was able to tap into a rich seam of latent interest by involving that audience more overtly in the brand experience. As a means of doing this, Lego invited its newly-discovered 'mature builders' to offer up their own building templates for others to copy. Run via a highly engaging and intuitive website – www.legofactory.com — this foray into engaging parents with the toy has spawned an enormous range of alternative designs for everything you can imagine building with Lego bricks. Not only is this evidently interesting for this new audience, but the positive externalities for the brand are considerable: now anyone thinking about building a scale model of London's Big Ben has the option of reviewing a number of alternative designs and inspirations, with all this additional value for those experiencing the brand created at virtually no cost to the brand itself, bar some photography and hosting costs.

And how did this all come about? Well, we believe as a result of Lego building and leveraging new levels of social capital (and who better to build social capital than Lego?). In the case of Lego, the brand embarked on trying to connect with those parents not solely as purchasers on behalf of their children, but as a potential community that actually experiences the brand and derives value from that experience. In short, the Lego example illustrates how brands can enjoy the benefits of co-creation and collaboration with their audiences, through turning the dial a little on the various forms of social capital. In fact, in quite a quirky fashion, Lego – considering the core user profile – carried out a nifty bit of bridging and linking social capital building to bring on board this new community, considering the clear hierarchy differences between children and their parents.

The Lego example demonstrates another economic benefit from social capital building with an external audience – more information flows into the business, courtesy of the brand's handiwork and network building. Not only that, it's more pertinent information and more timely information. And all of this without having to go fishing for it. Being able to gather data and information, uncover insights and act on those insights to the brand's and the audience's advantage are natural by-products of being credited with bringing people together and uncovering new areas and types of value for those people. In other words, being responsible for creating higher levels of social capital can often involve those responsible finding themselves very constructively in the middle of that social capital.

Internal and external audiences

Before looking at more specific areas where social capital is a good thing for society and business, it's worth reflecting on the broad internal benefits for the business and, specifically, a prerequisite that we feel many brands overlook.

Just as a brand offers consumers a short-cut to ascertain quality, consistency and a promise of reciprocity, so the same is true internally. Whilst maybe not displaying the exact same traits, the image presented by the firm and received by those who are engaged with it in some way plays a crucial role in clarifying the proposition which shapes the exchange that's about to take place. This internal image shapes – and is shaped by – the culture and ethos of the firm, which are, in turn, influencers of – and influenced by – the types and levels of social capital at play. In other words, a central identity gives rise to a multitude of bundled characteristics, all of which are presented to and received by different audiences.

To be clear, what we're not espousing is that these bundles can be whatever they want to be and that the business can create images that are inconsistent or contradictory. The theory should be that if faithfully drawn from the identity of the firm, there will automatically be consistency and complementarity (Figure 32). The key image presented to external audiences is the brand, and in the case of a corporate brand, this is a synthesis of many

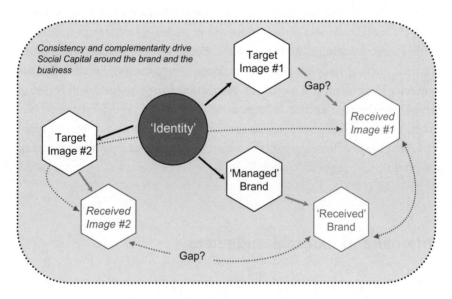

Figure 32: Identities, images and brands

of these corporate identity traits. In the case of a product brand, this is a synthesis of quality and provenance assurances, underpinned or guided by the salient attributes from the corporate identity.

The point is this: where these various images are not aligned, then stocks of social capital around the business will fall. Why? Because these contradictions or ambiguities will dominate the dialogue and thinking phases of the process, cutting off any route to building further trust.

Beyond direct economic benefits for societies rich in social capital, there are potentially positive outcomes in a variety of other areas, including education, neighbourhoods, health and wellbeing and even democracy itself. It seems we weren't too wide of the mark when we captioned this part of the book with a claim that social capital is the elixir of life. And a gentle walk through these areas throws up a host of ideas as to how similar benefits can be bestowed upon those firms with forward-looking brands that commit openly and credibly to restocking social capital.

Education

From an educational perspective, and in the context of society, social capital appears to be of extraordinary importance. If there is one overriding, compelling reason to have high levels of social capital, it is wrapped up in education. Children just do far better in terms of education where there is high social capital around them.[118] We're not talking in terms of pure academic achievement, but rather the more holistic, well-rounded sort of education children should have. As Putnam points out, in actual fact most research has focused on what happens to children's education when in areas of low social equity, and the results are quite horrific. So the message is clear – high social capital starts your kids on the right track, and acts as a compellingly useful barrier in stopping awful things happening to them, from which they may never recover.

In the business and brand context, we believe higher social capital also bestows educational benefits on those credited with raising the levels. Creating an environment where it is safe, productive and encouraged to learn is vitally important. It is key that those who work for the firm have the opportunity to learn and flourish, not only through more formal and scheduled events, such as training courses, but in a more fluid and informal manner, be that through colleagues with whom they share an office or others throughout the organisation or industry. In this respect, bonding capital is key to nurturing day-to-day learning and experimentation with close colleagues, and bridging and linking capital is key to connecting with others with alternate perspectives and viewpoints. All three forms of social capital are needed in order to expedite the discovery, sharing and dissemination of knowledge throughout the firm, with bonding capital encouraging in-depth, context-specific thinking and development, and bridging and linking capital ensuring these outputs do not get caught in silos, but are shared and built upon with others.

In other words, as the 'hard' assets of firms and their brands become more and more commoditised, and human capital becomes more and more important as probably the only source of enduring competitive value, it is high social capital that releases the potential of the human capital.

Neighborhoods

Linked to the benefits for education are the benefits to neighbourhoods within societies with high social capital. High social capital removes tendencies for neighbourhoods to backfire in terms of crime and violence. Looking specifically at the US, Putnam plots murder rates per capita per state against levels of social capital per state (according to his Social Capital Index).[119] The correlation is striking. Those states with the lowest levels of social capital show the highest murder rates per capita, and this murder rate steadily drops as the Social Capital Index rises. Jane Jacobs,[120] the US sociologist, spells out that the single most likely cause of social problems – including murder at the far end of the scale – is an urban environment which reduces the possibility for informal exchange and the development of social capital. Jacobs attacks twentieth century urban planning (in the US) for its apparent ambition to actually stop people mixing; this has had terrible results. For her, urban life has to present a myriad of opportunities for people to pass each other on the pavement, say hello to others tending their gardens, enter into an exchange in a local shop or see others in recreational spaces. In short, she says, we need all of these extremely informal and ad hoc exchanges – many of them purely phatic – in order to function properly.

Lifting these benefits across to the environment of the firm, the first thing we want to point out is that we don't think murder is a particularly common occurrence. But other serious crimes do take place – embezzlement and fraud, bullying, intimidation, racism, sexism, ageism – there's a whole list of offences that can play out in the work place. So having higher levels of social capital immediately seems like a good idea, if it can help remove these tendencies, and there's every reason to assume these tendencies will indeed diminish with higher levels. Removing the threat of these issues would also bestow greater levels of trust and confidence in those within the company, allowing them to more effectively reap the economic and educational benefits of higher social capital. And just as with these other areas of benefit, the internal image or corporate brand is vital in establishing the norms, codes and culture in which social capital can flourish. The internal image needs to establish the 'default' settings for those entering that environment.

Democracy

At arguably the most profound level, social capital can stimulate stronger democracy in society. Deeper and broader dialogue, and the subsequent shared thinking, has to be good for a liberal democracy, and social capital has the potential to 'awaken' all of us to reflect, consider, voice and debate our concerns not just for ourselves, but for those around us. Philosopher John Stewart Mill argued that without participation in public life:

> '[a citizen] . . . never thinks of any collective interest, or any objects to be pursued jointly with others, but only in competition with them . . . A neighbour, not being an ally or an associate, since he is never engaged in any common undertaking for joint benefit, is therefore only a rival.'[121]

From the perspective of the firm and its brands, encouraging a form of democracy can greatly improve the agility and response time of the business. Issues become apparent sooner, as do potential solutions, and the ability to source new ideas and suggestions, as well as gather feedback for either action or proposed action, all increase where social capital is high. In addition, an increase in social capital within the firm, as well as an increase around the firm, allows the relationship with employees and consumers to transcend the normal boundaries dictated by a traditional market, be that one for labour or products and services. Markets are governed by an exchange where both sides glean value. In other words, they are driven by selfish motives – as Adam Smith said:

> 'It is not from the benevolence of the butcher, the brewer or the baker that we expect our dinner, but from their regard to their own interest.'[122]

But where social capital is high, and there's a greater sense of participatory democracy, individuals will be less prone to think purely in terms of personal – and very probably short-term – gain, and much more in terms of what is best for everyone, most likely in the longer term. For employees, this becomes less about heading into the office 'just for the money' and more about 'what we can achieve together'; and for those who actually consume or experience the brand, it becomes more about 'how can I participate and collaborate, to make this more valuable?' rather than just 'what are my rights if I don't get what I expected?'. It is this idea of the move from consumer to citizen-who-consumes that underpins the transition of a brand to a Social Equity Brand. As we'll explore in the next part, whilst this is undeniably a step in the right direction, it is not necessarily a step into the unknown. Instead, it's a step into what is familiar but almost certainly forgotten territory.

Health and wellbeing

One area which seems to benefit enormously from higher levels of social capital is our general health and wellbeing. As this applies to us as individuals, the benefit to both society and business is clear. Not surprisingly, when people are asked how healthy and well they feel, there is again a strong correlation between high answers to those questions and high levels of social capital. People claim to be healthier and feel better where there is high social capital. But that could be just a case of them feeling better, or feeling healthy, as a by-product of feeling happier. And if social capital can make us feel happier – which plenty of research shows it can[123] – then that in itself is no mean feat; optimism is a great enabler, and the notion of a happy – alongside prosperous and productive – society is one that is gathering pace with economists and policymakers.

But there is also hard evidence that aside of how it makes us feel, in actual fact, higher social capital does indeed allow us to live longer. Putnam has plotted mortality rates per state with his Social Capital Index and arrived at a resounding negative correlation. In other words, if you live in a state with high social capital, then you're going to live longer.[124] That's good news for all those based in those social capital rich states (but bad news if their insurance companies get hold of the same graph, as they'll see their retirement annuities drop sharply as a result).

It also seems levels of trust – as an antecedent and consequence of social capital – can play a big part in how long we stick around. The ominously named 'Whitehall Studies' of British civil servants[125] looked at mortality rates amongst all grades of the UK's civil service. Strangely, the study was only conducted on men, but the results unequivocally showed that those in lower levels of the hierarchy were far more likely to die young from heart disease. The correlation was clear – the more senior you are, the less likely you are to keel over prematurely, with those at the very bottom more than three times more likely to die early than those at the top. And this is after diet and other health issues such as smoking had been controlled in the study. Striking though it is, one could immediately raise the issue of causality and claim the reason these men did not rise to the top of the civil service hierarchy is specifically because of their likelihood to fall ill early, reflected in other ways, such as energy, bullishness and general ability to tackle problems. But it appears the driver for an early death is actually the existence of the hierarchy itself.

In an experiment that proves the potentially divisive effects of stiff and inflexible hierarchies – and where the irony is not wasted, considering the previous study on British civil servants – researchers studied what happened to the health of monkeys who, within their well-defined communal hierarchies, had their positions or ranks within those communities upset or reordered.[126] It turns out the experience of being forced to accept a different position or rank within the group hierarchy is particularly stressful, regardless of whether the monkey is 'promoted' or 'demoted'. However, for those monkeys who were originally in superior positions, and then forced to take subordinate positions, the negative effects on their health were considerably greater: in fact those being demoted tended to suffer five times as much atherosclerosis (the build-up of fatty deposits inside the artery walls, leading to narrowing of the arteries and higher risks of angina and heart attack) as a result.

This is an extraordinary result – a marked and rapid deterioration in physical health as a consequence of forced change within a rigid and established social order. One possible explanation for this effect is the loss of control or influence for the low-ranking monkey (and the low-ranking civil servant) in that they are unable to steer or govern their own choices, such is the perceived rigidity of their hierarchy. This catapults them into a state of 'mental emergency', which in turn alerts the body to engage its 'fight or flight' mode. When this happens, valuable bodily resources are moved on to a war footing, with the result that other systems and processes, considered less valuable or necessary in that specific moment of impending battle or flight, are deprived of their attention. This results in a shut down of many of the body's natural repair and maintenance systems, which ordinarily shouldn't be a problem, since this shut down of maintenance functions and the re-routing of resources should only last for the time of the fight or the flight. But in the context of a stifling and unforgiving hierarchy, with limited or zero opportunity to affect change, this state could go on for a long, long time – in the case of the Whitehall civil servants, an entire working life, tragically. So, with essential maintenance functions out of action for that period of time, it is no wonder they had a far higher tendency to die younger.

Another factor that can bring about an early death seems to be trust – or rather a lack of it. We've discussed at length the advantages of high trust in terms of lower transaction costs, and how when trust drops, these costs increase. But it also seems people who are more prone to mistrust others are also more prone to die sooner.[127] That has to be the highest transaction cost of all, doesn't it?

So when it comes to health and wellbeing, it seems beyond doubt that social capital is a good thing. It's not that we necessarily die without it, but it does seem we're far more likely to die when it's not around us.

The implications for business hardly need to be spelt out. Aside from the number of person-hours and days lost a year to illness, even when people are at work, if they're weighed down and worn out by stress and concern over the way their world looks and the direction their life is going, then it doesn't take much to see how this is going to hamper their effectiveness and productivity. Whilst we acknowledge social capital may not be the only solution to safeguard against these issues, it certainly looks like a compelling one that can deliver a host of other benefits too.

To summarise, social capital has the potential to produce a wealth of benefits, for those who stimulate it and indeed those who happen to be bystanders and passive recipients. Social capital can encourage economic prosperity by enabling people to fulfil their true potential; social capital can improve education, by creating opportunities to learn and develop rounded social skills and empathy; social capital can create safer and more welcoming environments by removing prejudices and encouraging informal exchange; social capital can ramp up levels of wellbeing and happiness and keep us ticking along for longer; and social capital can light a fire under us to engage in greater levels of participatory democracy.

All of these benefits can be adapted to apply equally to business. Social capital can increase the quality and frequency of innovation, not just in terms of products, but in business processes and indeed business models; social capital can aid market expansion and diversification; social capital can generate local community support, providing a licence to operate plus access to informal channels for information, trends and emerging codes or norms; social capital can initiate, establish and nurture formal and informal partnerships and consortia; social capital can aid the recruitment, retention and effective advancement of talent; and social capital can engender more sustainable consumer loyalty and nurture more durable brand equity (Figure 33).

From this impressive list, it seems even the most aggressive and cynical lawyer would struggle to make a case against social capital being good for society and good for business, and the role brands can play in building it. And as we know, lawyers have a very powerful incentive to try and discredit social capital.

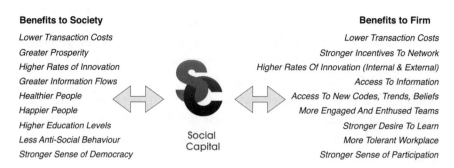

Figure 33: Benefits of social capital

But social capital is not all buttercups, hazy sunshine and a warm comfortable feeling inside. Sometimes, it seems, it can have teeth. And sometimes, it seems, it turns that bite upon itself.

Harmony and social capital

We started this book with a discussion about the purpose brands originally stepped in to serve, in that they were substitutes for the traditionally high levels of bonding capital that were present in their tight communities. In the absence of these trusted and established mavens, brands set out to make amends for the 'provenance costs' faced by now relatively enriched, mobile and, to an extent, isolated consumers. As this 'plastic' bonding capital fillip increased, so some less than pleasant side effects started to creep in. Where individuals had, by and large, been aware and respectful of 'the commons' in their recently previous community life, now they were becoming serial 'free riders', concerned primarily, exclusively even, with meeting their own utilitarian and hedonic wants and needs. The new consumer was complicit in the marginalisation and externalisation of considerations outside of these ambitions, as they became increasingly intoxicated by the seemingly unfaltering attention they received in these exclusive relationships.

This unchecked growth of bonding social capital clearly was not a good thing, and highlights the perils of social capital developing in a lop-sided way. To reiterate, whilst we talk about the negatives of the Era of Social Capital

Waning, we should also be talking about the negatives of the Era of Asymmetrical Social Capital. Without the necessary balances in place, certain forms of social capital can grow unchecked. When this form of 'social capital cancer' happens, it can chronically distort the benefits of social capital as a whole (there, we've said it: brands can cause cancer – the brand-haters would be proud).

This propensity for 'cancerous social capital growth' is most likely to happen with bonding capital, since, as we've touched on previously, this is the form of social capital that we find easiest to produce, and that seems to give us the 'hit' or comfort we crave from homogenous, like-minded groups. The very term 'comfort zone' is, in fact, a pretty accurate description of exactly what bonding capital represents.

There are plenty of examples of where bonding capital can start to attack the other forms of social capital, but possibly the most striking is in the context of one of the benefit areas we discussed earlier, and one that many see as the single most convincing argument that social capital is good for us and society: education.

Where I live with my family, we are surrounded by good primary schools. I mean surrounded – walk out of the front door and turn left, right or just walk straight on, and there's one within 200 m. At 3.30pm Monday to Friday, if you happen to find yourself on the street, you're suddenly surrounded by battalions of blazered children, obediently walking in lines, but with the occasional outbreak of giggling or shrieking, or a sudden halt in traffic on account of someone (invariably a boy) stopping to pick up a stick, pocket a fir cone or just gawp at a cat. It's quite a scene, and despite the chaos that it brings, is strangely calming and bucolic. There's something very 'right' in seeing children go to school, and especially when you know the schools are as good as they are. But this scene masks a terrible consequence of rampant and unchecked bonding social capital.

There's one state (free) primary school and five private (fee-paying) primary schools, and the most debated aspect between all of them is how to manage the balance between admitting children from local families and those from families farther afield. We live in a nice enough area, just on the underground system, but far enough out for you to 'decompress' on the way home, with more than its fair share of trees and grass, and a pretty laid-back attitude. To give you an idea, up until just a few months ago (and the first few pages of this book) we were home to one of the most secure Liberal Democrat parliamentary seats in the country, made even more unusual considering we are in London. So we're an easy going, international bunch who are, it appears, very aware of the benefits of 'engine oil' social capital as well as 'engine bolt' capital. Yet when it comes to the schooling issue, bonding capital seems to take control and all but stamp out any hint of bridging capital. People are, by and large, convinced the schools should be for local families only. This may be because house prices are high – for the very reason the houses are near the schools – but the fact remains that families in our area bind themselves into such tight homogenous groups when it comes to schooling that all the broader benefits of social capital are snuffed out.

Although this is presented as a slightly amusing and unabashedly middle class issue, it does highlight a dangerous aspect of unchecked and asymmetrical bonding social capital: a lack of tolerance. As it turns out, most researchers and academics reckon that high bonding capital is indeed the right environment for children to receive their education – in effect, the creation of their ideal comfort zone. But this only makes the dilemma more vivid. In most constitutions – formalised or not – countries espouse qualities such as freedom, liberty and democracy, but does high social capital necessarily encourage freedom and liberty? The challenge, it seems, is with bonding capital specifically, in that an overly strong sense of community could curtail freedom and indeed liberty – society's 'engine bolts' being overtightened.

This natural conflict between social capital and the benefits it tries to deliver is captured succinctly by Robert Putnam[128] where he talks about the banners of the French Revolution, emblazoned with the ideals of liberty, equality, fraternity (highly appropriate, considering Havas's origins). He surmises that fraternity in this case is an alternative name for social capital, but raises the question that if that were the case, can it really co-exist with liberty? Surely it's one or the other? And can you strive for equality at the same time as giving people liberty? Surely the former involves a 'levelling' and some form of control, whereas the latter represents the freedom to be whatever you can and want to be?

Hopefully there's a balance that can be struck. Putnam calls it a High Social Capital, High Tolerance Society or 'Salem without the "witches"'.[129]

Such a society has to be dependent on commercial actors (brands) working constantly to keep these aspects balanced and in harmony.

That said, the risks persist. If bonding social capital grows too quickly, it can soon start to crowd out the other forms, and in doing so begin to unpick the wealth of benefits that come from a more balanced and harmonious development. Brands must heed this caveat: brute social capital growth is not the objective, blunt building efforts will not be effective and such a route will not build a Social Equity Brand. Instead, a Social Equity Brand will recognise the dynamic subtleties of its environment and ensure a balanced, consistent and appropriate route to higher levels of social capital.

It does this through an effective Social Capital Strategy.

S ome may say we've taken our time to get to a more detailed investigation of what social capital is, and how it affects all of us every day. We'd counter that on the grounds that social capital is such an integral part of our lives, we have, in fact, been referring to it – or rather its benefits and costs – from the word go. In the context of brands, it is – we believe – impossible not to talk about social capital when discussing communications.

That said, in this part we've attempted to stop and stare directly at social capital, in an attempt to understand its anatomy and physiology. We've explored the forms of social capital (bonding, bridging and linking) and we've explored the strands or elements that make up those forms (the structural, cognitive and relational).

In an attempt to start to shape components of what we call a Social Capital Strategy, we've also extended the work of prominent academics to create what we feel is a process model, from which brands can start to understand the steps required to build social capital around themselves.

Despite its popularity amongst policymakers, political scientists and sociologists, it seems a clear definition of social capital is still proving elusive (maybe the social capital amongst those groups is not as high as it should be?). With this in mind, and considering the importance of establishing a definition that is tailored for the purpose of brands, we have proposed the following:

> 'The quality, depth, breadth and frequency of brand-inspired dialogue, exchange and interaction that occurs within a community. It is the benefits – both private (to the brand) and public (to the community) – that are generated as a result. And it is the resultant collective ability to maintain and enhance these processes and benefits.'

What we hope is evident in this ambition is a brand's commitment not to chase brute social capital growth slavishly, but rather to seek balanced qualitative growth, where each type of capital is nurtured, and each strand is suitably strong. Where this doesn't happen, social capital can turn upon itself, with bonding capital invariably seizing the initiative and going on the rampage. We've tried to illustrate the default dominance of bonding social capital, from the truces that sprang up from the rotting winter trenches of World War I, to the pedestrian congestion that occurs outside my front door every day at 3.30pm when the local primary schools disgorge their young learners. The irony of including primary schools and battle-grounds in the same sentence when talking about social capital is not lost on us.

Finally, we've attempted to show that the simple act of communication itself does not build social capital. Communication is not dialogue, and neither shared thinking nor trust necessarily emerges from that communication. In fact, we'd argue that invariably this is the type of 'conversation' brands have with their audiences: social-capital-poor shrill repetitions, in an attempt to cut through everyone else's shrill call for attention. This does not build trust. But it does put your teeth on edge.

When it comes to trust, if there's one aspect of its creation and preservation we'd reiterate, it would be that shaped by Onora O'Neill,[130] where a focus on accountability and transparency as a way to build trust is most probably misguided. Transparency can, at best, remove secrecy, laying that which is now transparent at the mercy of the onlooker. But trust is not compromised by such secrecy – that is carried out far more effectively by deceit. So, for brands to attempt to build trust through extolling transparency on behalf of their corporate guardians, the result will most likely be an emotionless and exhaustive relationship, riddled with even greater levels of ambiguity and confusion and dwindling levels of trust.

In pursuing this strategy, we genuinely believe brands will be destroying trust in the long term, and in doing so, undermining brand equity. Put another way, destroying opportunities to be valued destroys opportunities to deliver value.

We believe brand audiences want to believe – want to trust – especially when it comes to an issue as complex, demanding and terrifying as sustainability. Social Equity Brands will not only deliver on that need, but will always remain mindful that they are defined by that need.

And the benefits that can flow from this are considerable, not just to the brand, and not just to the audiences directly experiencing the brand, but rather everyone.

So, in a nutshell, here's our argument so far. Social capital represents a unique lens through which to view the purpose and value brands can adopt and deliver, as business battles to understand and get to grips with the myriad changes unfolding around it in this Era of Social Capital Rising.

More than just mitigating for risk and ensuring a licence to operate, exploring a brand's ability to nurture social capital, rather than faithfully repeat the firm's endeavours around sustainability, presents an opportunity for the brand to move front and centre in terms of delivering value both to its guardian and all those who come into contact with it.

In this Era of Social Capital Rising, the role of the brand is key. Not only can the brand help restock levels of social capital for the benefit of all, but it represents an enduring and irreplaceable licence to innovate for the firm. Without a brand – without a Social Equity Brand – the business cannot fully exercise its operational capabilities in this Era of Social Capital Rising.

That much, we hope, is clear, even if you don't necessarily agree with it. But it does prompt a series of questions:

1. What exactly, then, is a Social Equity Brand?
2. And what exactly, then, is a Social Capital Strategy?
3. And if this new breed of brand really can deliver these sorts of benefits to the business, and indeed all its audiences, just how do we go about measuring that?

Never let it be said we try and duck the big questions. We were saving the best until last.

So far we've presented a broad descriptive account of how we've got to where we are today. As we now move to a more prescriptive account of how we think we can move more effectively towards a more collectively and commercially constructive tomorrow, we'll do our utmost to give answers. Answers that focus ultimately on how to create a brand that is truly valued.

Part IV

Towards Social Equity Brands, and How a Social Capital Strategy Gets Us There

Our preoccupation with sustainability – or rather unsustainability – is a preoccupation with a symptom, rather than the cause. And like all obsessions with symptoms, a genuine and durable solution remains out of sight.

Instead, we've argued that the cause of our problems is the slow collapse in levels – and appreciation – of social capital. Actually more than that – we've argued the cause is a collapse and *loss of balance* in social capital. This loss of balance and quality has allowed us systematically to marginalise voices and externalise costs in the name of convenience when it has come to our exclusive and intoxicating relationships.

But where social capital is high, the propensity and desire to marginalise voices or viewpoints and externalise these costs or impacts is low. Why?

Because we know, understand, care and want to act. As our focus group mother succinctly framed it, 'When I throw something away, where is "away"?'

With high social capital, there is no 'away'. This should spell good news for brands, as we've argued these products of twentieth century industrial progress are in the very business of building social capital. More than that, brands cannot function *without* social capital – it is their oxygen. Social capital, when looked at in the context of brands, represents the potential conductivity of society, and the more conductive a society, the more likely it is that communication (including brand-led communication), and all its positives, will spread.

So far so good.

But historically brands were only really good at building one type of social capital – bonding social capital. As a response to unprecedented levels of migration, industrialisation and specialisation, this plastic substitute worked well to assuage 'provenance costs' that were rising as a result of people no longer being in – or belonging to – tight-knit communities where they knew how to seek guidance in making the most effective purchases to meet what were essentially utilitarian needs. To try and knock out these provenance costs, brands pursued what could be called exclusive 'dyadic' relationships with consumers.

And when these utilitarian needs evolved into hedonic wants (and very possibly hedonic needs), this preoccupation with such an exclusive, intoxicating and dominant form of social capital created the perfect breeding ground for materialistic tendencies. Where individuals had had exposure to linking and bridging social capital via their communities (both of which acted in concert with bonding social capital to offer the right balance of self and community), in this emerging world of the dislocated consumer drawn to the seductive relationship of brands, this distorted, lop-sided and bonding-dominant social capital mix meant these checks and balances were absent. Materialism could flourish unfettered.

Materialism, then, started to become the principal currency of these relationships between brands and their audiences in this period we have labelled the Era of Social Capital Waning. And whilst the quite perfunctory consequence of obsessing about material wealth is very possibly one reason for the subsequent collapse in social capital (leaving you less time to focus on rela-

tionships for a start), it seems the troublesome relationship between materialism and social capital is far more complex.

In *The High Price of Materialism*, Tim Kasser[131] draws on a number of
experiments that show high correlation rates between materialist tendencies
and insecurity, an inability to connect emotionally, a reluctance to be a part
of the community and a disinterest in volunteering. Those who score highly
on the materialist scales are also generally less happy and exhibit consistently
lower levels of wellbeing. So, beyond just taking away your time to connect
with family, friends and other loved ones, materialist traits really are very bad
for us. They're also bad for the creation, nourishment and maintenance of
healthy and balanced levels of social capital.

Whilst clearly seeded in the early decades of the twentieth century, even
today brands engage in practices that make it very hard for us to see the wood
for the trees when it comes to making decisions regarding being more sustainable consumers – becoming more sustainable citizens. Driven by ever-
increasing levels of competition, brands continue to pursue strategies built
around the notion of driving us to be rational, 'maximising' consumers. In
other words, gather, sift, analyse and discard information through as many
iterations as it takes, before we make the best possible choice. And, of course,
for every brand, the best possible choice we can make is to choose *them*.

There's been an explosion of research and writing in the last few years,
making almost unshakable arguments that we don't want to operate in
this way – that we're simply not *designed* to operate in this way. Where the
dazzle of scientific management techniques may have appealed for a period
as industrialisation and specialisation took hold, in reality we are emotional,
somewhat irrational types, who squirm and grimace at having to make tough
choices laden with detail and information.

And we've gone a little further to say that, in the context of sustainability,
we really *really* don't want to operate in this way. Why? Because exhaustive
searching throws up more and more trade-offs and opportunity costs, multiplied many times over in this context, due to the unavoidably ambiguous and
contradictory nature of sustainability. As we currently frame it, sustainability
is one enormous congealed mass of trade-offs and opportunity costs.

In short, as brands push us further and further towards making cold
rational decisions on sustainability criteria (via larger and larger numbers of

certifications, and louder and louder echoes of corporate endeavours), so the trade-offs and opportunity costs mount, and we walk away to make decisions on less stressful criteria – or through habit.

It's worth repeating that we don't think brands could have created a less efficient – a less sustainable – way of communicating and engaging around sustainability issues if they had tried.

Very likely brands are pursuing this route for a number of reasons: in response to the 'seriousness' of the issues; a desire from marketing managers to get closer to more established business functions; and the entrenched reluctance to tackle anything complex or negative in brand communications.

Pushing against these and countless others, we've argued that rather than leaning on an outdated rational consumer model to demonstrate legitimacy and accountability, brands must instead get very used to splashing about with emotion.

Emotion is enjoying a huge resurgence in communication circles (despite its wonderful 'messiness' in terms of execution and measurement) as it becomes more and more apparent how central it is to the way we work as creatures. Emotion-based communication presents us with an opportunity to lunge for one option over another, with seemingly no rational justification whatsoever. These opportunities to develop emotional biases allow us to by-pass (or, more accurately, drive straight over) the myriad trade-offs and opportunity cost dilemmas that a more rational and exhaustive search produces. The negative effects of trade-off and opportunity cost analyses are clear, and in the context of sustainability, these negative effects have the potential – we firmly believe – to create insurmountable barriers to consumer behaviour change.

We've argued that brands have to stop this approach – this obsession with a symptom, a desire to faithfully report corporate endeavours and a mission to get us to make purely rational, utterly informed and methodically calculated purchase decisions.

But it seems we are, by and large, a long way from this point. And consumers appear to agree. In the 2009 Greendex[132] study, carried out by National Geographic and GlobeScan, the clear majority of respondents across a broad mix of markets agreed with the statement that the media and advertising '. . . are encouraging us to consume in an environmentally irresponsible way'.

As well as sending a clear signal that brands are behind the curve on this, these data point to something else: that we're entering a period which British author Philip Pullman calls 'wakefulness'.[133] That somehow the motivations and mechanics of the systems around us are due a rebuild or reboot. And just as social capital ebbed away during the long previous swing of the pendulum, so it's beginning to rise in this new arc: this period we call the Era of Social Capital Rising.

In the early decades of the twentieth century, if there were a strap line to sum up an overarching consumer theme or purpose, it would have been 'I Need'. In other words, as we moved, worked and produced in new ways, brands had to respond to these needs. From the middle of the century, with rising affluence and expectations, this strap line evolved into 'I Want'. Hedonic wants emerged, allowing brands to find new ways to channel desire and ambition for their benefit.

And now? Well, we'd argue the strap line for today is fast becoming 'I Belong'. This sense of connection and inclusion is the ambition of the waking individual in this Era of Social Capital Rising (Figure 34).

In just the same way that brands recognised, responded to and led the 'I Need' and 'I Want' movements, so they must get behind and drive this emerging 'I Belong' movement, as part of this Era of Social Capital Rising.

To reiterate, we genuinely do not see this new era as the death knell for brands. Quite the opposite. It is the most extraordinary opportunity for rebirth. Brands have in front of them an opportunity to be valued genuinely by society, and in doing so create unprecedented levels of durable, high quality value for their corporate guardians.

Figure 34: Identity changes over the decades

Brands – certain brands – can be instrumental in creating and maintaining this Era of Social Capital Rising. Brands – certain brands – can be instrumental in meeting this balanced desire to belong. Brands – certain brands – are approaching a position where they can step out of the shadows of their guardians and be responsible for finding and encouraging innovative solutions to the sustainability challenges we face today; challenges that cannot be met only by supply-side ingenuity, but that are crying out for mass scale participation and collaboration. Brands – certain brands – recognise that the key to durable sustainability solutions – the key to their own durability – rests with replenishing and nourishing abundant and balanced levels of social capital.

These certain brands that recognise the opportunity, and their role, are what we call Social Equity Brands.

Throughout the previous chapters, we've touched on many of the traits or qualities that we recognise these brands need to exhibit. But in order to approach this process of transformation effectively and efficiently, a more detailed exploration of the anatomy of a Social Equity Brand needs to be undertaken.

It is to this task we turn first.

Chapter 10

A fter 166 pages of cataloguing and criticising brands over the decades, we've now a clear – and very possibly overdue – responsibility to offer a detailed impression of what we think a progressive brand should look like; the qualities and traits it should uncover and share with its various audiences.

As the underlying theme through this book, we've talked about the need for this new breed of brands to focus on investing in society for the long term, with high quality social equity. This translates into investments and contributions that lead to balanced, healthy and durable stocks of all three types of social capital – bonding, linking and bridging. To reiterate, this focus on social capital is key, since not only does its replenishment and nourishment hold the key to our finding solutions for the sustainability challenges we face, but social capital is also the *air that brands breathe*. They cannot survive without it.

And as brands (product and, increasingly, corporate) represent more and more value to firms, it seems obvious that there should be a detailed focus on maintaining this valuable and dynamic resource. As we've said before, we need to recognise that social capital is the key supplier for any business.

This is opposed to the more typical and traditional approach of brands; focusing on restrictive, exclusive and often intoxicating forms of bonding social capital to create dyadic relationships with a view to quick gains. It is this latter approach – and its subsequent encouragement of materialism as well as other negative outcomes – that we've labelled at times 'low quality (toxic) social debt'.

These comments, then, frame our definition of a Social Equity Brand:

'A Social Equity Brand is a brand that recognises both the private and public importance and value of investing in long-term, balanced stocks of social capital, as a means of uncovering, developing and activating collaborative, innovative and dynamic solutions to the sustainability issues we all face.'

But beyond a commitment to social equity and long-term balanced social capital development as a means to uncover solutions and create value, what is the more detailed make-up of a Social Equity Brand and its corporate guardian? What are its constituent parts? And what drives it forward? If we're to move towards this new approach – if brands are to present themselves as something 'brand new' – then we need to know what we're attempting to move towards.

To answer these questions, we've observed the characteristics and behaviours of a number of progressive brands and their corporate mentors, and have developed models, assumptions and theories that extrapolate these qualities into what we consider to be the generic anatomical study of a Social Equity Brand. In other words, what it is exactly that the brand needs to have under the bonnet that can help it become more constructive in building balanced social capital, and in turn yield better value returns for society and its corporate guardian.

It is important to say at this point that we do not, for one second, think this 'anatomical blueprint' is exhaustive. And in keeping with many of the themes presented in this book, it is hoped that those of you who have something to say – whether that be support, a challenge or indeed an addition – will do so via the final section that is available online (www.brandvalued.com). It is our genuine ambition to grow and evolve this anatomical study over time, as more data, insights and examples come to light.

The profile characteristics we're about to present – our Social Equity Traits – may not be immediately obvious within existing brand personalities, and we stop short of saying that all of them *need* to be present in order for the brand to move towards recognising itself and being recognised as a Social Equity Brand. Our reason for hesitation here is that whilst we believe we've created a detailed and consistent view of the anatomy of a Social Equity Brand, the physiology of a Social Equity Brand is undoubtedly extremely complex

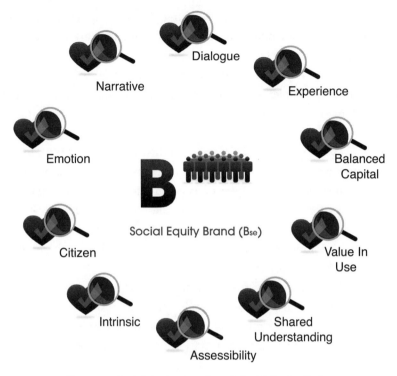

Figure 35: Social Equity Brands and Social Equity Traits

and dynamic. As such, specific contexts and conditions will play a significant part in the visibility and dominance of these profile characteristics.

But these caveats in place, we believe the following profile breakdown represents an extremely detailed, valid and constructive context within which to understand, debate and reflect on what exactly it is your brand has at its disposal with respect to harnessing the opportunities presented in this Era of Social Capital Rising – and what it can do to emerge as a Social Equity Brand (see Figure 35)

Social Equity Trait #1: Compelling narratives

This characteristic has cropped up anecdotally throughout the book, probably more frequently than most of the other traits listed here. As we've touched on time and time again, if there's one thing people are drawn to, it's a good story, and the need for brands to embrace, shape and share narratives with their audiences when it comes to sustainability cannot be underestimated. Why? Because narratives are an extraordinarily powerful way to help people find meaning in complex situations. Metaphors and analogies are, in effect, sense-making micro-narratives and their potency in shaping or framing understanding or opinion is beyond doubt.

Narratives can help us make sense of confusing or fast-moving situations, which, when we consider the dynamism and complexity of sustainability, is key. We've touched on the dangers of data and information-led initiatives and the propensity for these to cause us to buckle mentally under the weight of trade-offs and opportunity costs: narratives (working in conjunction with our second Social Equity Trait) offer an effective way to side-step these negative qualities that become barriers to behaviour change.

Besides helping make sense of complex and dynamic issues, narratives are also central to the construction and maintenance of social capital – all forms of social capital. Narratives present opportunities for people and groups not only to understand in their own way, but to adapt the narrative to pass on to others, who in turn can understand in their own way. In other words, narratives encourage dialogue, through contextualising a filtered array of complex issues, to make them relevant and appealing to a particular audience. Moreover, the very act of filtering information – and as a consequence creating biases within the account – generates trust between story-tellers and audiences (who then become story-tellers to new audiences, and so on).

As we've detailed, trust is both a key output of social capital and a key input. As such, narratives not only contribute to the development of social capital, as people and groups create, share and adapt stories, but they become more widespread and recognised as social capital increases. In other words, as social capital increases, so softer, more implied societal codes expressed through narratives start to exert dominance over cold, enforced covenants, expressed through rules and regulations. And the more these codes become established, the more powerful additional narratives become in embellishing and augmenting them.

So narratives are an essential tool not only for helping us make sense of the myriad environmental and social challenges we face and for eking out possible solutions, but also for building and maintaining social capital. The existence of narratives is a key *ingredient* for increases in social capital stock, and their existence is a strong *indicator* of the health and balance of social capital.

But like any good story or narrative, there are a number of criteria that have to be met. We've mentioned the need for effective narratives to both contextualise the salient issues for the audience and to filter the possible content legitimately in order for the emotional biases to be accepted and trusted. To meet these and other criteria, we've identified five distinct aspects of a successful brand-originated narrative in this sustainability context. We call them our Narrative Accelerators.

Narrative Accelerator 1: Compelling Author

Obvious as it may sound, is your brand actually entitled to be leading the narrative? In other words, are the various traits that make up the images being communicated to the appropriate audiences in line with the type of narrative proposed? This question touches on the complementary relationship that needs to exist between external facing images to consumers and other third parties, and internal images presented to employees and suppliers. To clarify, we're using images to describe the collection of identity attributes that are presented to distinct audiences, recognising that the projected – 'target' – image may not sync up with the received image.

Increasingly, as the value consumers expect from a relationship with a brand is more and more shaped by the alignment of personal and brand values, the need to develop a consistent corporate brand that supports and underpins the various product brands is rising. It is no coincidence that we have seen so many large companies dust down, revitalise and push forward their corporate brands in the last few years. Once the mainstay of internal communications architecture and corporate communications, corporate brands are now being recognised as a powerful asset by which companies can instil a range of qualities or values across an entire portfolio of product brands, allowing consumers to 'see beyond' the product and understand the machinery and motive of the organisation behind. Well that's the theory, but as we'll discuss at a little later, this, in itself, presents a host of challenges. Despite claims, it does not rely solely on transparency.

But images to one side, if the narrative is to be believed, shared and acted upon, then the author has to be credible. And considering this narrative needs to be shared in a multitude of formats with a variety of audiences, this credibility has to be consistent across all faces of the business and its brands. To ensure this is the case, it requires a careful re-analysis of the corporate identity and its various images (brands) and an understanding of how these identity traits relate to or fit in with the sustainability debate as relevant for the appropriate audiences.

In short, can the brand tell this story?

If it can, then a second interesting issue arises. In nearly all commercial cases, these identities are formed around essentially utilitarian purpose – in other words, the identities are there to support a commercial identity set up to meet a need or a want (and ideally more effectively and profitably than its competitors). But if the firm attempts to build a narrative around salient sustainability issues, and then share this with key audiences through the appropriate images, its overall identity may start to become more *normative*.[34] Whilst a little conceptual, this can have a significant impact on the identity of the organisation, in that it shifts from utilitarian to normative, which in turn has consequences in terms of consistent communication outside of these issues. In other words, if the firm takes a strong position on issues around sustainability and creates a vivid and sense-making narrative for its audiences, then this position has to shape the wider communication efforts.

Narrative Accelerator 2: Gripping Plot

This is a natural follow-on from the above, in that for the narrative to be relevant, effective, valued and trusted by the various audiences, then not only must the author be credible and appropriate, but the story must be too. We've looked in detail at how we as individuals can get lost in a sea of data and information that is often offered up in the name of transparency in order to build trust. But as is hopefully clear by now, our position on this point is very different, in that we feel that whilst it may be far more complex, the route to longer term, durable trust is via narrative and its associated effects (see Social Equity Trait #9 for more on this).

But how does the brand decide what to include in its sense-making narrative? Which characters will feature? How will they interact? What principal events will unfold? And, indeed, how will it all end?

Whilst we are not claiming the brand can have control over the narrative arc, in what has to be such a collaborative process, it is nonetheless important that those managing the process determine the frames of the narrative – to suit the audiences, the issues and, of course, the firm – and have a clear idea of where it *could* go as the narrative comes to life, is shared and then reversioned for new audiences.

Narrative Accelerator 3: Genre

As part of ensuring the brand is creating a compelling narrative for the right audiences and at the right moment, decisions need to be made about narrative genre. Right now, most communication around environmental and social responsibility seems to sit in 'dry factual', 'overly long biography' or just plain old 'horror'. None of these, we'd wager, are good genres from which to build the sorts of sense-making narratives we need to both bolster social capital and instigate the process to find innovative solutions to our problems at source.

Instead, we need to see more imaginative uses of wider genres – crime, comedy, tragedy, even romance. In short, the genre has to fit the audience and the brand in order to create the context in which to form the plot. Whilst we've moaned about the sheer scale and complexity of the sustainability debate throughout most of this book, in this particular case this scale is a great asset, since it can easily accommodate any number of narratives from any genre we care to pick.

If we refer back to our consumer segments as part of Havas's Sustainable Futures project, we can immediately place this use of genre into context. Let's consider the Devotees – for this segment, surely romance would work? And the Hostages? Well, such is their angst and confusion, maybe some well-placed and light-touch humour could help? And for Sceptics and Critics? Crime, thriller and 'who done it?' spring to mind.

Crashing around our segments and attaching blunt genre types is, of course, just a broad-brush example, but it does serve to illustrate the importance of stepping back, looking at the various components and then considering which genre may most effectively play host to our brand-led narrative that could have the greatest impact on our audiences.

Narrative Accelerator 4: Jeopardy and Conflict

It's a paradox of modern brand communication. On the one hand, everyone who works in advertising and media recognises the importance of a good story. And away from advertising, everyone knows that within the story arc, you need jeopardy and conflict (and hopefully resolution) to keep people interested.

So why is it that advertising and brands are so averse to embracing jeopardy and conflict in their stories?

Of course no-one wants to be the harbinger of bad news, but that's not to say jeopardy and conflict can be ignored. Like it or not, any story without these siblings is leaning towards being dull.

Regardless of genre, regardless of plot, regardless of author, all brand-led narratives have to recognise and embrace jeopardy and conflict.

This is especially true when we talk about sustainability, since the debate itself is riddled with these two slippery characters.

Jeopardy and conflict engage audiences. And, as we've seen, emotional engagement is key if we're to move beyond the brittle regurgitation of corporate efforts in this space, and allow brands to uncover and deliver the value that lies beneath.

So there's no escape – any brand-led narrative has to recognise and feature jeopardy and conflict. And whilst an overall resolution is nowhere to be seen, it is important that there is some form of resolution in the narrative: resolution in the form of the brand identifying wins, developments or other outcomes, which, whilst not obfuscating the major issues still ahead, move us all in the right direction, even if only by a step.

Narrative Accelerator 5: Editorial Openness

This is the last of our Narrative Accelerators. And, like the four before it, seems pretty obvious when we write it down. Brands as authors have to become more comfortable with a loss of editorial control over these new capital-building narratives.

And whilst it may sound simple and obvious, this is probably the most important criterion that needs to be met in terms of effective narrative building and sharing. The option and opportunity to revise, reversion and retell these narratives are vital if social capital is to flourish in a balanced and constructive manner.

In every small pocket bound by bonding capital, the context is a little different, and those who acted as the primary audience for the first telling of the story from the brand must feel able, comfortable and enthused to take this story, make it their own and share in their own environments. It is only with editorial openness that these sense-making narratives can travel across the bridging and linking divides and flourish within a wealth of bonding environments. It is only with such openness that the most salient, engaging and enduring narratives will emerge.

Again, this is something traditional brands are not used to doing – and not comfortable doing. But this acceptance of loss of control – this willingness to lose it – is vital. It will only be in the true setting free of these narratives that their stories will yield the long-term value to both society and those who are credited with initiating them.

Social Equity Trait #2: The power of emotion

Again, this has been a recurring theme throughout this book. Emotion – once banished from any communication efforts in a bid to move us all to being rational data-sorters and decision makers – is now recognised as a major lever with which to engage audiences. This may muddy the relationship once again between those within the firm that steer the communication efforts of the brand and the other departments or functions, but the use of emotion in engaging audiences around these issues cannot be underplayed. As we've shown previously, emotion is increasingly being seen as a 'gatekeeper' variable when it comes to the potential benefits or value someone anticipates from entering into a relationship with a brand. In other words, increase the emotional aspect of the burgeoning relationship and the potential value of that relationship goes up too.

In a world where consumers are always being quoted as finding sustainable alternatives less than efficient or attractive when compared to their more traditional counterparts, the incentive to use emotion to override these reactions is staring us in the face.

As we've discussed, when it comes to matters of sustainability, brands are frequently playing the role of faithful communicator of their corporate guardians' initiatives. In other words, repeating the operations-led work of the firm, hoping this demonstration yields some appreciation from the audiences. This is not only emotionless – with dry, factual accounts of operational successes – but also focuses exclusively on the firm and its behaviour, rather than on the consumer *and their potential behaviour.*

With this complete absence of emotion, is it any wonder supposedly sustainable options (often determined so purely by packaging and labelling) fail to generate the predicted utility levels needed to trump established products and services?

In short, when it comes to connecting around these issues, most brands are not leveraging the potential benefits of a more emotional connection.

Social Equity Brands recognise the importance of emotion – and indeed the responsibility. Combining emotion with the power of narrative (especially plot and genre, as detailed above) requires a significant degree of discretion and bravery from this new breed of brands if they are to avoid criticism for skewing or distorting the issues for their own gain. The key here is recognising the beneficiary of the gain. In keeping with an objective to build higher and more balanced levels of social capital, Social Equity Brands are never interested directly in their own gain. This is not to say that they are philanthropic, but rather that their gain is alongside that of society's – or certainly the communities with which they engage. In other words, the desire to communicate – emotionally and through narrative or otherwise – is driven by an intrinsic desire to build social capital. As we've already expressed in our working definition of social capital, there has to be a recognition of both public and private benefit from social capital building, and Social Equity Brands recognise the need to balance the two.

Jennifer Aaker[135] demonstrates the importance of emotion in the audience–brand relationship through a fascinating experiment with online users interacting with a new photo-sharing and printing company. With one group of users, the company's brand was developed to signify emotional attributes of stability, security and sensibleness. For this brand, storing, sharing and printing photos was incredibly important as a way to catalogue and remember the important events in our life. The brand positioned the services on the website as supporting what could almost be seen as a responsibility we all have to remember our lives. Conversely, the second group interacted with a far more light-hearted brand, celebrating spontaneity and offering users the chance to share these vibrant records of life instantly. It's important to stress that behind the branding and copywriting, the actual experience on the site was exactly the same, with identical functionality.

With these 'personalities' established, both groups used the site for several weeks, uploading photos, creating albums and then choosing to email or print collections to friends and colleagues. However, within each user group, they were further divided into two, with one group enjoying uninterrupted use of the service and the other experiencing a failure in the service after several weeks. For the latter group, they lost their photos. As would be expected, regardless of brand personality or the emotions involved in the relationship, both sub-sets of users were suitably frustrated to lose not only the use of the service but also their remotely stored images.

But what's interesting is what happened next. The service was duly resumed, and lost images were recovered. And from that moment on for the rest of the trial, for those using the more light-hearted and fun brand, their closeness to the brand actually improved as a result of the incident. But for those using the colder, more austere and sensible version, their closeness never returned. In other words, the emotional connection with the brand (as a result of matching brand value sets with individual value sets) worked to create more value for certain users of the site.

The ramifications of this interesting experiment for brands and social capital building are also significant. As we've already set out, jeopardy and conflict are key parts of any effective narrative, and narratives are vital if we're to rebuild levels of social capital. By ensuring audiences have the right emotional image and connection, the brand has an increased licence to incorporate jeopardy and conflict in its communications without any potential damage to the brand – quite the opposite in fact.

So, where many say that sustainability is fast becoming a licence to operate, we would go further and say that in the context of sustainability and social capital building, *emotion in brand communications creates a licence to innovate*.

Social Equity Trait #3: From consumer to citizen (who consumes)

There's plenty of evidence that suggests shopping has become a ritual in which we seek to identify our own identity,[136] and via brands, the very act of consumption creates meaning for us, either as individuals or as part of a group.[137]

Depressing as this may sound, it does offer a glimmer of hope, in that increasingly consumers are not consuming because of the material benefits of the product, but what they perceive to be the values of the brand around it. In other words, values are arguably as important as value.

In the context of this emerging Era of Social Capital Rising, we can start to see how Social Equity Brands can build relationships with their audiences based on value sets that transcend the normal brand–consumer relationship.

In short, Social Equity Brands focus not so much on the consumer, but the person who happens to be in the frame of mind to consume at that moment. The subtle difference is that this person is so much more than a consumer, before and after this moment of pure market interaction. They're a father, a mother, a son, a daughter, a carer, a volunteer, a hobbyist . . . the list is endless. In short, they are citizens.

Social Equity Brands recognise the multifaceted nature of each member of their community, and look to create value in their attempts to build social capital by understanding the myriad needs, wants and ambitions these individuals have. When we consider brands' historical preoccupation with such a narrow profile of their consumers, both psychologically and temporally, the opportunities to create additional value – both public and private – from this shift in perspective are incredible. Social Equity Brands will be interested in people even if that interest cannot yield an immediate tangible return, for the reason that Social Equity Brands are committed to raising stocks of social capital first and foremost. In other words, Social Equity Brands view individuals not as some malleable consumer from whom to satisfy extrinsic ambition, but rather a well-rounded citizen whose ambitions can be met with a more intrinsic approach and outlook.

It's a shift in perspective that we believe means firms and their brands are no longer in the B2C (Business to Consumer) business. *Everyone's now in the B2Ci (Business to Citizen) business.*

And whilst we have neither the time (nor the ability) to climb into a detailed debate on the impact of arguing that we need to be seen as citizens rather than consumers, there are two major consequences we'd like at least to introduce.

Firstly, as consumers we constantly obsess about our 'rights' – that there are a number of conditions that act to protect us from unscrupulous business. Whilst we do not deny the importance of these consumer rights, we believe they lead to a culture where we – the consumer – are absolved of any responsibility in our purchasing decisions. In other words, if there's a legal market for something, then we are excused from needing to carry out any personal due diligence on that market, since we're protected by an army of rights. This is a terribly consumer-oriented mentality – just take a look at the reactions of people who feel they are wronged as consumers. But as citizens (who may consume) the emphasis has to shift, or at least broaden, to one that recognises and encourages our personal duty to make sure we're making the right decision. In other words, just because there's a legal market, and just because we're protected by Visa, does not mean we should necessarily consume or experience that product or service. As citizens, we have duties as well as rights.

And second, if Social Equity Brands attempt to understand their audiences as citizens rather than consumers – understanding before and after, background and foreground – these brands must offer the same in return. In other words, the before, after, background and foreground of the experience they represent. This translates into letting the audience understand the identity and motives of the organisation as a whole, which underpin and support the specific proposition of the brand – so a thorough understanding of the corporate identity. Social Equity Brands recognise that the social capital lens can be – must be – looked through in both directions (see Figure 36).

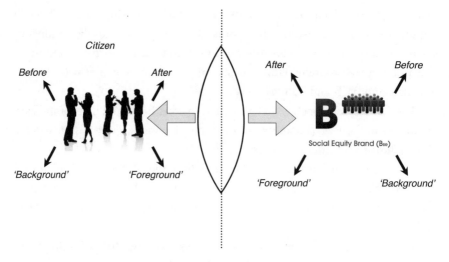

Figure 36: The importance of reciprocity

Social Equity Trait #4: Value-in-use

Straight off the bat, we want to say this is not our term, but instead describes the groundbreaking work carried out in the last five years by a number of marketing academics.[138] But the reason we're drawing on it is that we feel it has significant consequences for the development of social capital (and the sourcing of innovative solutions to many of the environmental and social challenges we face).

As we've already referenced, Vargo and Lusch[139] talk about a number of principles that are shaping the future of marketing, including the arguments that all economies are now service economies and consumers are co-producers of value. Underpinning all of these arguments is the premise that value is not embedded in a product, but rather is derived from using the product. As incredibly sensible as this may sound, this is contrary to the established view of production and, by association, marketing. And nowhere is this better illustrated than in the now-popular example of why we buy power drills.[140] When we walk into a hardware shop, we're not really looking to buy a power drill with a 1/16" drill bit – we're looking to buy a 1/16" hole in the wall. In other words, right under our noses, people have been deriving value-in-use, rather than simply realising the value embedded in the product at the moment of purchase. And if it's the hole we want, rather than the drill, then aren't there far more effective and valuable business models – for the consumer and the provider – waiting to be created?

On a far larger scale, the entire car industry is predicated on the conceit of value embedded, rather than value-in-use. This may well be a by-product of the industry largely representing the arrival of scientific management with Henry Ford's Model T production line and its operand resource obsession, but it persists to this day. The manufacturer crises of 2008 and 2009 are all we need to cite to argue effectively that the industry should have abandoned this approach. It simply doesn't make sense – either to the consumer or the manufacturer.

The reason this concept of value-in-use is so important in the context of Social Equity Brands and the creation of greater and more balanced levels of social capital, is that it recognises all of the value that can come from inter-acting, sharing and adapting. In other words, if there were some form of 'value curve' from the moment of purchase, the argument of value-in-use recognises that this curve rises steeply once the product is 'out there' being used (and shared and adapted). This, in turn, encourages social capital to flourish (as a result of the sharing), which, in turn, creates a virtuous circle, in that as social capital increases, so the opportunities to create greater value-in-use increase (see Figure 37).

This value is captured in the way users adapt or customise the product or service to meet their shifting needs, with this value being as much a product

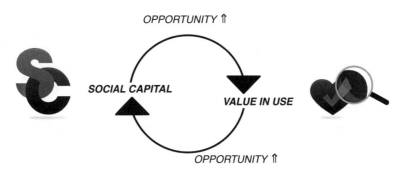

Figure 37: Social capital and value-in-use

of the immediate usage context as it is the context within which it was designed or made. What's more, through constant iterations of value-in-use, the product becomes better at delivering what exactly people want – or certainly more flexible, in order to be adapted to what people want – as and when their wants adapt and evolve in turn. Returning to the car example, I drive an Audi A6 estate. It's a wonderful car – smooth drive, well-engineered and very reliable. But it's also an estate. We bought an estate to fit in children, bags and an increasingly broad variety of other 'support kit' when going away. The problem, though, is that we are in the car as a family probably no more than once a month. The rest of the time, it's just me. So the car is the wrong car for us the clear majority of the time. Research suggests that upwards of 90% of the energy produced by a car is used just to push the car itself down the road.[141] This is certainly the case with just me in a large estate, so the 'value' derived seems predominantly for the benefit of the car. In effect, I've become a chauffeur for my own car. And at my own expense.

What's more, this obsession with value embedded destroys so much advantage for the company and brand. Again, in the case of car manufacture, despite lavishing years of R&D, design and manufacturing expertise on new models, in many cases the manufacturer sees less than 20% of the total revenues from a car model flow back to them over the lifetime of the vehicle (when you factor in servicing, repairs, fuelling, tax, insurance, etc.).[142] Less than 20% seems a lousy return on all that effort – certainly not good 'value' for money.

There's another striking example of an industry fixated – at great personal cost – on an outdated model of physical resources rather than value, far closer to home: marketing services and advertising firms. Still these firms focus largely on exclusively 'owning' the resources to be deployed on clients, with a price tag to match that exclusivity – so selling the power drill, not the hole. Where's the option to simply access those resources as and when necessary – as and when the client needs the hole – with the price tag to match?

Value-in-use is also a powerful supporter of the argument to dematerialise products, which is a key tenet of the broader sustainability debate. In both the power drill and car examples, the value is in what the thing can do, rather than the thing itself (although we acknowledge with cars there is a hefty dose of materialistic and hedonic satisfaction for many owners). And in both cases we're seeing interesting business models evolve which are more oriented around a value-in-use proposition, such as car clubs and garden tool clubs.[143] As an interesting side comment, apparently the typical power drill is used for just 12 minutes, on average, across its life span (10 years)[144] – just stop and think of the wasted value in owning that, and how that value could be unlocked with higher levels of social capital.

The same is true of cars. Zipcar, the pioneer of car sharing in the US, uncovered an interesting insight when polling its users – it found that whilst cost and hassle savings were big drivers for satisfaction with the service, members also cited the ability to choose from a range of vehicles as a big plus. So, if driving into town, a small two-door hatchback would be ideal (maybe even electric to avoid congestion charges and get free parking); if away for a romantic weekend, a sporty convertible; or if off with the family, a comfortable touring estate. The point is that the member is able to maximise the value they get in use from the service, by picking the right vehicle for their specific needs or wants. Now compare that to the car almost certainly sitting idly outside your house right now. Can you really say it delivers such versatile and tailored value depending on your specific needs?

Even ad agencies and marketing firms are adapting, with new challenger firms emerging with utterly new business models that see them borrowing from these arguments for dematerialisation and value-in-use approaches. The result is a new type of agency that is not only more agile, flexible and current than most, but also able to tap into world-class resources (around the world) at a moment's notice, without the eye-watering price-tag for clients.[145]

Social Equity Trait #5: Dialogue

We've made a habit of landing on over-used words and phrases in this book. The three big ones that we've collided with so far are 'sustainability', 'brand' and 'trust'. To that list we're now adding 'dialogue'.

Dialogue is a very well-worn term when discussing new era brand communications (to replace the old school monologue model), and it should come as no surprise that this is a key characteristic of a Social Equity Brand, since dialogue is one of the foundational pillars of our process model of social

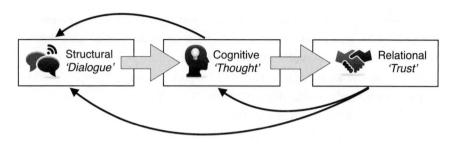

Figure 38: Social capital process

capital. This model argues that all social capital development needs to start with dialogue (which then leads to new and shared mental models, and ultimately trust – see Figure 38).

Much of the conversation around the need for dialogue focuses on the opportunities presented by social media, and we're certainly in agreement – social media presents an unprecedented opportunity for dialogue between brands and their audiences.

But we'd argue this does not go far enough. Whilst the role of a brand to create an enabling space for this intricate, granular dialogue to take place between it and its constituents is important, this is, in its heart, an updated and sophisticated form of bonding social capital building. In other words, it is still enabling a bilateral relationship to develop between the brand and its audience, albeit in real time and via interactive technology.

What will separate Social Equity Brands out from the rest, when it comes to initiating dialogue, is that they will do so by nurturing linking and bridging environments as well as bonding environments. So, rather than dyadic relationships by whichever media, it becomes a focus on 'triadic' relationships, *regardless of media*. More than that, Social Equity Brands will ensure this dialogue takes hold in these environments even once the brand is absent. But that is not to say that the brand is forgotten – the credit will still flow to the brand for initiating or shaping the dialogue.

So, dialogue, in the context of Social Equity Brands, includes the rich, varied and dynamic dialogue that takes place amongst a far broader cross-section of stakeholders, many of whom would not even consider themselves consumers of the products or services that that brand identifies with. This broader, almost 'anti-targeting' approach to brand-led communication is starting to be explored amongst marketing academics, and is being tagged 'stake-holder marketing',[146] recognising its overlap with what has traditionally been the sole domain of corporate communications.

But that is not to say that this wider orbit of stakeholders cannot derive value from the dialogue initiated by those brands. It is this almost vicarious relationship between the Social Equity Brand and this wider community that results in far more value being generated ('in use' and 'in context'), with richer social capital and its associated benefits as a result. With this shift in value, the opportunities to engage with a far wider audience become far more vivid.

The key element here is the brand being able to shift the purpose or direction of the dialogue away from the firm and its efforts in moving towards more sustainable practices, and instead towards enabling the audience to establish its own motivations, ambitions and solutions (see Figure 39). As we've already mentioned, the current default setting seems to be brand communication predicated on the faithful and dense reproduction of corporate endeavours, hoping that these reports inspire consumers to engage and reward with loyalty. It's pretty clear this is not working, and Social Equity Brands will move beyond this, ensuring the motivation and consequence of any dialogue is to engage and empower the audience (stakeholder) in *their* context, not the firm's. In other words, it becomes less about 'we the firm – haven't we done well?', and more about 'you the individual – what can we help you do?'.

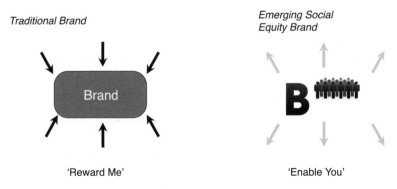

Figure 39: 'Traditional Us' vs 'Emerging You'.

Social Equity Trait #6: Shared understanding

Following on from the importance of developing dialogue within a broader, deeper definition, Social Equity Brands also recognise the importance of developing shared understanding around the issues we face. Whilst this may sound obvious, in most cases this is a complex task, considering the start points, ambitions and motivations of distinct and disparate audiences.

This is further exacerbated by the fact that most brands today consider the primary role of communication to establish greater loyalty from their targets, and as such are committed to skewing the communication to achieve this. As we've said from the word go, this is a negative consequence of this intense, often intoxicating, form of plastic bonding social capital created by brands.

And whilst we've argued for the effective use of narrative and emotion in order to engage brand audiences – these communities of awakening citizens (who consume) in this Era of Social Capital Rising – the need to educate and inform is equally as important. Social Equity Brands recognise the need to establish platforms of shared understanding, since it is only with these platforms in place that audiences can accurately assess the materiality of the issues they face.

For brands to do this requires a fundamental shift in outlook. Rather than focusing on the traditional and narrow bonding capital scope of a relationship with consuming audiences, Social Equity Brands will recognise the need and opportunity to communicate – and collaborate – with their traditional competitors, in order to establish these stable platforms of shared understanding. We've already seen glimpses of this practice, where competitors come together in order to build a common platform (before then abandoning this collaboration for a return to competition), such as the sustainable fishing initiative, the Marine Stewardship Council[147] or the efforts to introduce more sustainable laundry and washing behaviour with the AISE.[148]

Social Equity Brands will recognise the need to establish these collaborative efforts as the norm, rather than the exception. In other words, their commitment to build and nurture social capital will not be restricted solely to their audiences who derive value from their products and services, but will also embrace their peers. And whilst the immediate reaction may be that this destroys competitively derived benefits, we would argue this is more than offset – both immediately and in the long term – by the increases in collaboratively derived benefits. And by this, we mean all those benefits that are derived from being credited with building higher and more balanced stocks of social capital – so a focus on value rather than on product or service.

Social Equity Trait #7: Balanced social capital

In our efforts to build the argument that sustainability – or rather unsustainability – is a symptom (albeit a hugely significant one) of our current crisis, rather than the cause, we've constantly championed the replenishment of social capital. But a brute increase in social capital won't get us to where we want or need to be. Instead it has to be a balanced increase in social capital – all forms of social capital.

Social Equity Brands recognise this need – that if we're to leverage the opportunities to find innovative solutions to the problems we face, and in doing so create the maximum levels of public and private value, social capital has to increase across the bonding, bridging and linking axes. So as well as building dialogue, shared thinking and trust directly with audiences, Social Equity Brands will strive to link similar audiences and introduce disparate groups of communities. This is a marked departure from the focus of a traditional brand (Figure 40).

A broader view of the importance of balance within the forms of social capital will ensure that new ideas are shared, challenged and adapted, without the temptation to silo or protect innovation. Whilst bonding capital is key to establishing the efficiencies, familiarity and even informality, bridging and linking capital allow for the inflow of alternate perspectives, contexts and opportunities.

There are already excellent examples of some brands having moments of reaching out to restock bridging and linking capital, rather than relying on the traditional dominance of bonding capital. Initiatives where firms and their brands collaborate with governmental or supra-governmental bodies allow the marketing departments to bring their audiences into contact with new perspectives via linking capital – and efforts to bring to the attention of their

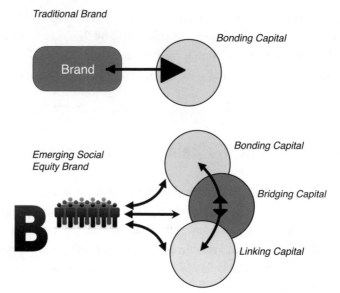

Figure 40: Brands and capital

consuming community the conditions of other communities are bridging capital at work.

A focus on all forms of social capital rather than just bonding capital can nudge the brand towards engaging in what some academics call social marketing.[149] By social marketing, we're talking about attempts to influence '. . . a target audience to voluntarily accept, reject, modify or abandon a behaviour for the benefit of individuals, groups or society as a whole'.[150]

With this definition, it's easy to see how this can be interpreted as 'de-marketing',[151] since the focus can be on stopping people consuming. But whether it's labelled social marketing or de-marketing, this approach is essentially a recognition of needing to build all forms of social capital. If traditional marketing is 'bonding capital marketing', then social marketing is 'bonding, bridging and linking marketing'.

With a shift away from the bonding capital dominant approach, Social Equity Brands have to find a way to balance what is good for an individual with what is good for the immediate community, society or indeed a community on the other side of the world. Bridging and linking capital provide those all-important checks and balances to ensure bonding capital does not run away with itself, intoxicating those who are a part of it. And whilst this may panic some brand managers that they're going to stop selling as much stuff as they used to, we have this practical response: yes, maybe you are. But is it the sale you're after or the value that the sale creates?

We think it's the latter, in which case by focusing on building more balanced social capital, the amount of value that can be created increases – maybe not in the form of immediate sales, but in terms of reputation and equity, which can, in turn, be converted into a variety of forms of value, depending on objectives (premium pricing, extensions, new markets, etc.).

This highlights the relationship between social capital building and marketing. If marketing is focused on delivering sales today and building value in the long term, then social capital building *supports* those actions today and *drives* those benefits for the long term.

Social Equity Trait #8: From 'accessibility' to 'assessability'

This is probably the simplest of these ten characteristics to outline – and probably the most important.

Over and over we see brands, on behalf of their corporate guardians, attempting to lay bare the full extent of the efforts being made at an operations and logistics level, in order to justify claims around sustainability. The plan – we assume – is that in return for exposing all in the name of corporate transparency, their audiences will respond with greater levels of loyalty and respect for the business and its brands.

As we've discussed earlier, whilst transparency may go some way to appease a glut of mistrust, it's unlikely in our humble opinions that it will actually build trust. Why? Because trust fails not because of secrecy, but because of lies – and transparency does nothing to remove the desire or ability to lie.

Social Equity Brands recognise this shortfall and understand that if durable trust is going to develop between it and its audiences, it is not enough to simply make itself accessible.

Instead, it needs to make itself 'assessable'.

In other words, Social Equity Brands attempt to find ways not only to present sufficient information to their audiences, but to establish means by which those audiences can then use that information constructively. Social Equity Brands arm their audiences with the right tools with which to understand the information being presented to them.

As is the case with many of these attributes, this ability to assess – rather than simply access – the brand and its owner is often done through the use of narratives, helping audiences make sense of the issues and the firm's positions on these issues.

Social Equity Trait #9: Intrinsic trumps extrinsic

We've already introduced this distinction between intrinsic and extrinsic motivations, but we think it warrants a little additional discussion.

Traditionally, all brand activity has been extrinsically motivated. In other words, everything a brand does is geared ultimately to meet another goal – to secure a sale, initiate a transaction or open up a new revenue stream. Ironically, when we talk about materialistic behaviour, this very trait from brands is spectacularly materialistic. Materialists often engage in relationship building purely in an attempt to meet some other objective. In other words, the relationship has to yield some tangible value besides the value in the relationship itself. When looked at like this, it's no wonder brands have been so involved in the slow decline of social capital; never mind what consumers have been doing, the behaviour of brands themselves has been the epitome of materialism.

Intrinsically motivated behaviour, by comparison, is typified by an interest purely in the direct benefits of that behaviour. So, rather than making friends with someone in order to get a promotion or to ensure that person will do you a favour at some point in the future, intrinsic motivation would see that friendship being forged purely for the fun, warmth and intellectual stimulation the relationship brings. Imagine that.

Social Equity Brands recognise the importance of being driven by intrinsic motivation when appropriate. This approach fits well when overlaid with the other characteristics, so many of which are specifically not driven by a desire to snatch a short-term pecuniary gain from an audience, but to enjoy the value from the relationship itself.

The challenge, however, comes when the brand monetises this intrinsic motivation. Which, of course, at some point it has to – we are pragmatists after all, and recognise that this new breed of brand is not some extreme and permanent form of cause-related marketing.

The response to this dilemma, we believe, lies in the original ambition of the action. If the brand is genuinely committed to raising the quality of the relationship through dialogue, shared thinking and trust, then for benefits to flow ultimately to the brand as a reward for having this ambition is fine. This does not compromise its original intrinsic motivation, since the (financial) rewards are flowing as a consequence of this ambition, rather than being the ambition.

We're aware there may be a little water being let in with respect to that response, and it's something we'd like to hear other people's thoughts on (via www.brandvalued.com). But that said, the need for brands to demonstrate intrinsic motivation consistently, and at the same time keep an eye on delivering value ultimately to their firm (as well as to a wider public) is a tricky line to tread.

As an example of where not to tread on this line, at a recent conference we listened to a branding and innovation consultancy proudly explain how they'd developed a new revenue stream, and ultimately business model, for a well-known mass luxury car manufacturer. Their idea had been to take the brand traits of superior engineering and a commitment to safety, combine it with the target market of new families and create a range of similarly highly engineered baby and children's seats for the cars. Furthermore, the same engineers who would service the vehicles (keeping them safe) would fit and service these chairs at the same time. The consultants were delighted at what quickly blossomed into a strong revenue stream.

Now, for us, whilst there was clearly a market for these car seats (sold at eye-watering prices, it has to be said), this approach was extrinsically motivated and horribly damaging to the integrity of the brand. In short, profoundly un-Social Equity Brand-like. With the company's reputation built around safety for you and your family, to unabashedly pursue new revenues from exploiting a natural desire to protect one's family when driving laid bare the brand's extrinsic motivation.

To reiterate, we are not claiming the brand should have given these seats away. But had it started from the position of attempting to extend its commitment to safety, to include awareness around correctly fitting a car seat, with engineers willing to review the seat at the service, then the brand would have been acting with intrinsic integrity. And had the branded, exclusive seat range been born from customer feedback, with better knowledge, dialogue and trust for the brand to ensure all aspects of safety were at least discussed and understood, this would have been much better. Acting intrinsically does not have to mean there's no external gain from the action or behaviour. It just means it is not the primary ambition.

Social Equity Trait #10: It's the experience that counts

This characteristic sums up many of the previous characteristics described, and combines them into almost an overarching approach that Social Equity Brands subscribe to. Social Equity Brands recognise that for social capital levels to rise, and for innovative, durable solutions to be found to many of the challenges we face today, brand audiences need to be released from the 'maximising relationships' so many brands – most brands in fact – try to establish. This slavish relationship created under the banner of (plastic) bonding social capital has to be modified. No-one is more aware of this than the architects of Social Equity Brands.

Maximising, as we've shown, not only soaks up too much time, leaving less to spend on other, more important activities and relationships, but also riddles us with panic, angst and buyer's remorse. The maximising ambition encourages trade-offs to be analysed and opportunity costs to be considered, resulting in horrendously compromised experiences that can never effectively parry the inevitable blows of disappointment. And that's before we even address maximising's tendency to encourage materialist behaviour and the arsenal of challenges that it brings with it.

Social Equity Brands will encourage 'satisficing' instead: that when it comes to choosing the product, a short, cursory review via a trusted source (ideally the brand itself) will suffice. It'll be 'good enough' – with 'good enough' actually being excellent. In other words, 'good enough' means excellent, but without the pain of search, or rather the pain of being *obliged* to search.

Again, like so many of these traits, this may strike fear into the heart of polished, seasoned marketers. Does a move towards satisficing mean an end to loyalty?

Our answer is no. Quite the opposite. Because in pursuing this strategy, Social Equity Brands are realising that within higher social capital lies a wealth of untapped value – value that audiences can experience and subsequently credit the brand for uncovering. To put it bluntly, happy, healthy brand audiences must be a good – and eminently more sustainable – thing.

A shift to recognising the value in social capital itself – in relationships, exchanges, thoughts and trust – is utterly in sync with the notion that real value comes from use and context, not from those who administer the brand. Through nurturing social capital (and by ridding relationships of the maximising ambition), Social Equity Brands will find a wealth of new competitive advantage amongst this blooming social capital. What's more, they're forms of advantage that are near impossible to mimic, thanks to their often informal and nearly always fluid and ambiguous nature.

Recognising that it is all about the experience, imagine you're heading to a concert to see your favourite stadium band. It's a massive event, and the concert experience is extraordinary. You come out and, flushed with the experience, buy a tour T-shirt from a small stall outside the venue. We believe traditional brands focus on the T-shirt sale – a moment of monetary exchange, attached in some way (ideally) to a wider experience or value. But Social Equity Brands are in the business of delivering the concert – the panoply of emotions that combine to make it a valuable experience – made unique by your interpretation of it amongst a community of others. Of course, Social Equity Brands will not ignore the merchandising opportunities (the physical product, in this case the tour T-shirt), but is this where the real value lies? No – to find that, we need to explore and celebrate the experience.

To reiterate a point made at the beginning of this chapter, this list of characteristics is certainly not exhaustive, and many may be conspicuous by their absence in the make-up of what are otherwise shining prototypes of Social Equity Brands. But the list as a whole paints what we believe is a more vivid and detailed picture of what an archetypal Social Equity Brand may look like.

But there is still a gap: a gap between the development, uncovering and ramping up of these characteristics and the actual construction, support and nourishment of social capital. In other words, how does a brand that exhibits a comprehensive raft of these characteristics actually put to them to good use, to steer how it creates social capital? How does it build public and private value, as well as sparking innovative, collaborative processes to find solutions to the challenges we face in a resource-constrained, sustainability-aware world? What is the device or architecture that takes this make-up and applies it to the brand's business of engaging and interacting with its audiences? What is in the box with the '?' in Figure 41?

The answer, we believe, is a Social Capital Strategy.

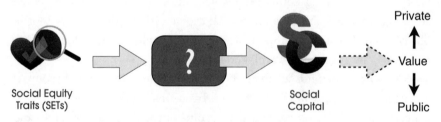

Social Equity
Traits (SETs)

Social
Capital

Private

Value

Public

Figure 41: Linking traits to capital to value

Chapter 11

In the previous chapter we outlined a number of qualities or traits that we believe Social Equity Brands, by and large, exhibit in one form or another – qualities that allow us to glimpse their modified DNA, separate them from the crowd and hold them in good stead to become recognised and rewarded engines of social capital. The list is far from exhaustive, primarily because we don't claim to have all the answers in what we feel is an emerging role for brands, and we're sure not all characteristics need be present at all times.

But accepting that these qualities coalesce into some Social Equity Brand 'archetype', the question that now stands up in front of us is this: how can a combination of these characteristics manifest itself in the day-to-day business of the brand, and constructively contribute to the creation of social capital and its resultant public and private benefits? In other words, how can these traits be linked to the creation of new value through influencing how the brand engages with its audiences?

The answer – the link – is the creation of a Social Capital Strategy (Figure 42).

A Social Capital Strategy represents a holistic and manageable way to interpret the salient Social Equity Brand characteristics effectively and leverage them to maximum effect in terms of creating social capital and its array of benefits.

Considering we're talking primarily about the interaction and relationships the brand forms with various audiences (both internal and external) and the ambitions and consequences of those relationships, the immediate reaction is to say any strategy to increase social capital should be masterminded

| Social Equity
Traits (SETs) | Social Capital
Strategy (SCS) | Social
Capital | Value
Public |

Figure 42: Linking traits to capital to value via a Social Capital Strategy

and administered by the Marketing Department. After all, as we've said over and over, all marketing and brand communication has always been a form of social capital building. So we agree with this argument – but with caveats attached.

Historically this process has prioritised the almost 'steroid-like' growth of bonding capital, and in this new Era of Social Capital Rising, this updated role requires the balanced growth of all three forms of capital. In addition, social capital levels need to rise in both the external and internal audiences around the brand and its various manifestations.

This need to create a strategy that encompasses social capital growth internally and externally, with those traditionally targeted via the Marketing Department, those traditionally engaged via Human Resources and those traditionally managed via the Corporate Communications function, not surprisingly prompts the thought of a marketing-dominant hybrid function within the business – the Social Capital Department (see Figure 43). Whilst it may not physically exist within the business (yet), the creation of a strong Social Capital Strategy should certainly call on the skills and experience found within these three departments.

Figure 43: Social Capital Department

That said, with input from these departments or functions, the role of creating and actioning the Social Capital Strategy falls first and foremost with the Marketing Department – it is, after all, responsible for shaping the relationships the brand forms with external audiences. But it is worth exploring the core differences between the skills and perspective required for a traditional marketing strategy approach and those demanded for the emerging Social Capital Strategy approach. We're not advocating one gets replaced with the other – rather one is reshaped and supported by the other. In essence, a brand-centred Social Capital Strategy should underpin the broader marketing strategy across two key dimensions – value today (through sales) and value tomorrow (through brand-building). (See Figure 44.)

Historically these dimensions have been predicated on a rational, scientific approach to the consumer acting logically, alone and solely in their self-interest. They are the result of a product- and transaction-focused mindset, formed from the notion that repeated transactions today are all that is needed to drive brand value tomorrow.

This may not sit well with some, as we're now talking about marketing strategy, rather than brand strategy – and building Social Equity Brands is certainly all about a new type of brand strategy. But we strongly agree with the argument that the traditional marketing mix, as the basis of marketing

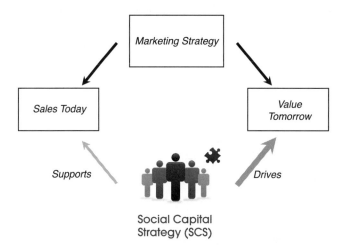

Figure 44: Social Capital Strategy and Marketing Strategy

strategy, was the starting point for strategic brand management. This is because the brand literally came into existence in order to drive sales, overcoming what we have labelled 'provenance costs'. In other words, the marketing mix was the 'how' of strategic brand management (and to many, it still is). Heding and Knudtzen[152] clearly make this point, supporting it with a meta-analysis of the research that shows that the 'economic approach' to brand management[153] had (and still has) as a central tenet the traditional marketing mix focused on product and transaction.

It may sound clunky and short-termist when described like this, but this really is the case – and very importantly remains so for many brands to this day. Many brands still focus predominantly on 'single-transaction' efficiency with consumers, where the purpose of the brand is to remove or at least lower those transaction costs for consumers in whichever way they can. They do this by applying the levers of the marketing mix: the 4Ps – product, place, price and promotion.

Introduced by Neil Borden[154] and then 'packaged' as the 4Ps by E. Jerome McCarthy[155] in the mid-6os, the 4Ps have gone through a few revisions over the years as a way to keep them central to many brand management strategies. Relatively recent additions (from the 1980s onwards) have included a P for People, recognising the importance to the quality of the sale experience of employees. And there has even been a sixth P in Planet, recognising some consumer interest or value in products and services that are mindful of natural resources and impacts. But regardless of how many Ps are put in, the marketing mix model remains product and transaction focused, with the result that traditional – but persistently pervasive – brand management techniques built on this foundation continue with an obsession on the momentary and functional.

This continued importance of the traditional 4P marketing mix approach is interesting considering the widespread criticism the model receives in both academia and practitioner circles. Whilst maybe no longer referred to explicitly, the impact and continued value of the marketing mix approach to brand management is undeniable. It seems the 'tidiness' of a more scientific and rational approach to marketing, where much of the control is considered to still reside with those who manage the brand, is something marketers are still reluctant to let go of. But with the scientific and rational approach, there comes an inevitable linear rigidity, which is chronically out of sync with this emerging era of wakefulness.

In this new Era of Social Capital Rising, the decision-making process whereby brands and their guardians mix and play their capabilities to the benefit of their audiences (and ultimately themselves) has to be very different. In line with the increase in breadth, depth and granularity of what a brand now needs to consider, it should come as no surprise that this whole process is now far more complex and dynamic.

In an attempt to bring some clarity to these new demands – these new pressures to find ways to leverage the capabilities and values of the firm and its brands – we've identified five key components of what we believe is an effective Social Capital Strategy – the strategy through which to build a Social Equity Brand.

To reiterate, we believe a Social Capital Strategy brings a degree of rigour and process to the connecting tissue between day-to-day requirements and longer-term value objectives in this Era of Social Capital Rising.

So we're arguing for a transition from an extrinsically motivated and transaction obsessed short-term approach predicated on a number of product-centric variables, to one that is more intrinsically driven, long-term and predicated on five relationship and experience-centric variables. The '5Is' are: Interconnectedness, Inclusiveness, Ignition, Interest and Imagination (Figure 45).

The '5Is' represent our attempt to upgrade and broaden the marketing mix: to inform the 'how' of modern brand management strategy, making it relevant, constructive and durable in terms of building effective brands in this new era. The 5Is model understands the need to build balanced and long-term social capital, not just instant bonding capital; recognises the importance of creating thick and rich value from a variety of experiences, rather than thin and momentary forms via product consumption; and appreciates that building social capital both within and around the business requires a broad set of skills not always found in the marketing function (but certainly found within the rest of thc organisation).

In short, the 5Is represent a fluid series of proof-points by which progressive brands can begin to understand how they can move towards recognising and celebrating the characteristics of a Social Equity Brand archetype by

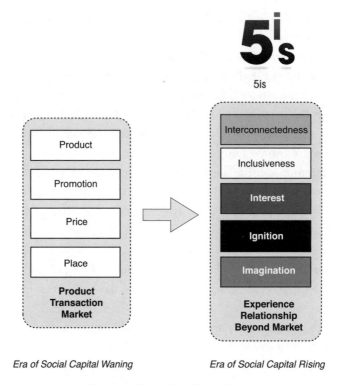

Figure 45: From the 4Ps to the 5Is

creating higher social capital and all its benefits. In just the same way market-ers have related their efforts to the various 'Ps' to ensure they're working as efficiently as possible, so we believe this new generation of social capitalists will be informed by these '5Is' to ensure that all they do in terms of the brand engaging with various audiences is aligned to build social capital, generate public and private value from that social capital and uncover innovative, col-laborative solutions to the challenges we face. As a bridge between reversioned brand identity and emerging market expectations, the 5Is combine to form a comprehensive and flexible set of indicators by which progressive brands and their skilled teams can assess if they are leveraging these new-found capabili-ties to create higher levels of social capital and everything that goes with it.

As a note of caution, however, we do not, for one second, believe that the 5Is can be so cleanly applied as a series of tests against which brands can gauge their efforts in this new era. These are not binary 'yes–no' conditions to be met, but are highly interpretative. The very nature of this new 'messy' era requires marketers to use more qualitative techniques in order to understand what they're managing to achieve, and to focus on what they should be aiming to achieve. Where the 4Ps are defined by quantitative techniques such as regression analysis from large datasets, the 5Is are informed by techniques such as ethnography, netnography and phenomenology within far smaller groups.

Interconnectedness

The first question a Social Equity Brand needs to ask is whether it fully understands its relationships with its peers. And after that, is it really leveraging those relationships?

To put it another way, how aware is it of the symbiotic relationship it has with its broad competitor set, and how much more value it could generate by leading more collaborative efforts within that set?

For most brands, the tried and tested approach for marketing is to try and reach their consumers more efficiently and effectively than their competitors. Consumers have finite attention spans and limited needs, so grabbing their attention as swiftly as possible and trying to establish this exclusive bonding capital with them is considered key. Just the very use of the term 'target' tells us all we need to know about how established marketing operates. As we laid out in an earlier chapter, this approach is almost certainly as a result of traditional brands considering their limited ability to influence consumers. As we've argued, on an individual brand level, all a traditional brand can hope for is to channel already existing demand in its direction. And if all goes to plan, keep channelling it, time and time again.

This approach by traditional brands is not only in keeping with an outdated view of value being wrapped up in the actual product, but it also highlights the sheer insecurity brands have about the genuine uniqueness of these products. This clamour to secure pole position in terms of building exclusive bonding capital between it and its audience is, we believe, a clear signal that the potential value from this process is pretty thin, brittle and ultimately transitory.

It's also very confusing. In the jostle to get the prime position, brands fragment their version of the story in order to appeal to what they consider to be distinct consumer segments. So for some, the message is predicated on quality, others price, others still availability. And on it goes – higher fragmentation, deeper segmentation, greater choice. The result is a marketplace chocfull of messages sliced and diced according to who's going to receive it, where and when, multiplied by the sheer number of brands involved. Suddenly the shocking statistic that we opened this book with, of us being pummelled by 3000 messages a day, doesn't seem so far fetched.

This confusion as a result of 'x' messages, multiplied by 'y' targets and then multiplied again by 'z' brands becomes even greater in the context of sustainability, as traditional brands try and appropriate one particular aspect of the debate they deem relevant to their targets, and one that is being tackled by the firm. The result is a sea of certification options and conflicting messages claiming salience for the consumer within a context that refuses to be reduced to pithy binary options.

Where traditional marketing strategy – and the 4Ps of marketing – focuses on trying to establish some form of efficient exclusivity over competition in an attempt to transact, a Social Capital Strategy focuses on developing value in broad, nonexclusive environments, in an attempt to relate meaningfully.

As such, a better Social Capital Strategy demands a better understanding of how the brand could collaborate with peers in order to make these relationships with brand audiences more rewarding – both publicly and privately. So how can recognition of this interconnectedness create richer, deeper and more frequent forms of dialogue, more established levels of shared understanding and ultimately more trust in those originating the dialogue and the stories they tell?

Certainly this recognition of interconnectedness has been used to good effect on occasions. As already highlighted, collaborative efforts such as those to raise awareness and understanding of laundry washing temperatures, as well as sustainable fishing and forestry practices are well covered. But in each case, once the standards have been established through collaboration, each participant has returned to a competitive stance. In other words, it is the exception rather than the norm. For Social Equity Brands, recognising this interconnectedness – leveraging this interconnectedness – should become a more normal, ongoing process.

One way that this collaborative stance can work more effectively for Social Equity Brands is through the recognition that this interconnectedness may

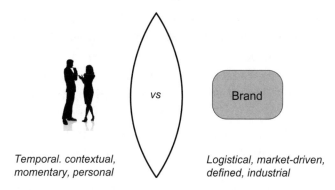

*Temporal. contextual,
momentary, personal*

*Logistical, market-driven,
defined, industrial*

Figure 46: Consumer view vs business view

be more powerful – may yield more public and private benefit – if the peer group is seen through the eyes of the user, rather than the established perspective of the firm. In other words, understand what it is the user wants at that moment in time and define the group by that need or ambition, rather than more traditional market factors (see Figure 46). This view challenges how we define our competitor sets and, as already discussed, can help shed light on why consumers may act the way they do and so often appear fickle and inconsistent.

An example of this approach here in the UK is EDF, the French energy company, working closely with a number of car manufacturers (including Toyota) to find ways of delivering effective, affordable and scaleable electric transport alternatives within London.[156] In this case, EDF is working closely with the manufacturers as well as governmental and planning departments to eke out a viable solution via smart grid technology and near-ubiquitous charging points. In other words, EDF recognises the potential to uncover greater and more long-term value by appreciating and leveraging its interconnectedness with other firms and entities, all of whom come together to answer a specific need or want of the end-user. In this particular case, the benefits that will be created for EDF and indeed all of the other interconnected entities are pretty clear to see.

Renault Nissan has also been leveraging this interconnectedness in Israel, through being a founder partner in its Better Car programme.[157] Working closely with energy suppliers and the government, this case study of collaboration and interconnectedness caught our attention for a single insight it uncovered from dialogue with potential users. The debate about all-electric vehicles is dominated by the concern over the mileage possible from a battery charge, and the fact that this limits where you can go in the car (at least with a hybrid you can always switch to gas to complete the journey). So when would electric cars have battery options that would last longer (and take less time to charge)? Everything seemed to suggest that the mainstream acceptance of the all-electric car was being held back by a perception that battery technology just hadn't arrived yet.

But dialogue initiated by this consortium of interconnected businesses and government departments found that underneath this well-worn concern was a far more interesting – and solvable – concern. When asked how far they thought an electric car could travel on one battery charge, most respondents had a pretty good idea (thanks to this concern being discussed frequently in the media), but when asked how far their own petrol or diesel car could travel on a full tank, far fewer people knew the answer. Why was this? Well, one answer could be that for petrol or diesel, you simply don't *need* to know the distance you can travel, as service stations are never more than about ten miles from wherever you are. In other words, a potential solution to removing this barrier for adoption lies not in waiting for battery technology to catch up, but rather in making electric recharging points as ubiquitous as petrol stations.

As it happens, the benefits of interconnectedness also led to novel ideas about swapping batteries rather than charging batteries (leading to 'refuel' stops that are even shorter than those required to fill up with petrol) and adopting a mobile phone business model of users buying the cars (the handset) but leasing the battery technology (the network), meaning new technology could be used in the car straight away, and the issues over battery disposal were no longer the consumer's concern.

In short, all of these areas of value were uncovered by those within the consortium recognising not just their interconnectedness, but the benefits of exploring that interconnectedness as a means to create higher social capital through dialogue and shared thinking. Businesses and organisations that ordinarily would not consider themselves in the same market, focused on an end-user perspective and in doing so uncovered opportunities to not only create considerable private and public benefits, but to also make considerable inroads with one of the most pressing and complex aspects of the sustainability debate – mobility. Recognising, developing and extending interconnectedness offers an opportunity for the protagonist to create more durable social capital and release more value.

Interconnectedness can also be uncovered and leveraged by looking at the needs and wants of users bound by a moment. In other words, understand – again from a user's perspective – how one particular need or want is shaped by – and shapes – the need or want that immediately precedes or follows it. It could be that by widening this context just by a matter of moments, opportunities to interconnect and create value could increase. Anthony Tjan – a blogger on hbr.org – makes this argument beautifully with his 'Three Minute Rule',[158] laying out the argument that if companies looked at what their consumers were doing immediately before and after their scheduled involvement with the brand, new opportunities to create interconnected value would spring up. One example in particular makes the point well: a supermarket uncovered a consumer insight that when entering the supermarket and having the option to pick up a basket or take a trolley, people are often chronically optimistic about how little they need to buy and choose to take neither. Then, half-way round the store – and as their hands are getting fuller and fuller – the thought of backtracking to the door to get a basket after all is just too galling. So they don't buy anything else, simply because they cannot carry it. In other words, a decision they made just a few minutes earlier determines the outcomes and value of the subsequent encounter. The solution? Placing a stack of baskets in the middle of the store, rather than having them all at the entrance. Imagine then, the additional value that is just sitting there for those brands that engage in understanding how they're interconnected to the brand-induced experiences that are immediately wrapped around their own experience.

Inclusiveness

At first glance, inclusiveness may sound suspiciously like interconnectedness. It's not.

When we talk about recognising inclusiveness within a Social Capital Strategy, we're making a nod towards what could be called an 'anti-targeting' or 'anti-segmenting' approach to brand building, communication and marketing: in other words, a move away from focusing on one particular profile at the expense of all others.

Segmenting and targeting, as we've discussed, go hand in hand with an approach to marketing strategy fixated on building high-speed, plastic and exclusive bonding capital with audiences. Anything and everything outside of that narrow relationship – be that aspects of the target's life or those who are not targeted – is considered immaterial.

In contrast, a move to build a compelling Social Capital Strategy as a means to create richer, deeper and more balanced social capital considers all profiles and all characteristics important. In short, inclusiveness is all about recognising that everyone can feasibly find value in what a Social Equity Brand stands for – even if the specific products are in themselves not valued by those audiences.

Inclusiveness recognises that value resides in relationships – in their constituent parts and in their outcomes. Inclusiveness can only come into

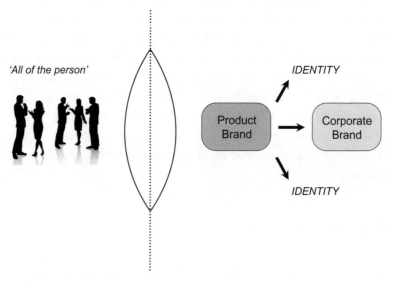

Figure 47: All of the person, all of the brand . . .

play when the brand is more intrinsically driven. At this point, when the relationship is the value, not solely a means to value (through transaction), the purpose of engaging as broad an audience as possible, and as deeply as possible within that audience, becomes clear.

As already mentioned, in a recent broadsheet interview here in the UK, Dr Rowan Williams, Archbishop of Canterbury, talked about our short-sighted fascination with only those parts of our lives that were 'productive' in the economic and market sense.[159] With similar arguments to those made by Senator Bobby Kennedy in 1968[160] when he questioned the sovereignty of GDP as a national measure of progress (see Chapter 2), Williams was lamenting the marginalisation of all those other parts of our lives that fall outside of what markets, business and indeed society deem 'valuable'. This is inevitable if the focus remains on the velocity of transaction and the dominance of product.

But Social Equity Brands recognise that it is about exchange and relationship, not transaction; and experience and service, not product. As such, an inclusive approach to all audiences simply makes more sense – with a wider and deeper audience, there are more opportunities to create value.

It doesn't matter that in some cases audiences do not want to buy the product, because the product is simply a blunt manifestation of a wider value proposition (think back to the tour T-shirt vendor earlier in the chapter). But there will be a myriad other ways that value can be uncovered for them, whether that's through stronger dialogue, shared thinking or indeed trust in the brand. Social Equity Brands are as concerned about levels of trust amongst those who do not consume them as they are about their loyal users.

So inclusiveness has two dimensions – depth and breadth.

Firstly, there is the focus on the whole person, not just the consumer (as we've detailed in our characteristic that sees citizens rather than consumers, and the growth of the B2Ci brand). This is what we call *inclusive depth*.

And second, there's the focus on more people – people who would not ordinarily be considered in any way valuable to the brand. As we know, in this emerging Era of Social Capital Rising, everyone is valuable to the brand, and the brand can deliver value to everyone. This is what we call *inclusive breadth*.

And whilst depth and breadth are different aspects of inclusiveness, they share one important quality. Both are focused on broadening and increasing the quality of the exchange and relationship, which means less time focused on consumption and product. In other words, a move away from the 'maximising product' focus of old, and a move towards a 'satisficing product' focus.

And these same dimensions apply to inclusiveness when it comes to internal audiences too. Understanding those who work for the brand beyond their presence from 9–5, along with engaging with their wider social group and community, are key ways by which to build stronger dialogue, thinking and trust, and unlock the public and private benefits that come from that.

A striking – if now overused – example of this inclusiveness in action is Unilever's Real Beauty campaign.[161] Initiated by Dove, the campaign quickly grew into a medium and platform through which all women could discuss the pressures they or their daughters felt by the superficial attention placed on looks by society. Talking to an audience way beyond its consumer base, the campaign developed workshops and online forums, and committed to engaging a significant number of young women and girls to understand and shun the potentially divisive effects of the modern beauty industry. Here was an example of a brand creating what appeared to be an intrinsically motivated initiative that transcended a brand–consumer mindset, and not only spoke to women as women (rather than female consumers) but to women who ordinarily would not be Dove consumers. The product almost became peripheral to the campaign, with the brand recognising the value in dialogue and new thinking (and social capital) around these issues.

But with this commitment to create inclusive depth and breadth with these audiences comes a greater demand for reciprocity from the brand. To put it bluntly, if the brand wants to engage on these new terms, then it's only fair that these audiences can engage with the brand on the same terms.

In other words, what does the brand do when it's not in the marketplace, when it's off duty?

This recognition of product brand limit, and the need to offer deeper and broader access for audiences, is supported by the anecdotal evidence that shows how many firms are building stronger corporate brands as a way to demonstrate values and ethos that go beyond the confines of a particular product or service.

So when it comes to inclusiveness, it is not simply a case of making sure audiences are wider and deeper, so as to create more value, but rather a case of making sure sufficient breadth and depth from the brand (corporate and product) are available to those audiences, allowing them to uncover value (Figure 47).

Ignition

Put simply, Ignition focuses on the prominence and centrality of the role the brand is playing in the building and nourishing of social capital. In other words, is the brand pivotal in this building process? Is the brand the spark that is causing it to happen?

It's important for a Social Equity Brand to be the spark for the creation of more social capital for several reasons. Firstly, this is what Social Equity Brands do – it's central to their reason for being, since they recognise that the more social capital there is, the more value there is, and the more likely it is that innovative solutions will be found for the challenges we face. And as we've argued, the trust–social capital relationship can become a virtuous circle, as higher levels of trust lead to higher levels of social capital, and higher levels of social capital present more opportunities to demonstrate trustworthiness (see Figure 48).

And second, a lot of the value that is created from higher social capital flows to those credited with creating the higher levels. In other words, it's good to be the ring leader when it comes to social capital.

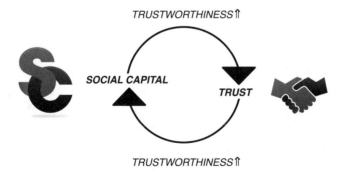

Figure 48: Social capital and trust

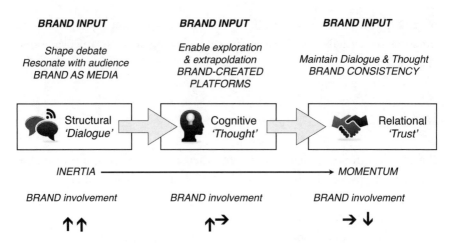

Figure 49: Social capital and brand input

Recognising that social capital creation is a process (see Figure 49) with distinct phases, the question is, then, how does the brand act as this ignition spark for each of these phases?

Adding an additional layer to this process from the versions shown earlier, we argue that as the social capital development process matures, so the potential direct involvement of the brand diminishes, as momentum builds and the system draws more and more energy from its own action, rather than needing external support. This is in keeping with the idea of it being a virtuous circle, where more trust creates more opportunities to trust, with more value created. It is also in keeping with the brand being an ignition device for the whole process, in that once the machine is ticking over, the reliance on this ignition process falls away.

With this in mind, igniting the dialogue phase is arguably the toughest. To overcome inertia due to ambivalence, disinterest or just false or erroneous information, the brand needs to be in a credible position to spark interest in the specific debate. The brand needs to initiate the dialogue through being able to shape the aspects of the debate to resonate with broad audiences. What's more, this resonance has to be genuine, deep and durable – this is not a sharp clap of the hands in order to create hype and fad for a fleeting moment.

During this period of what may be quite heavy lifting for the brand, in order to be instrumental, it needs to become a legitimate form of media for awareness to develop around the debate. As a form of media dedicated to the debate – or certainly parts of it – this role of media cannot be built on exclusivity, but rather the brand must also consider its relationship with its peers or those considered peers by its audiences. In other words, its interconnectedness.

To ignite the shared thinking part of social capital creation, the brand then needs to expedite the process whereby audiences can begin to explore and shape the debate beyond the information given as part of the dialogue phase. Responsibility for driving the development of social capital is moving away from the brand and towards the newly engaged audiences in this phase. But even though these audiences may be engaged, it is not necessarily the case that they are enabled. This is the role the brand must play at this stage, leveraging its core characteristics and capabilities to ensure it's providing opportunities for audiences to complement dialogue with salient action; in other words, to shape it for their own purposes and for their own collaborative efforts.

As a far more interactive phase, the brand needs to be credited with creating the appropriate and believable platforms and forums upon and within which this thinking can take place. Again, interconnectedness and inclusiveness are extremely important here.

Moving to the trust phase, the brand's involvement here is reduced further. But there is still a requirement from the brand to ensure the dialogue and thought phases remain active and fertile, which in turn requires it to remain trusted and respected by its audiences. As such, the brand must ensure consistency in all of its other communication efforts – product and corporate – with the position it takes on the debate.

This is far easier said than done, with some of the most progressive brands to date falling foul of this consistency element, and in so doing, stalling their ability to act as durable ignition devices for the growth in social capital. A striking example is one we've already mentioned – Unilever. We've mentioned the extraordinary efforts and results of the Real Beauty campaign in terms of building dialogue, thinking and trust within a broad community. But whilst this was going on, Unilever was also selling Lynx (Axe) deodorant for men. And in their campaign for this deodorant, they portrayed the geeky user of the spray as being able to attract beautiful women as a result – beautiful women who were literally unable to help themselves but chase the freshly deodorised guy along a beach, whilst wearing skimpy bikinis. Was Unilever consistent with its Dove audience? Certainly not. Was its intrinsic motivation for the Dove campaign called into question? Very probably. And did it reveal a dilemma regarding the values and beliefs of the parent brand? Certainly.

Referring back to our inclusiveness litmus test – and the need for that inclusive depth to go both ways – it is no surprise that Unilever is now a champion of developing a strong corporate or parent brand to underpin and support its product brand positionings.

Interest

If brands are to be trusted as engines of long-term and balanced social capital – to be credited as engines of long-term and balanced social capital – then they have to take a genuine interest in their audiences; in other words, a long-term and holistic view, which is intrinsically rather than extrinsically motivated.

We've already discussed the intrinsic/extrinsic issue, as well as the short-termist, transaction and product-obsessed approach still favoured by many, if not most, brands today. This approach seems so out of place in what we've labelled this Era of Social Capital Rising, yet it persists.

Today, it is not about how to grab a consumer's interest long enough to build just enough of a relationship to transact with them. It is about how to take an interest in that person that is genuine, long-term and mutually beneficial.

In the Era of Social Capital Rising, it is a shift from momentary attention to *continuous interest*.

Rather than relying on a fleeting, shallow and brittle interest in the consumer, a Social Capital Strategy focuses on that interest being continuous, thick and flexible (see Figure 50).

The reason for this shift in focus – from momentary attention to continuous interest – should be obvious. Only by taking this level of interest will Social Equity Brands really be able to understand where their audiences seek

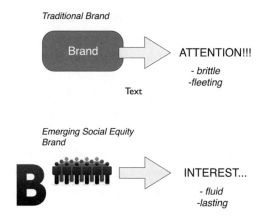

Figure 50: Attention vs interest

value – and, more importantly, where they are unable to seek value today. Interest, then, is the passport to understanding where and when these pockets of under- or un-realised value reside.

More than this, interest can create value. If we recognise that collaboration and co-creation are important outcomes of a Social Equity Brand's involvement with its audiences, then interest is the primary input. We've already mentioned a few examples of where brands have stopped to take stock and deepen their interest in their audiences – Danish toy brick company Lego is a good one, where their interest around their traditional core target consumer (children) uncovered a considerable stock of unrealised value with the parents of those children.[162]

And when we start to talk about sustainability, then the importance of a deeper and more lasting interest in the brand's constituents becomes even more obvious, since aspects of sustainability touch so many parts of our lives and are present in so many of the decisions and opinions we hold away from our day-to-day consumption behaviour. As such, if brands want to be constructive in building stronger and more balanced social capital, they cannot afford to be absent from all these other aspects of people's lives.

This may, of course, ring alarm bells for many, as brands attempt to become even more embedded in our lives. But whilst such alarms should go off if this were the behaviour of a traditional, brittle brand, Social Equity

Brands need to work hard to convince their constituents that they are not the same – they are not motivated or driven by the same short-term, bonding-capital approach.

If we remember the original role of brands – to offer some way to bypass provenance costs as a result of confusing, complex and distant practices – then this role could not be more important today. If brands can invest in understanding not their consumers, but the citizen (who consumes), then they stand a far better chance of proving valuable in terms of creating the right environments to foster dialogue and thinking, as these constituents try not only to understand, but improve the provenance of the decisions they make every day.

Examples of brands moving from an attention model towards an interest model are popping up everywhere – and not just in developed, post-materialistic societies. As we've already seen, in Kenya for example, Equity Bank has successfully set itself up where all major international banks had decided to abandon. Taking a deeper interest in the lives of those who could be customers of the bank, the bank has created a new business model around this more 'continuous interest' (rather than the attention approach still prac-tised by other high street banks). The bank quickly realised that where others saw untrustworthiness within potential customers, what was really on display was an inability to demonstrate trustworthiness. With this insight from its deeper interest in its constituents, Equity Bank set about lending to small businesses and budding entrepreneurs using social capital as capital. And Equity was quick to spot the virtuous circle we've pointed out several times already – that higher levels of social capital give rise to more opportunities to demonstrate trustworthiness, which in turn raises social capital stocks even higher. One other aspect of Equity Bank that should be made clear is that, unlike some other micro-loan operations, Equity Bank has never sought any donor finance or support. The bank used the creation of social capital – pri-marily through a stronger and deeper interest in its environment – as a source of business innovation and competitive advantage. The results are impressive – to reiterate, its default rate sits at just 3% compared to an industry average of 15%.[163] If ever there's a compelling case for using social capital as a means to uncover and create new value, to a brand's and firm's advantage, then surely this is it?

Closer to home, another example of a brand recognising the importance of the interest model, rather than the attention model, is Pepsi with its 'Refresh' project.[164] We're not, for one second, saying that Pepsi is necessarily a Social Equity Brand, but we do recognise that this initiative is an excellent example of the brand taking a more long-term and broad interest in its constituents – not just its consumers, but the people behind its consumers, and the networks and communities to which they are attached, with an ambition to build dialogue, talk and ultimately trust, over and above any other benefits. As it happens, Pepsi's Refresh project is also a great example of the brand recognising the importance of Inclusiveness (wide audiences and deep conversation) and Ignition (platforms, media and forums in which the dialogue and thinking phases can develop). So maybe Pepsi is emerging as a Social Equity Brand after all.

Imagination

Imagination is the fifth and final of our proposed 5Is that underpin the development of a Social Capital Strategy and collectively act as a litmus test to ensure the brand is leveraging its own capabilities, ambitions and beliefs most effectively to build social capital, create new value and find opportunities to unpick and remove many of the challenges that fall under the banner of sustainability.

Imagination is also what brands should excel at.

Traditionally, this use of imagination has focused on dazzling or intriguing a consumer long enough to snare them in the plastic bonding capital provided by brands. And make no mistake, there have been some truly dazzling examples of imagination in this context. But as competition has increased for the consumer's attention, so this objective has required ever-more shrill and sensationalist interpretations of imagination. The result is the cacophony of brands we hear about every day, wherever we are and whatever we're doing. Increasingly, imagination is confined to finding ways to cut through.

It should come as no surprise to hear us argue that Social Equity Brands should use their imagination in very different ways.

For Social Equity Brands, Imagination is primarily about identifying how best to bring the dialogue and shared thinking aspects of the social capital process alive. Why? Because the more vivid, rich and vibrant these aspects, the stronger and higher the levels of social capital, and the greater the public and private benefits from that social capital.

If the objective of a Social Equity Brand is to nurture and nourish social capital, then Imagination is a foundational step in meeting that objective. And just as dazzling imagination has worked well to meet the historical ambition of building bonding social capital, so a more balanced and enduring form of Imagination will be needed to restock social capital across the bridging and linking dimensions as well.

Imagination is needed to understand why social capital may be low in the first place. The previous section's example of Equity Bank in Kenya is also a shining example of using Imagination to understand why other banks were not operating in that market – why trustworthiness was in such short supply. So Imagination needs to shape the development of initiatives to demonstrate the deeper and more durable levels of Interest the brand has in its constituents.

In its heart, a Social Equity Brand wants to build social capital, as its focus is on building value through these increased stocks – value for society and, in no small way, value for itself. Recognising that social capital grows through a cyclical process – from dialogue, to shared thinking, to trust – Imagination plays a crucial part in initiating the dialogue and keeping the thinking fresh (see Figure 51).

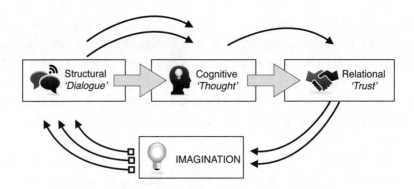

Figure 51: The role of imagination in the social capital process

At the outset, the brand needs to draw on all the creative resources it has at its disposal to understand how best to position the debate in the most salient context for its constituents. This cannot be done with marketing and brand teams alone. As we suggested at the beginning of this chapter, for a Social Capital Strategy to work effectively, inputs need to be sought from Human Resources and Corporate Communications departments, since these functions have a significant part to play in building and maintaining social capital levels with the various audiences of the firm. Collectively, the team responsible for building social capital through the brand must be convinced the approach to building dialogue and subsequently shared thinking is the most effective possible, with that effectiveness shaped dramatically by the use of collective Imagination. In short, does the approach bring the issues to life for the constituents and energise the discussion and co-creation processes? When couched in these terms, it is an easy step to see how we link Imagination to the use of narratives and emotion, as two key traits of a Social Equity Brand.

This is a real departure for brands. Historically, imagination has been used to create some sense of exclusivity between brand and audience, be that some inside knowledge, some tacit reference to a club or some phatic expression that suggests loyalty and belonging. But for a Social Equity Brand, Imagination is about encouraging openness, rather than exclusivity (see Figure 52).

And before seasoned marketers with impressive CVs start wincing at the thought of all that proprietary imagination seeping out into the public domain, we'd like to put forward one final argument for the collaborative approach. As we've stressed over and over throughout this book, one of the most durable

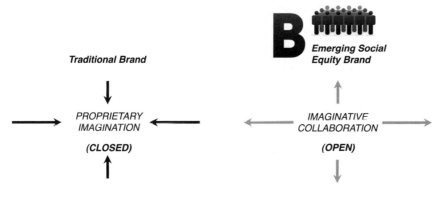

Figure 52: 'Proprietary imagination' vs 'Imaginative collaboration'

and protectable advantages in developing social capital is the credit bestowed upon those considered responsible for that development. This credit can manifest itself in a number of ways – trust, loyalty, access to information and informal nonmarket authority are just a few examples. And even though our definition of Imagination is one where collaborative processes – both inside and outside the firm – shape the development of social capital, the opportunity for the brand to be recognised as the principal author is still strong. In other words, being seen to have the foresight and ambition to work towards higher social capital is what brings the rewards. And as these rewards climb with higher levels of social capital, so the incentive should be there to strengthen social capital levels in whatever way possible.

Imagination from the brand in the context of social capital is a byword for bravery and confidence. Where it's been used in the past to obfuscate the evident for short-term exclusive gain, in this Era of Social Capital Rising, Imagination needs to represent a willingness to simplify, clarify and share. How can these issues be made more palatable, engaging and solvable within a more inclusive environment?

If the brand genuinely has confidence in the power of its Imagination, then it will not obsess about ownership of the process but will be more focused on – excited by – the prospects of public and private value created.

Inside and out

This chapter has started to lay out how we see the relationship between the traits and characteristics of Social Equity Brands and the way those brands interact, stimulate and respond to their environments for mutual benefit. This relationship – if it's to be as effective as it can be – is determined by the creation of a Social Capital Strategy.

It is also key to recognise the equal importance of internal and external audiences. Much has been written about the importance of recognising internal teams in brand initiatives, but in the context of Social Equity Brands, and a Social Capital Strategy, their importance cannot be overstressed. Employees are the life-blood of a Social Equity Brand – just look at the soft, amorphous nature of the '5Is' and the Social Equity Traits. Social Equity

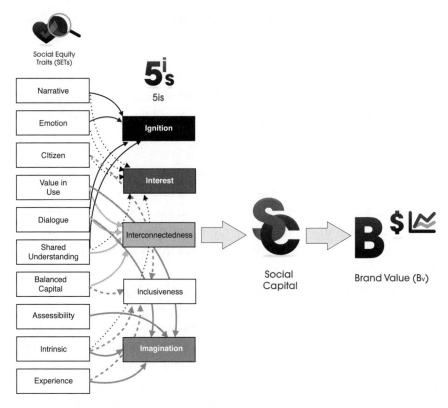

Figure 53: Pathways between the SETs and the 5Is

Brands are built from the inside out. Put another way, people build social capital.

To illustrate this building process and the flow from characteristic to input or driver for the Social Capital Strategy to the creation of social capital, we've shown some of the linkages and pathways that bridge the outputs of the last two chapters in Figure 53.

As is to be expected, a quick look at the linkages shows how interrelated these characteristics are with the pillars of a Social Capital Strategy, and indeed how interrelated the 5Is are. The idea of a clean, stable linear model is out of the question – in today's hyper-connected, dynamic and complex world, such thinking needs to be abandoned. In many ways, this one diagram illustrates the 'messiness' of this new era marketing that so many traditionalists prefer to ignore in their desire to remain linked and respected by the more established functions within the firm. But this 'messiness' also represents the sea of opportunity that is out there – opportunity that brands are perfectly placed to uncover and seize with the right motivation, ambition and outlook. We don't, for one second, reckon we've captured all the linkages and indeed the feedback loops in the diagram, but even with this level of interpretation, the complexity – the 'messiness' – is clear.

As we argued in the previous chapter, we've no claim to make that our 5I process is exhaustive – this is an evolving process, after all. But as a set of acid tests to ensure an ambition to build social capital is being delivered on a day-to-day basis in terms of how the brand operates, we think they're extremely valuable and a great launch pad from which to adopt and adapt for specific circumstances.

In the book so far we've tried to stitch together an argument that links brands to social capital, and have highlighted where that relationship has sometimes been good and sometimes bad. But whatever its state, and like it or not, the relationship persists. In parallel, we've argued that the current brand approach to sustainability is probably the most unsustainable approach possible, with entrenched brand behaviour pushing us further and further from more sustainable consumption and more sustainable lifestyles. We've tried to map out where we think brands have been going wrong, with respect to emotion, 'maximising', exclusivity and bonding capital obsessions among other behaviours.

In then trying to highlight the opportunities we believe lie ahead for this new breed of brands, we've sketched what we believe is a pretty comprehensive outline of what these brands need to look like, and how they can present and use those qualities to make their experiences in their host environments as constructive as possible – to both them and their widest audiences.

All the way through, we've jostled to say the following: that social capital – talking, thinking, trusting – is an inherently important thing for us all to do more of; that brands are best placed to encourage this activity; and that in doing so, brands as well as us will benefit, as higher and more balanced social capital squeezes out the very behaviours that lead to unsustainable behaviour. In short, a focus on building social capital is the most effective route for brands to deliver long-term value to their organisations, long-term value to their consumers (who we consider more importantly as citizens) and, uniting these two, long-term and innovative solutions to the mounting issues we face.

This much, we hope, is clear.

But one last question remains in our conceptual framework. Even if social capital is good for a brand, its guardian and society in general, in all the ways we've attempted to outline, how does the firm actually measure increases in social capital around it? What exactly is it we're trying to measure, what does it look like and how do we know when it's moving in the right direction?

It is this question of measurement that we explore and discuss in more detail in the final chapter.

Chapter 12

The prospect of measuring social capital – and the effects of social capital – is quite daunting, primarily because it is something that has not really been measured before.

Actually, that's not strictly true. Social capital – in the context of firms and their brands – has never been the *main* focus of any research or measurement, but we believe it has, and does, regularly pop up in various guises in and amongst a wide range of metrics and results. As we said right back at the beginning, social capital swirls around brands and indeed business, so it's not surprising bits of it show up in our peripheral vision here and there when we're focused on something else. For example, many of the key indicators of brand health are linked to social capital – word of mouth, trust, advocacy and loyalty for example. And Corporate Communications lifts the lid on certain aspects of social capital when entering into dialogue with various stakeholder groups.

But these fragmented, often accidental glimpses of social capital and its consequences will do nothing to help brands become Social Equity Brands and maximise their impact on society and their guardians. For this to happen, we need to have more focused and tailored approaches to research and measurement. We need to be looking specifically for social capital.

Bringing social capital to the centre of a research and measurement process is complex for a number of reasons.

Firstly, most of the measurement needs to take place in situ and in context, far away from the brand. As well as having to 'get in amongst it', measuring social capital also calls for a far more intuitive and nuanced measurement process, otherwise much of it would wither under the bright lights of more established and 'massive' techniques.

Second, to measure social capital effectively, we need to measure the strength and quality of the relationships between individuals or groups within the network, not the individuals or groups themselves. So we have to focus on the *connections*, not the *nodes*.

And third, any measurement of social capital has to be linked to a broader brand and organisational strategy in order to gauge the value derived from creating higher social capital stocks. In other words, what is the ambition of the brand and its guardian in terms of creating value for itself from its investment in social capital? As is the case with brand equity, equity in itself is not value (although in mainstream practitioner environments the terms are often used interchangeably). Instead, the equity – or credit – has to be converted into value in some way. And the same goes for social capital and the equity investments – how do the brand and its owner want to convert that equity into value?

This need to have a focused strategic aim sits at the start of the measurement challenge around social capital. The other areas then follow, namely: the ten Social Equity Brand characteristics (SETs); the 5Is; the subsequent investments in the sources of social capital (dialogue, thinking and trust); the resultant core stocks of social capital; and then the brand's 'spending' of that social capital as a way to create value (and to meet the initial objective or aim). This process naturally falls into three sections, and is laid out in Figure 54. But to reiterate our note of caution from the previous chapter, we should not be lulled into a false sense of security that the measurement of social capital can be linear, quantitative and massive (as is so often the case, even to this day, with much brand strategy research work). Instead, measurement devices must rely on mixed methods. Exploratory qualitative techniques should include ethnography, netnography or phenomenology to get under the skin of the brand and its contribution to social capital levels. And then quantitative techniques can support these insights through volume to uncover trends and patterns. Those who manage the development of Social Equity Brands must be comfortable engaging a range of measurement tools.

'Area 1' essentially falls outside the scope of this book, considering it is highly dependent on the context, capabilities and wider goals of the company.

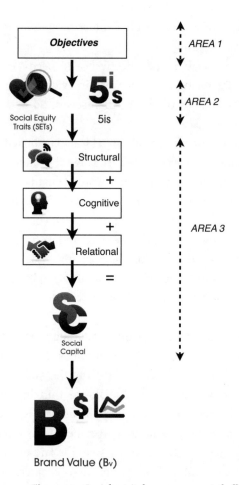

Figure 54: Social capital measurement challenge

But suffice it to say, the importance of linking organisational and broader brand objectives to the investment and measurement of social capital should not be underestimated. A commitment to social capital building cannot be a fringe, isolated activity, but rather must be central to and dependent on the broader strategic ambition of the firm and the brand.

'Area 2' focuses on measuring two key areas introduced in this book – the characteristics of the brand and the commitment to leverage those characteristics in the way the brand engages and creates value with its constituents in its environments. As such, those responsible for building and implementing the Social Capital Strategy need to establish regular assessment sessions drawing on internal teams and external stakeholders as and when, to ascertain how effective the brand is being in marching towards amassing a more comprehensive set of Social Equity Traits (SETs), and how well those are being put to use in the day-to-day behaviour of the brand, via the '5Is' litmus test. We've already established the main elements of each of the 5Is, and these should act as a starting point for brand teams to adapt in context. We would argue, however, that any review sessions to ascertain how the brand is progressing in terms of characteristics and regular demonstrations of those characteristics, should be flexible and collaborative, rather than rigid and quantitative. This is for the straightforward reason that the boundaries of these qualities, and the effects they can have on the day-to-day business of the brand, are blurred and many, respectively.

The really thorny and complex area, however, is 'Area 3'. In here are all the challenges with respect to finding the strength and quality of the relationships not just between the brand and its constituents, but between constituents where that relationship is created, fuelled or shaped by the behaviour of the brand. To try and navigate through this, we'll take each component of social capital at a time, and then attempt to understand where the brand and its guardian fit in this complex network of relationships – since this position is as important as the stocks of social capital in terms of offering opportunities for the brand and its guardian to benefit from this social capital uplift.

Measuring the structural component – Dialogue

With all of these components of social capital, we need to separate out the bilateral component – between brand and citizen (or group) – and the multilateral component – between citizen (or group) and other citizen (or other group). The temptation is to focus on the former, as it is easier to identify and far more aligned to the type of research and measurement a brand is used to. But to fall into this trap would result in swathes of social capital – and

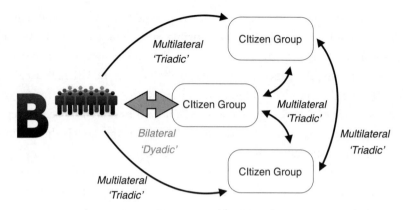

Figure 55: Complex and ambiguous relationships within stakeholder marketing

value – being ignored in any review and analysis. So we need both (see Figure 55).

The bilateral dimension requires the brand to draw up a comprehensive list of all those with whom the brand has a relationship. In line with the Interconnectedness and Inclusiveness aspects of a Social Capital Strategy, this list almost certainly needs to be longer than initially thought. In this Era of Social Capital Rising, the reach and influence of the brand is considerably greater than it used to be. It's also considerably more dynamic, demanding that this identification of relevant stakeholders for the brand needs to be carried out and updated on a rolling basis.

For the multilateral dimension, probably the most effective way to establish something approaching a comprehensive list is to run a series of pilot studies amongst the identified bilateral stakeholders, focusing on surfacing nominations from those stakeholders for others to join the process. This may well be an iterative process until a more stable multilateral list is in place (see Figure 56).

With respect to what to explore within this part of the process, we need to adapt and embellish the work that already exists in more formal stakeholder engagement processes.[165] In short, we're trying to get to a point where we can gauge the degree to which the brand is always associated with the issues, concerns, challenges or opportunities that have been adopted and framed by the brand (using its Social Equity Traits and built into its wider brand objec-

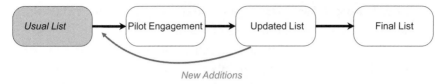

Figure 56: Compiling multilateral brand stakeholder lists

tives and strategy). In this respect, the multilateral dimension is crucial to measure, considering the editorial importance of many of these issues. In other words, how effective is the brand in shaping editorial and other indirect channels between audiences?

If the brand is being consistently and constantly associated with the debate, and is seen to be actively and constructively contributing to and enabling dialogue, then we are starting to understand just how active the brand is in creating this first phase of social capital.

Data from the stakeholders within the bilateral and multilateral relationships can be combined in a number of ways, possibly by stakeholder, showing how active the brand is in creating dialogue around a number of issues; or by issue, exploring how active the brand is with a number of stakeholders.

Measuring the cognitive component – Shared thinking

Naturally, it is not enough just to gauge the frequency of dialogue – we need to assess the quality of the dialogue. In other words, how this dialogue is acting as the catalyst – the first phase – in leading to more informed and shared thinking around the issues and challenges deemed salient by the brand and its environment. Specifically, brute increases in dialogue will not necessarily create richer and more balanced social capital. This is visible every day when we trudge into work in the avalanche of messages from brands trying to establish some form of dialogue that are devoid of any attempt to find common ground from a 'thought perspective'.

Instead, dialogue has to lead to new and complementary ways of thinking – manifested in new social codes, visions or ambitions.

Recognising how this thinking can manifest, questions asked to stakeholders in both the bilateral and multilateral environments need to focus on whether they feel the brand has shaped their opinions or helped them engage in issues. Questions should also focus on whether the outcome of the dialogue with the brand – or as a result of the brand – has allowed them to contextualise the issues, challenges or opportunities. So, in a nutshell, purpose and clarity.

An important way to gauge whether this shared thinking has taken root with different constituents is whether it has led to collaborative endeavours, since these can only get a foothold if the dialogue has set up shared mental models or frames within which the brand and the constituents can collaborate.

Measuring the relational component – Trust

Trust is the crucial end-game when it comes to brands becoming Social Equity Brands and building stronger stocks of more long-term and balanced social capital.

Trust is the incredibly vague, amorphous and fickle component that also acts as the powerful return loop, ensuring the social capital continues to replenish itself, encouraging more dialogue, more shared thinking and even deeper, wider levels of trust – both the thick, specific flavour and the thin, generalised flavour we've discussed previously (see Figure 57). But its nebulous nature should not deter us from trying to pin it down and quantify it in some way, so as to know whether the process to create social capital is resulting in greater levels of trust.

As a means momentarily to nail it to the floor, we should also remember that trust is a key component of brand equity, often expressed through loyalty and advocacy for the brand. In this specific context we're talking about the trust the brand fosters in its environments as a result of how it approaches the process to build dialogue and shared thinking around the myriad sustainability issues and challenges we face. So if we can measure the degree to which these aspects of brand equity are being driven by the perception of

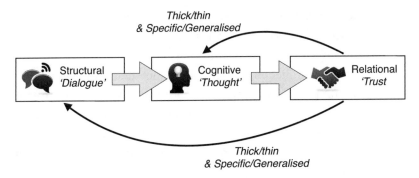

Figure 57: The role of trust in nurturing social capital

improved dialogue and shared thinking, then we have the beginnings of understanding how much trust is entering the relationship between the brand and its constituents.

This is precisely what we have done within Havas's ongoing research project, Sustainable Futures. As one of the outputs generated from collecting detailed, sustainability-focused data on a wealth of high-profile consumer-facing brands across a range of markets, we've been able to produce a proprietary metric – the Sustainable Futures Quotient. As the name suggests, it's a weighted and blended output that signals the future potential of the brand in this area, with this potential shaped in no small part by the amount of trust bestowed upon the brand by those with whom it interacts.

The Sustainable Futures Quotient – SFQ

As we've said over and over throughout this book, we feel brands have approached the whole sustainability debate in nothing short of a disastrous way. For starters, they have continued to obsess about getting us to act as maximisers when it comes to choosing brands, causing us stress and anxiety and taking away opportunities to engage and invest in more balanced, natural and frankly more important relationships that underpin more durable, high quality social capital. On top of this, when it comes to sustainability issues, and those specific issues that are considered to affect the firm (more often than not determined by internal analysis, rather than consulting peers and other third parties), brands have become slavishly devoted to acting as loyal mouthpieces for their corporate guardians.

This faithful regurgitation of fact and science into an environment so desperately wanting context, emotion and any other device by which to engage is an extraordinarily dysfunctional combination of brands destroying their potential usefulness for their guardians, through the very act of trying to cosy up to those guardians to demonstrate their value. It has to be the brand–sustainability paradox.

So to try and look beyond and around this paradox, from the wealth of data we collect every year within Sustainable Futures we created our proprietary quotient – the Sustainable Futures Quotient (SFQ). As introduced back in Chapter 8, and blended from perceived performances across a range of sustainability issues and the trust shown towards the brand in that context, the SFQ represents a quick but detailed snapshot of whether trust in what the brand is saying and doing is necessarily flowing from what the brand is *seen* to be saying and doing. In other words, if the brand is acting purely as a rowdy and unthinking cheerleader for its corporate guardian, and so not invoking strong dialogue and shared thinking, then, chances are, trust derived from these efforts will be low.

And in the clear majority of cases, this is true.

To understand what the SFQ really tells us, it is worth taking a few moments to understand what's being blended, and how they're blended.

As part of the investigation into every brand and its perceived sustainability performance, Sustainable Futures amasses perception scores across a raft of sustainability attributes. As we've discussed, these attributes were originally arrived at by exploring the ways any organisation can derive value from five sources of capital: Natural Capital, Human Capital, Asset Capital, Financial Capital and Social Capital.[166] The last one is a little misleading, since in this context it represents a judgement made by consumers with respect to how much social capital is in play around the brand (but with this judgement itself a product of broader social capital).

Recognising that these attributes were fashioned out of a conceptual capital model, the attributes were then reordered into six more understandable groups or clusters through Factor Analysis: Marketplace; Environment; Community; Workplace; Economy; and Governance and Ethics. With every brand, the research records a rich composite score for each of these clusters. In other words, a score that depicts consumer perception in that market as to how the brand is performing across a number of attributes that make up that cluster. Recognising that some clusters have more attributes than others, these six results are then weighted and combined to form a single result – and one half of the SFQ.

The other half of the quotient comes from exploring brand equity in this context, captured by measuring two fairly generic proxies – general impression and advocacy. As already mentioned, we fully recognise that these may not be the most pertinent brand equity measures for many brands, but in what is a multi-market, multi-sector and multi-brand piece of research, consistency and relevance across all of these sectors and brands are necessary, hence our focus on these two. And to date, seeing how effective equity is – as defined by these proxies – at predicting some very established benefits of increased levels, it seems we've not given up too much in terms of accuracy in the name of being consistent and relevant across so many sectors.

By looking at the strength of relationship between these equity proxies and the various sustainability attribute clusters, we are able to arrive at a coefficient that represents the overall contribution to brand equity being made by those attribute clusters collectively (and individually when needed). In other words, how influential are these performances to brand equity? How much faith are consumers placing in these performances, so as to influence their cognitive and affective reactions to the brand? How much are they trusting the brand in these contexts?

This weighted coefficient – in effect the 'flow' of trust from constituent to brand as a result of these perceived performances – is the other half of our Sustainable Futures Quotient. When blended and weighted with the performance perception scores and rescaled out of 100, we arrive at an overall quotient for that brand (see Figure 58).

What the SFQ allows us to do immediately is look behind the relatively obvious perceptions held by consumers and start to explore how these perceptions are driving trust. More specifically, if the brand is driving strong, engaging and relevant dialogue, which in turn is leading to shared ways of thinking and possibly collaboration, then this is being reflected in higher SFQ scores on the trust side of the quotient. The flip side of this is that even though there

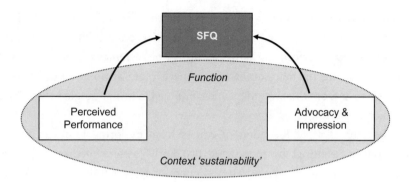

Figure 58: Make-up of the SFQ. Sustainable futures.

can be relatively high perceived performance scores (so one half of the quotient), low trust scores (as seen by contributions to brand equity) can hobble the SFQ, sending a clear signal to those who manage the brand – Interest, Ignition and Imagination from the 5Is within the Social Capital Strategy test are all likely being underdelivered.

In Figure 59 we've reproduced the SFQ league table for 2010 (we've already shown the 2009 results earlier – see Figure 30), showing which brands held the top twenty slots for each year. We'd add a note of caution here, in that the real value of the SFQ is really as a tracking device for the same brand over time, rather than as a benchmarking device across firms, especially when those firms are in such different industries. We should also point out that these results are aggregated at the global level, so in doing so have swallowed up many of the more intricate insights we get to see at individual market level. But that said, those brands dominating the SFQ tables – and deriving the most brand equity from their stance towards helping their audiences understand, explore and engage with the issues (so building social capital) are consistently retailers and CPG brands. But are any true Social Equity Brands? Not yet.

Bringing talk, thought and trust together

In the previous three parts, we've introduced a view on how brands may try and get to grips with whether they're actually working in the right ways to

	Brand	Sustainable Futures Quotient (SFQ)
1	Ikea	71.7
2	Danone	71.4
3	Google	71.0
4	Kraft	71.0
5	Unilever	70.8
6	Nestlé	69.6
7	Procter & Gamble	69.3
8	Volkswagen	69.3
9	Apple	69.1
10	BMW	69.0
11	Philips	68.7
12	Sanofi-Aventis	68.7
13	Auchan/Alcampo	68.4
14	Coca-Cola	68.4
15	Microsoft	68.3

Figure 59: SFQ 2010. Sustainable Futures 2010.

build social capital via the three components we introduced earlier in the book. As should be clear, just initiating the dialogue phase of our process model is not enough to ensure social capital grows in a healthy and balanced way, in that the process can easily stall even after a monumental push on the dialogue front.

Boutilier[167] highlights the risk of high contact/communication efforts that result in low mutual trust and understanding (see Figure 60). Returning to this diagram, two things immediately jump out.

Firstly, and to reiterate what he calls a 'Conflicted Relationship' – high contact but low trust and understanding – seems to sum up most bran

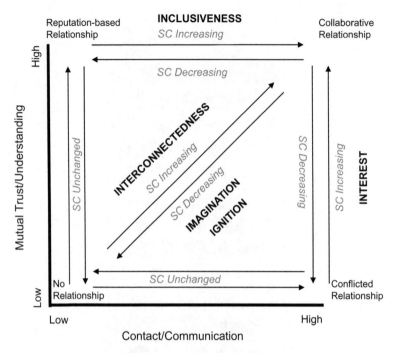

Figure 60: 'Relationship matrix'. Overlaying the 5Is as means to stimulate social capital. Reproduced by permission of Greenleaf Publishing.

communication efforts today. The argument seems to be that if we can just get you to register us more often, then this will build trust and understanding. Not so – if anything, such a tactic just pushes the state of the relationship further along the *x*-axis, increasing the amount of conflict.

The second thing that jumps out is the direction of shifts that create higher levels of social capital within the relationship. In each case, we can overlay our 5Is to see how they can be instrumental as pillars for a strategy to increase social capital.

Boutilier makes the point with this diagram that the structural component of social capital (the dialogue) is distinct from the other two elements (shared thinking and trust). This is in line with our view, in that we see dialogue as the essential precursor to the development of social capital (in our process model), but not the guarantee. Social Equity Brands have to work harder on this.

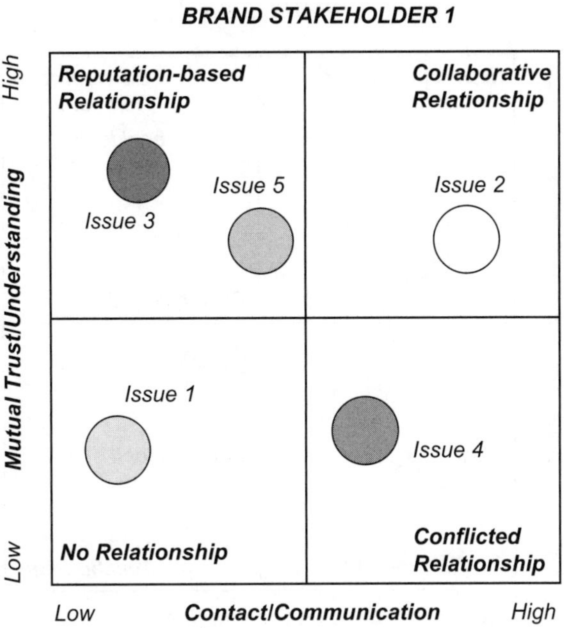

BRAND STAKEHOLDER 1

Figure 61: Social Equity Brand issue mapping

With this in mind, we can lightly adapt this to create a 2 × 2 matrix that can be used by brands to map their levels of social capital – and their journeys to create more social capital. In other words, it can represent both a static snapshot and a process for the brand. What's more, as we mentioned earlier in terms of slicing and dicing data gathered on social capital building efforts, the brand can create these matrices per stakeholder or per issue. So with the former, all the issues that are considered relevant for one stakeholder can be mapped on the grid (Figure 61), highlighting not only imbalances but the possible routes to resolving those imbalances.

When it comes to mapping by issue, again the brand can plot the balance of each component that is in play with each stakeholder, with additional analyses or overlays to then ensure that there is also a balanced array of relationships in terms of bonding, bridging and linking (see Figure 62).

What becomes clear from these matrices – whichever way they are plotted – is this: for brands to be creating high social capital, relying on reputation

BRAND ISSUE 1

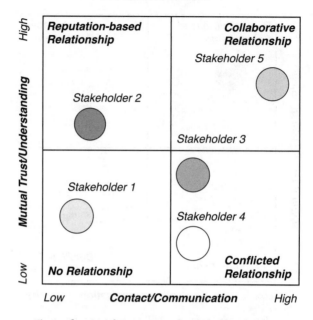

Figure 62: Social Equity Brand stakeholder mapping

is not enough. Reputation is a representation of historical consistency, often created and supported by third parties. Whilst valuable, in the realms of social capital, and specifically being rewarded for creating social capital and its public and private benefits, reputation is passive. Instead, the brand has to be active; constantly active.

Social capital and brand locus

So far we've laid out some options in terms of how the brand may begin to understand whether it is creating, nurturing and maintaining balanced social capital stocks within its many environments. Starting with understanding objectives, constantly reassessing its commitment to the Social Equity Traits, and how these play out in terms of the Social Capital Strategy and its 5Is litmus tests, we've gone on to reference and adapt other, wider social capital models to show how the brand can get a handle on whether dialogue, thought and trust levels are rising and indeed coalescing into higher social capital around them. But the last remaining question to answer here is what exactly does 'around them' mean? In other words, if social capital is amongst and within a network of relationships, how important is it for the brand to understand where in that network it sits? The answer, we believe, is very.

Understanding where in the network the brand sits, and the relationships or characteristics of the network around it, is important in understanding what the brand can do not only to build stronger and more balanced social capital, but to ensure that the public and private benefits of those higher levels are optimised. So, in other words, a key measurement requirement for a brand when it comes to social capital is not just how much and how balanced the stocks of social capital are, but *where are we within those balanced stocks?*

One conceptual model[168] for assessing networks from a company's perspective suggests they are determined by two qualities – density and position (for our interpretation when it comes to brands, see Figure 63). Firms (and brands) that are central to dense networks are what are called 'compromisers' because, despite being central, their influence is matched by the quality of the relationships around them. Conversely, being central in a low-density network shifts the firm (or brand) to being a 'Commander', thanks to there being far fewer links to challenge the authority of the business. Being more marginalised within a low-density relationship creates a 'Solitarian', as neither the firm (or brand) nor the rest of the network is particularly engaged. And finally, being on the edges of a high-density network makes the firm (or brand) a 'Subordinate'. Not good news. Importantly, we strongly believe this is where many brands are ending up, as this Era of Social Capital Rising is unfolding around them.

So the three external components a brand needs to understand and measure when it comes to social capital are:

1. Blended quality of relationships within the network (dialogue, thought and trust).
2. Density of the network around the brand.
3. Position – or locus – of the brand within that network.

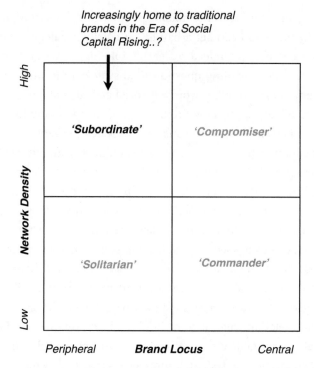

Figure 63: Density/locus mapping (see Rowley T.J. (1997))

It's worth exploring the combination of these three elements in a little more detail, since they combine to influence how the brand can spend its credit for creating social capital, which in turn has a significant impact on whether a Social Capital Strategy can meet its objectives. In other words, the network density and brand position is a moderator between building social capital and deriving value from social capital (see Figure 64).

All density–position variations within networks of actors really come down to the idea of a core–periphery relationship.[169] How big is each component, how are they linked and where is the brand amongst it all?

Returning to Boutilier,[170] he sketches a series of broad core–periphery variations, with increasingly strong cores and variations in the make-up of the peripheries (see Figure 65).

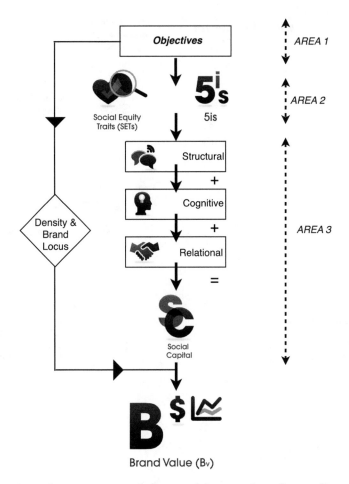

Figure 64: Measurement challenge and the network moderator effect

As we move from top to bottom, we can see that the core strengthens. The left column shows a periphery that becomes more and more connected, whereas the right column shows a periphery that remains fragmented ('isolated and individualistic').

What is of real interest here is the last variation – what Boutilier calls the 'Cohesive Balance'. In this state, the 'holes' in the periphery are minimised (in other words, the peripheral stakeholders are well connected and not solely dependent on going through the core). Why is this state important? Because

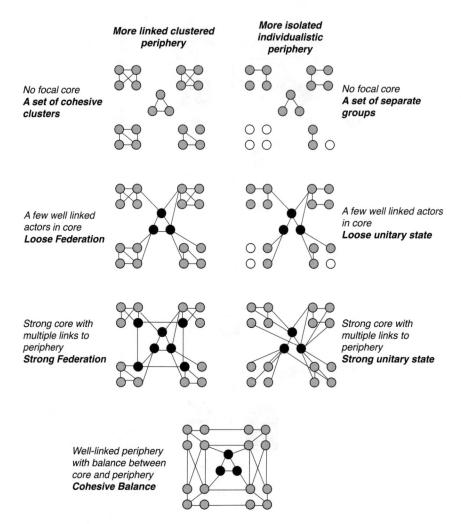

More linked clustered periphery

More isolated individualistic periphery

No focal core
A set of cohesive clusters

No focal core
A set of separate groups

A few well linked actors in core
Loose Federation

A few well linked actors in core
Loose unitary state

Strong core with multiple links to periphery
Strong Federation

Strong core with multiple links to periphery
Strong unitary state

Well-linked periphery with balance between core and periphery
Cohesive Balance

Figure 65: Network configurations. Reproduced by permission of Greenleaf Publishing.

it most likely represents the best environment in which sustainable development can flourish. In other words, the strongest and most balanced array of social capital – with the brand pivotal in the creation and maintenance of balanced and durable social capital.

Of course, it's important also to understand not just the number of ties between actors (as shown) but the quality of those ties (as we've sketched in

*Well-linked periphery
with balance between
core and periphery*
**Social Equity Brand
Network**

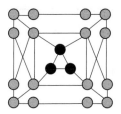

Figure 66: Social Equity Brand Network

the adaptation of Boutilier's work earlier), so finding a way to overlay the specific relationship measures onto each of the appropriate links in these core–periphery network charts is important. But that said, there is almost certainly a strong correlation between the density and make-up of the network (Cohesive Balance) and the quality of those relationships, since without the latter the former would be unsustainable.

Recognising that the Cohesive Balance network arrangement represents the optimal blend in terms of connectivity and brand role, we call this specific make-up the Social Equity Brand Network (Figure 66).

However, if we head back to the 2×2 matrix in Figure 63, once again our experienced and seasoned marketers may be scratching their heads trying to fathom whether this network layout really is the optimal place for a brand to be. After all, this falls squarely into the Compromiser segment. Surely we want Commander?

From where we sit, we would say no.

Commander is where brands have sat historically, fixating on their exclusive, intoxicating bonding capital approaches. Like it or not, bonding, bridging and linking capital levels are all on the rise within this emerging Era of Social Capital Rising, so for brands the choice is simple. Accept relegation to be marginalised as a 'Subordinate', relying on ever slimmer and more brittle forms of value creation for an increasingly connected and frustrated audience (in other words, for many, business as usual). Or recognise and embrace the new order and work hard to be central and vital to this new array of high-density networks.

Which leads us to say – rather predictably – that we feel the Compromiser label is a little out of date and pretty misleading. If compromising means

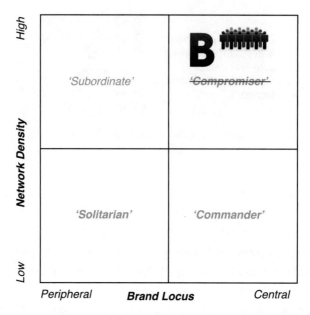

Figure 67: Density/locus mapping – Social Equity Brand locus

collaborating, sharing, engaging, thinking long term with peers and audiences, starting debate and building new ways of thinking, then we've another name for the type of brand that falls into that quadrant.

It's a brand new name.

It's a Social Equity Brand (Figure 67).

We've tried to build an argument throughout this book that in this emerging environment for business, the primary focus for brands should be on building social capital. This is for a number of reasons, the most striking being:

1. A focus on social capital is a focus on the root cause of so many of the problems we face today (rather than a focus on sustainability, which is, we feel, a symptom of collapsed social capital), so a better way to find long-term, durable solutions.
2. A focus on social capital – even out of the context of sustainability as many currently define it – is good for all of us, in terms of health, wellbeing and happiness.
3. A focus on social capital is good for the brand, since it nourishes the very thing that determines the environment in which it exists and hopefully thrives. It should be the ultimate long-term objective for any firm, via its brands, in an increasingly hyper-connected and values-aware world which we call the Era of Social Capital Rising.
4. A focus on social capital ensures the firm and its brands are looking at the optimal combination of generating long-term public value and private value.
5. A focus on social capital should play directly to the unique strengths of well-managed and progressive brands, creating innovative, imaginative and engaging ideas from which collaboration, long-term solutions, appreciation, closeness and loyalty all spring.

The value in nurturing networks – and diverse networks at that – crops up in arguments from a number of sources. Robert Metcalfe[171] – the founder of 3Com – came up with a compelling heuristic for the value in networks (specifically telecommunication networks), saying the value of any network is the square of the number of connected actors in that network. In other words, if a brand can grow the size of the network, the value within that network rises exponentially:

Metcalfe's Law:

$$Value \approx n^2$$

where n = number of actors in network

On a slightly different tack, John Kao[172] – the US-based innovation specialist – talks about the power of creativity in networks, and specifically how this 'creativity stock' rockets the more diverse the network is. In other words, if the brand can grow the diversity of the network, access to creativity rises:

Kao's Law:

$$Creativity_n \approx f(Diversity_n)$$

where n = network

Combining these together (in a horribly unscientific way, so apologies for that), we can see how these observations or heuristics can be applied to the argument for brands not only building and nurturing *more* social capital (more actors connected = greater value), but building *balanced* social capital (linking and bridging to complement bonding = greater creativity):

$$Social\ Capital\ Value_n \approx f(Diversity_n + n^2)$$

In short, it's more support for the growth of balanced and diverse social capital – and more support for brands being drivers of this growth. In a world moving towards value-based everything, building social capital is the route to the most durable, exciting and rewarding type of value on offer.

In this part we've attempted to move beyond the myriad arguments for why this is a good thing, and explore how this can come about. In other words, what brands must look for within themselves, and then how they must use those insights in their day-to-day activity to ensure social capital development remains at the top of the agenda, not just for society's sake, but for their own long-term survival and success; to marry these two extremely complementary ambitions under the banner of a Social Equity Brand; to focus on becoming valued.

In many cases this is going to require some hefty genetic modifications for brands. In the periods of deep reflection to understand what the brand stands for in today's social capital rising world, many marketers will reach the unsavoury conclusion that the brand has been built on short-term, quick-fix ambition, with fleeting and shallow value for those who come into contact with it (both externally and internally). For these brands, the work required is extensive – and necessary. Where their brand management strategies have been predicated on an unswerving economic viewpoint to lower transaction costs for clinical exchanges between consumers and the brand, there is now a need to embrace the more fluid, dynamic and unquestioningly messy world of the new consumer and the context they themselves define. Where, in the Era of Social Capital Waning, brand strategy was predicated on a rational and controlled marketing mix approach, in the Era of Social Capital Rising, this new approach to strategy must be built upon a new equity-creating ambition. And where the classic marketing mix offered some guidance to brand managers as a means to effectively drive brand strategy in that era, we hope the 5Is framework, as an undergirding element of a Social Capital Strategy, can also provide guidance and help to make sense of the myriad emerging roles brands now need to adopt.

If the traditional marketing mix approach represented a rigid recipe for brand managers to follow, then the 5Is and a Social Capital Strategy call out for the 'flavour to taste' approach.

That said, for many brands we genuinely believe it will be not so much a challenge of re-engineering, but a process far more intuitive and natural – remembering.

The truth is that many brands were originally created to protect inherent qualities that the firm felt separated them from the crowd – qualities that would set them down the road to being Social Equity Brands today. Some of the most enduring brands today were born from highly paternalistic practices at the outset – Cadbury's, Quakers and Boots (the prominent chain of UK chemist shops), for example. With each of these companies – and the brands they developed – huge care was taken to look after employees and their families, the communities where factories were located, and to ensure production and distribution processes were equitable. In other words, these brands were inadvertently leveraging the 5Is of our Social Capital Strategy process. Maybe these brands were truly progressive in spotting – and hedging against – the beginnings of the Era of Social Capital Waning.* Were they hedging against the hedgers?

Whatever the route taken, any brand that is looking to survive and thrive in this Era of Social Capital Rising will need to navigate towards becoming a Social Equity Brand. Only by focusing on this objective will the brand be instrumental in – and credited for – helping all of its constituents collaborate to find solutions and opportunities in today's world. This is the only route to becoming valued.

Our view of what we label a Social Equity Brand sits at the far end of a continuum of approaches to brand management offered by researchers and academics.[73] In these reviews of the literature, there are approaches that focus on the 'Economic' (prioritising low transaction costs for consumers)[74] through to 'Relational'[75] 'Community'[76] and 'Cultural'[77] approaches (see Figure 68).

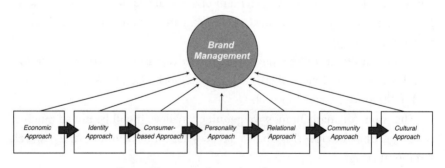

Figure 68: Approaches to brand management

*With changes of ownership for these iconic firms and their brands – both to international competitors and private equity partnerships – maybe the process of remembering will be a little more convoluted and complex than first thought.

With each approach we see support for a combination of the Social Equity Traits we advocate. But we see a brand management approach focused on social capital – and its informing Social Capital Strategy – as adding to this research in two ways.

Firstly, we see the social capital approach as a way to combine distinct elements from the other approaches. Rather than being seen as a series of distinct and mutually exclusive brand strategy options (and very much driven by some chronology or sense of evolution), a social capital approach allows brand managers effectively to cherry-pick aspects from multiple approaches, with the overarching ambition of building capital. A focus on sales today as well as brand building via relationship and community investment is an example of such a hybrid management approach.

Second, it is our belief that our vision of a Social Equity Brand sits beyond what is considered to be the most progressive approach to brand management today. Although the importance of community, relationships and even cultural fit are undeniably important for a brand, in our view a Social Equity Brand transcends the 'cosyness' of community, redefines the scope and importance of relationships (both thick and thin, near and far) and recognises that even within rich and established cultures, the very recognition and celebration of other values, perspectives and norms is key. As such, we believe a social capital approach to brand management, via a Social Capital Strategy, represents a development of the existing theoretical approaches to strategic brand management (see Figure 69).

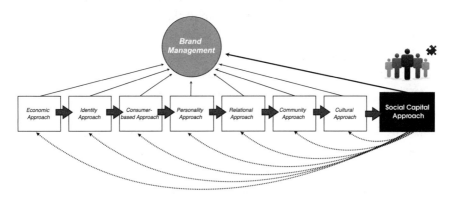

Figure 69: Approaches to brand management with the social capital approach

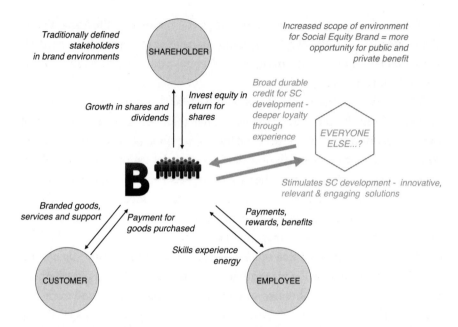

Figure 70: New stakeholders for Social Equity Brands. Reproduced by permission of John Wiley & Sons Ltd.

In his book, *Marketing Genius*,[178] Peter Fisk discusses the opportunities the brand has to create value, with these opportunities focused on Shareholders, Employees and Customers (see Figure 70). Whilst we do not doubt the importance of these stakeholders for the brand, to us this representation is only part of the picture; for a Social Equity Brand, value obligations and opportunities lie also with Citizens (who specifically do not consume the product), NGOs, governments and indeed society as a whole.

With all this increased activity and general 'messiness' around the brand in terms of what it needs to do and in terms of redefining itself and its relationships, both internally and externally, we've sketched out in this section a series of characteristics or traits that we believe are dominant (but not constant) in Social Equity Brands. These are our Social Equity Traits and are there to provide some sort of guidance, benchmark or objective as brands start on this journey.

But whilst these qualities undergird a Social Equity Brand, the challenge still remains as to how to convert these traits into constructive behaviour that fosters social capital within the brand's environment. In other words, how can this Social Equity Brand anatomy deliver public and private value beyond just being a 'feel good' badge on the door?

To help in finding some hard edges and routes through this complex and fundamental transition, we've proposed the rudiments of what we call a Social Capital Strategy. Updating and shifting the focus of the more traditional, product- and market-led marketing strategy (predicated on the 4Ps of the marketing mix), a Social Capital Strategy is experience-, relationship- and value-led, and represented by the 5Is – Interconnectedness, Inclusiveness, Ignition, Interest and Imagination. A Social Capital Strategy does not nullify a reliance on a marketing strategy, but rather guides it and provides context. It aims to help recognise the new environment in which the brand must respond to increasingly vociferous calls to create value today, and to meet the increasingly demanding expectations for value tomorrow.

And in the final chapter of this section we've grasped with both hands the most painful nettle possible: the subject of measurement.

Measuring return on marketing investment is complex at the best of times, partly because of the nebulous nature of marketing benefits and frequently because of ambiguous objectives behind the spend in the first place. What's more, the benefits of traditional marketing spend are predominantly felt in future years – Peter Fisk thinks up to 70% of every marketing dollar spent delivers value in years beyond that which it is accounted in.[79] When it comes to measuring the effects of a Social Capital Strategy and the brand's investment in social capital, these challenges are multiplied.

So on top of this messiness in terms of how a brand needs to interact and engage with its environments, we also have the challenge of what finance and procurement would consider distant – and heavily discounted – benefits.

But this is the way of the world now. No meaningful and durable collaboration and innovation is going to emerge from systematic incremental processes. No real sense of engagement and empowerment is going to emerge from faithful CSR reporting from the brand. This gloriously messy, nebulous and exciting environment is the new normal for brands in this Era of Social Capital Rising.

But nebulous and messy must not mean unaccountable. With this in mind, we've laid out a blueprint for how those managing progressive brands can start to unravel the measurement and efficiency challenges of creating a Social Equity Brand. From setting up systematic reviews as to whether the Social Equity Traits are becoming more dominant, to running through iterative conversations within the 5Is framework, we've tried to initiate a dialogue on how to measure these developments.

When it comes actually to measuring stocks of social capital, we've offered a process with which to explore how central the brand is in each of the components of social capital – components that, in our view, form a process and virtuous circle. By being able to single out contributions and involvements with each element, the brand is in a better position to understand how it can leverage its abilities more effectively to complete the circle and move past pinch points in the process.

Specifically we've shown how the structural (dialogue) component is fundamentally different to the cognitive (thought) and relational (trust) components, highlighting the issue that extensive dialogue does not necessarily lead to higher social capital.

When it comes to trust – the crucial feedback loop in social capital development – we've shown how Havas's proprietary and dedicated global research project – Sustainable Futures – is constantly providing rich data from which we can start to understand at a forensic level just how much trust is swirling around the brand when it comes to issues constantly being raised in this period of citizen-led 'wakefulness'. Each component or strand of social capital can be shown on a 2 × 2 matrix, allowing those who oversee the brand to immediately spot where there are structural holes in their efforts to build social capital.

Blending these distinct elements together into a measure of relationship strength, durability and value, we've also introduced the importance of considering the density of those relationships, and where the brand sits within that network of relationships – the brand locus. Highlighting the importance of being able to place the brand within the network map, this process allows the brand to visualise the end goal of becoming a Social Equity Brand, where it's centred and valued in a rich, diverse and interconnected network.

In a more traditional context of all-out competitive marketing in the Era of Social Capital Waning – where brand ambition was the rapid creation of exclusive and intoxicating bonding capital – this position is labelled 'Compromiser'. As the pendulum swings back, and as the fundamental role and expectation of brands within society shifts, we genuinely believe this position is not one of compromise, but rather opportunity.

It's the natural home of a brand that recognises the value in being valued – a Social Equity Brand.

Part V

Broadcast Off, Dialogue On – Invitation to Form Bonding, Bridging and Linking Capital (Apply Online)

So that's it. That's our Brand Valued narrative. Well almost.

In line with our own recommendations, we hope it's opened up the debate a little, starting to make people think and discuss – not just within the advertising, media and marketing industry, but beyond. We hope we've framed the debate in a way that has proven engaging, at least some of the time.

And very importantly, we hope it's made the case that the role brands could play in this exciting transition in our societies is enormous, influential and incredibly valuable. It continues to be our fundamental belief that the opportunity in front of brands today is beyond comparison. And so is the responsibility.

In this Era of Social Capital Rising, it really is time to recognise that brand value and brand equity are dependent on the brand being valued. To reiterate:

Brand Valued	Brand Equity	Brand Value
(Bvd)	(Be)	(Bv)

But our narrative has to be only the beginning. As we've said over and over, for social capital to increase, narratives have to encourage dialogue, dialogue has to encourage new ways of thinking and problem solving, and these new mental models need to generate greater levels of trust, leading all the way back again to even deeper, wider and more valuable dialogue. So this book is really just the beginning of a narrative that depends on the collaboration of others.

As we said at the outset, this final section of the book is for others to write. This is where we attempt to become a collaborative platform for discussion and new thinking.

In getting to this point, we hope we've followed our own advice and focused on ramping up the 5Is of our own Social Capital Strategy with this book.

We've focused on Interconnectedness, drawing on parallel research from psychology, sociology and taking as broad, deep and longitudinal a view of the relationship between social capital and brands as we felt possible.

We've focused on Inclusiveness, trying to make the debate as relevant to as wide an audience as possible, recognising the possibilities in front of brands to move beyond their historical role and create considerable private and public value for the long term.

We've focused on Igniting the debate, framing it in a way that hopefully makes it more exciting – more relevant – for brand managers and teams to realise what they could possibly do to raise social capital – what they could uniquely do to raise social capital – and the results it could have.

We've focused on Imagination, aligning all the unique qualities that brands have at their disposal and the myriad ways those could be put to such exceptional use in restocking social capital; unique qualities that could place brands once again in the vanguard of social change – and for all the right reasons.

And finally, we've never lost our focus on Interest. Our interest in this area, our interest in the role brands can play, is genuine and heartfelt. We started this book with a rallying call to all brands to unleash their potential to become better at everything they do; that the current climate and the seismic shifts coursing through commerce and society represent not a crisis for brands but an opportunity for rebirth. 255 pages on, we remain committed to that belief.

We constantly see committed, creative and intellectual brilliance from many associated with brand communication. Brilliance that is too great to be devoted to old-school communications alone. Brilliance that can be harnessed to bring about the colossal demand-side, mass scale behaviour change we need amongst us. As such, our interest is genuine and unquestioningly intrinsically motivated. And what's more, we think that innate intrinsic commitment is beating just beneath the surface within those who manage the world's most impressive brands today. It just needs surfacing and directing.

So with all of our arguments laid out, our ambition bare and our narrative told, we throw it over to anyone and everyone to add comments. We welcome challenges, disagreements, support and amendments; most of all, we welcome case studies and examples, where brands are considered to be on the right path to being a Social Equity Brand – and where they're not.

To that end, we include an opening gambit in terms of ten prominent and progressive brands that we feel are marching towards becoming Social Equity Brands (and for different reasons). In no particular order, we've given each a short report drawing on characteristics and Social Capital Strategy elements.

As a genuine act of collaboration, amongst the tightly bonded community of the communications industry, the increasingly bridged communities of business, NGOs and civil society, and the linked institutions of national and supra-national policy shapers and makers, we hope, in a small way, that this book starts to build some social capital – balanced, long-term social capital.

Because it's only through social capital that we're going to find solutions to the myriad challenges we face, be they commercial, ecological, financial, social or personal. And it's only through a focus on social capital that brands will be truly and durably valuable to the firms that own them, and valued by the societies that support them.

We look forward to the conversation.

Please join it at: www.brandvalued.com.

Ten brands heading towards becoming Social Equity Brands – a primer for conversation

As a primer for further debate, here are ten brands (and really in no particular order) that we feel are moving in the right direction. Before offering a short explanation for each as to how it's made it into our list, there are four points we'd like to make.

Firstly none of these is a Social Equity Brand. Yet. In some way, we feel they are moving forward, either at a corporate brand level or with a product brand showing the way. And there are certainly inconsistencies in their performances. But at the risk of using a very hackneyed escape clause, recognising that this is a journey for all brands, these are ten that we feel have started on the right foot, and are taking steps in the right direction (even if these steps are intuitive rather than planned as advocated in this book).

Second, as is immediately obvious, all bar one of these brands is associated with large multinationals. This is the case as we're keen to highlight high-profile examples of progress, but also to make the point that big is not automatically bad when it comes to social capital; that their scale and experience can be the perfect partner for the agility and hunger of newly created brands.

Third, the notes on each of these progressive brands are just that – notes. We have no detailed inside knowledge as to their motivations, ambitions, objectives or strategies. As such, we can only look at public benefits and offer conjecture with respect to private benefits – in other words, how possible increases in stocks of social capital are being converted into specific value for the brands involved. As we highlighted in the last chapter on measurement, this link between public stock and private value is as dependent on the position of the brand within the network as it is on the overall levels of capital within the network – density and position.

Finally, the short openers for each brand could be construed as missing the point; focusing on some initiative or campaign when the business itself is engaged in so much more. But to reach that conclusion is, in itself, missing the point. This short list of constructive brands heading towards Social Equity status is compiled on the criterion that in each case the brand is stepping away from the corporate endeavours and focusing on social capital development (see figures 9 and 10, Chapter 4).

In short, with each brand in our provisional top ten, there's been something in their recent behaviour that's caught our interest and encouraged us to look a little deeper. In each case, we've picked out which aspects of our Social Equity Traits they seem to be showing (or developing) and then looked at how those traits seem to be driving some sort of alignment to the 5Is of our Social Capital Strategy process.

Finally, this list has been put together primarily with knowledge and opinion within a very small, bonding capital-intensive, group. We hope the contributions from others will help bring in the much-needed balances of bridging and linking social capital. And make the list longer, more detailed and a more effective catalyst for debate.

Brand 1: Danone

Having said we've pulled this list together purely from distant observation, and with no direct involvement with the business and its brands, it's not the case with Danone, since a number of the company's brands are looked after by various Havas agencies in different parts of the world. And whilst not engaged with the group specifically on issues around sustainability (or social capital) we have noticed a strong and valuable commitment from Danone to use their knowledge, skills and network to build social capital through improved dialogue and understanding, specifically around a number of issues important to the brand, and us all.

Leading the communication of the personal importance of diet and wellbeing, and how production techniques and logistics can impact on nutrition and safety for us and our families, Danone has been instrumental in providing a highly relevant and engaging context within which we can explore and influence these issues. Focusing on wellbeing, Danone is attempting to empower us to take more responsibility for our health and, more generally and by association, wellbeing and happiness. We only have to look at Danone's own language around these issues to immediately see how *Inclusiveness* and *Interest* are central to their brand strategy: 'For All' is one of the key pillars of their guiding mission to 'bring health through food to as many people as possible.'[180]

Whilst many have said it is easier for food companies to make the sustainability debate relevant for their consumers, due to the link to personal wellbeing, Danone certainly seems to be stepping away from the competition when it comes to developing dialogue via the use of narrative, encouraging shared understanding and recognising its consumers more as citizens, with concerns, values and ambitions beyond the market.

Away from highly developed markets, Danone is also leveraging its capabilities in poor rural communities, working with Grameen Bank to provide better and more nutritional starts for children in Bangladesh, highlighting its intrinsically motivated commitment and interest to find ways to meet the challenges faced in this and other chronically under-resourced regions. Whilst this may feel like more of an operations-led approach to solving chronic sustainability issues, it must also be recognised that it is only through such a powerful – and socially oriented – brand that these challenges can be effectively framed, made sense of and tackled in such an effective way. As we will see with others in this list, whilst efforts in sustainability may well bolster brand image, the relationship is more complex; using the brand to embody long-term social motives can also drive and improve wider corporate performance. In other words, a Social Capital Strategy not only places social capital and its development at the heart of the brand, it also places the brand and its potential at the heart of the business.

Brand 2: Unilever

Unilever has popped up a couple of times within this book – once applauding its efforts with respect to the Dove Real Beauty campaign, and once with a question mark over its intrinsically motivated commitment to this campaign, considering its portfolio of other brands and their communication.

Unilever is, we believe, one of the most committed companies when it comes to using its brands to create social capital and explore collaborative solutions to the challenges we face. Certainly the Dove brand is an excellent example of this commitment, but much work also seems to be unfolding at the corporate brand level.

Anchored around the principle corporate trait of 'vitality' (as a possible way round the Axe/Dove dilemma), Unilever is working hard to craft relevant and engaging narratives, raising awareness and education levels through brand-initiated dialogue that is then firmly in the hands of external audiences of enabled citizens.

With the reinvigorated corporate brand creating and leading initiatives with respect to key production challenges (palm oil, for example), Unilever is championing ongoing *Interconnectedness*, as well as *Inclusiveness* via its consumer-facing education campaigns. And by finding ways to make the debate real and relevant for diverse audiences, the corporate brand is demonstrating a commitment to find *Imaginative* ways to *Ignite* the social capital building process. Nowhere is this corporate brand-led focus more apparent than in the recently launched 'Sustainable Living Plan'[181]. Using the corporate brand to encapsulate a multitude of initiatives, the plan intuitively recognises the true power of the brand to engage, encourage and support others in its strap line: 'Small Actions. Big Difference.'

One example is their Project Shakti initiative. Whilst not linked directly to the brand, the project's aim to raise entrepreneurial skills amongst women in Asia is a direct assault on low levels of social capital in the region. By encouraging an entrepreneurial spirit amongst women, dialogue, exchange and new thinking follow, creating higher levels of trust within communities and in turn more opportunities to demonstrate trustworthiness. In other words, it unlocks previously hidden and frustrated pockets of social capital.

I was fortunate enough to share the stage with Unilever's CEO, Paul Polman at the 2011 WBCSD conference[182] where we discussed the challenges and opportunities for brands today, and Paul stressed the importance of *Inclusiveness, Interconnectedness* and *Interest* as the key drivers for the corporate brand's activity. It was refreshing and captivating to hear the CEO of one of the world's largest FMCG companies (where two billion times a day someone uses one of their brands), say that Unilever cannot do enough on its own, and talk about the need for greater sectorial and cross-sectorial collaboration for the sake of genuine and lasting positive impact on lives.

What was also profoundly clear was Paul Polman's intrinsic motivation towards these actions, in many cases to the concern of his executive board. Clearly the emergence of Social Equity Brands depends upon business leaders with vision and courage. It is also worth mentioning that any quick scan will reveal how Unilever is already enjoying considerable increases in reputation and equity thanks to this commitment from a reinvigorated corporate brand to build rich and balanced social capital.

Brand 3: Pepsi

In many ways this US-global brand really should be in the business of building social capital. After all, a clear number of their product brands are all about social exchange and a celebration of diversity and shared experiences. Pepsi makes it into this initial list, though, for its groundbreaking Refresh project[183].

We've discussed it several times throughout the book, but to summarise, Refresh represents for us a quantum leap forward in terms of using narrative and emotion to engage as wide an audience as possible in this debate. These two characteristics combine to create the most impressive *Ignition* sequence imaginable.

In short, the narrative is simple: what do you want the story to be?

Creating an open platform through which literally anyone can engage to pitch for funds to support either existing or new socially constructive initiatives, Refresh then allows others to vote on the proposals before the brand commits funds to the endeavour. Funding can be from $5000 up to $250,000 for any one project.

By allowing everyone and anyone to shape a narrative that is personal and engaging for them, then encouraging the development of that narrative amongst like-minded protagonists, through to offering the perfect platform for linking and bridging capital-fueled relationships to add their voice to the debate, Pepsi has cooked up a compelling process for stoking all forms of social capital in a balanced way. In short, the benefits of higher social capital could not be more apparent and appealing for all those involved.

The highly *Imaginative* approach (not to mention risky, considering the withdrawal from conventional TV advertising to finance it) and the seemingly genuine *Interest* in seeing how it can use its scale and might to enable pockets of individuals to coalesce and create reams of value, genuinely strikes us as a company and brand that is finding its intrinsic motivation. Robert ter Kuile, Director, Environmental Sustainability and Public Policy, further demonstrated this motivation when we spoke at the WBCSD Montreux event in early 2011, discussing the work PepsiCo is undertaking to educate and engage communities in developing markets around solutions for iron deficiency in young women[184].

Whilst Pepsi's main competitor may have spent a large chunk of the twentieth century wanting to teach the world to sing, Pepsi, it seems, is making great strides in this century to teach the world to talk, and listen.

Brand 4: Walmart

We've been back and forth a little on including Walmart. Whichever side of the fence you sit on, it's impossible not to recognise that Walmart is a dominant player in the wider sustainability debate, if for no other reasons than the sheer number of people that shop at its stores everyday, the sheer size of its supply chain, or its iron-like grip on all those who work within or around it. For better or for worse, when Walmart moves, everyone notices.

And move it certainly has. There's no doubt that Walmart is now charging at sustainability, clearly recognising the inexorable pressure this issue is having on its business. Two of its efforts jump out; namely its impending sustainability index[185], and the sustainability consortium[186].

Looking at the latter first, this is an impressive initiative to bring together a number of specialist organisations – commerical, academic and public – to reach some sort of durable consensus on what sustainability means in the context of thousands of products. It's a colossal undertaking and really Walmart must be applauded for striving to leverage such *Interconnectedness*, and for efforts to increase bridging and linking capital. From a B2B perspective at least, this is a monumental commitment to *Ignite* the debate.

And with respect to the former – the sustainability index - again this is a blockbuster of an initiative, especially when we consider the diversity of what Walmart actually sells. To be honest, how the index will manage to distill down to a single graphic the impact of any and every product in store is beyond us, but ten out of ten for biting this much off in the first place.

It's this second initiative, though, that has also caused us to vacillate, for the simple reason that it's a commitment to more data and cold analysis and accessibility, rather than narrative, emotional biasing and 'assessibility'. This is not an initiative based on dialogue, but rather one anchored in transmission, distilling everything down to a single score, and so absolving those who use it from any sense of personal responsibility. In other words, treating us still very much as consumers, rather than as citizens-who-consume. That said, it is clearly early days for Walmart in this journey, and respecting their need to protect their core proposition, we're very keen to see where this all goes next.

Brand 5: Equity Bank

As a local Kenyan bank, Equity Bank is our one non-multinational brand to make it into this initial list, and is probably new to you, unless you've spotted it in the press over the last year, read journal articles from Stanford or Harvard, or have managed to get through the rest of this book, where we've referenced it several times[187].

For us, Equity Bank is a fascinating case study and a real stride towards a true Social Equity Brand. We accept that Equity Bank is not probably a brand in the more traditional sense of the word, and its success is more down to its business practices. But so central is social equity to its purpose, vision and extraordinary success, it makes it into this initial top ten with ease.

Equity Bank has not only focused on increasing social capital, but has made that focus central to its overall strategy. Equity Bank's entire business model is built on increasing social capital and the virtuous circle that results from social capital creating trust, trust creating higher social capital, and so more opportunities to demonstrate trustworthiness.

As such, Equity Bank has the development of balanced and long-term social capital at the very heart of its business ambition. Through leveraging social capital, Equity Bank confers enormous responsibility on to those it lends to, with excellent results – not just for those able to start their own businesses as a result, but the bank itself, with 50% market share, 4000 new accounts opening a day and a debt default rate at a fraction of the industry average.

Recognising the importance and opportunity in enabling swathes of the community that other, less imaginative, players considered unengaged and disinterested, Equity Bank's intrinsic motivation is plain to see – it has well and truly *Ignited* the process to build social capital, and the outcome of its work is inescapably shaped by an unswerving commitment to *Inclusiveness*, *Interest* and *Imagination*.

Brand 6: Vodafone

It seems very obvious. Surely a progressive telecoms brand must make it into a list that looks at brands that are, among other things, building the capacity and desire to enter into dialogue?

Obvious it may be, but Vodafone is the only brand in this sector that has caught our eye in terms of using its brand to encourage the development of rich and balanced social capital.

Vodafone places its consumer at the heart of its innovation and new services processes, and is committed to using its technology and network to allow us all to live more fulfilled, balanced and sustainable lives. In their 2009 sustainability report[188], the company says they're committed to using technology to deliver sustainability. We'd word it slightly differently; that they're committed to using their technology to bolster *social capital*. Increased dialogue, improved thinking and enhanced levels of trust, all round. Vodafone's skills and commitment are a perfect fit for a brand focused on nourishing social capital.

Looking at the internal brand audiences, Vodafone's 'World of Difference' programme[189] has allowed hundreds of employees to develop their thinking and leverage their desire to be stronger, more influential citizens via year-long placements with their chosen social enterprises and charities. Not only does this programme encourage social capital development within the communities playing host to these volunteers, but the initiative itself stokes social capital development within the organisation.

Externally, Vodafone's Money Transfer programme – branded locally as M-PESA in Kenya[190] (and more recently, the new service, M-KESHO) – has proven to be an extraordinary force in nurturing social capital. In much the same way as Unilever's Project Shakti, and Equity Bank in Kenya, M-PESA has unlocked the potential and desire to exchange, think, collaborate and build trust. To date there are more than 17,000 M-PESA agents operating in Kenya and it's estimated the initiative has created more than 30,000 new jobs. These jobs alone, and the network effects they create, act as the infrastructure for the development of social capital, bringing economic development and improved wellbeing for all those involved as opportunities are able to be seized to create collaborate services and initiatives for both public and private benefit. Again, whilst some of these initiatives may appear less brand-led than others, Vodafone's Director of Sustainability, Chris Burgess, makes a compelling argument that without a strong brand shaping and informing these initiatives, such efforts would remain fragmented and piecemeal. More than that, they would probably never be accepted as innovative approaches to development challenges due to little inherent trust in the entity behind the initiative. In Chris Burgess's words, a strong brand is a vital ingredient for the success of these initiatives that demonstrate what he describes as Vodafone's commitment to both 'lifestyles and lifelines'[191].

Brand 7: Toyota

Mobility is a hot topic for all of us and is never far from the top of the agenda for business, society and government as we look ahead. Plus we've touched on the apparent short-sightedness of the auto industry a couple of times in the book, so if one car manufacturer was to make it into our initial list of fledgling Social Equity Brands, we could have guessed it would have been the creators of the Prius – Toyota.

But whilst Toyota is included here, it is not, we have to say, because of the hybrid phenomenon that carries their name. Instead, the brand is here thanks to its 'Ideas for Good' initiative[192].

Here's a great example of a strong corporate brand leveraging one of its key strengths for collective benefit. Toyota is known for its commitment to using cutting-edge technology to create vehicles that are more effective and efficient, but in this initiative the focus is to use their technologies to make the *world* run effectively and efficiently. In their words, '...use Toyota's advanced technologies on more than just cars to make a better world'[193].

In many ways, this brand-led initiative is Toyota's own Refresh project, in that submissions from anyone on ideas for innovative uses of technology are reviewed by Toyota's own 'gurus' before there's a period of community voting and a series of winners announced. It's a compelling vehicle to engage and educate a wide audience in the challenges we face, with the brand perfectly placed to not only enable this conversation and exchange, but to be seen to use its might and ingenuity to action solutions that have bubbled up through dialogue and shared thinking. Whether it's Toyota's technology improving sports safety, running more energy efficient roller-coasters or lending vital help in natural disaster zones, there is no doubt that this brand-led initiative is building richer and more balanced levels of social capital through engaging us all as forward-looking citizens. The Toyota brand is focused on *Inclusiveness, Interest, Imagination* and – most appropriately for a car manufacturer – *Ignition.*

Brand 8: GE

These days, no sustainability listing or commentary is complete without GE and its Ecomagination[194] programme, it seems.

As a separately branded initiative, reaching out beyond core GE customers and consumers, Ecomagination has been extraordinarily successful in raising awareness, provoking dialogue and – very importantly – creating a strong and durable revenue stream for the company. Such is GE's ubiquitous presence in the US, it is not unlike Walmart in terms of its instant effect on social capital when it chooses to get behind something.

Ecomagination has created a number of useful tools and a strong platform for all to discuss, share and evolve ideas on energy usage and more sustainable practices – issues that extend far beyond the current capabilities of the brand's parent organisation. We particularly like the simple but very effective tool for tinkering with home energy use[195], acting as a great primer to get people engaged in trying to reduce their energy consumption in the most obvious places.

In short, with Ecomagination, GE has created a brand that has become a medium for all things sustainability and a brighter future - and in doing this, the medium is directly fueling the development of positive social capital.

Within the Ecomagination brand experience online, users are able to explore a broad range of issues and opportunities on a global scale, connecting with like-minded individuals or groups wherever and whenever. It's the potency of bonding capital, coupled with the balance, diversity and broader context only made possible through bridging and linking capital. This brand-led juggernaut is leveraging *Inclusiveness, Interest* and *Imagination* to *Ignite* and enable debate and discussion amongst a myriad of communities and interest groups.

Away from their consumers, the Ecomagination initiative is also capturing the hearts and minds of other businesses. Never shying away from extolling the commercial benefits of the initiative, GE is making continuous inroads towards long-lasting *Interconnectedness* and, in raising the bar, is raising social capital levels amongst its peer group as discussions develop around how best to innovate.

Finally, in terms of internal audiences and the power of social capital, GE is also active, having recently announced the launch of an internal, marketing-focused social network[196]. Recognising the value of having bonding-heavy teams who easily and quickly derive value from linking and bridging environments, GE's 'MarkNet' initiative demonstrates that the company is as committed to building and leveraging social capital within the company, as it is to building it around the company.

Brand 9: IBM

There's no doubt that International Business Machine's CEO Thomas John Watson Sr (1874-1956) was an extraordinary salesman, who took the company from strength to incredible strength in the early decades of the twentieth century. In fact, on reporting his death, the The New York Times went further and said Mr Watson would probably be remembered as 'the world's *greatest* salesman.'[197] He's also remembered for a prediction he apparently made in

1943, that there would be a market for at most five computers on the planet. Despite being a mainstay of almost every light-hearted jibe about the inability of business to look ahead, with a little digging around it looks certain this prediction was never made[198] (and was instead most likely 'adapted' from another speech made by Watson Jr, on the potential market for the IBM 701 Electronic Data Processing Machine in 1953[199]). But even if Watson Sr had stuck his head out and made that prediction when it is claimed he did, it would have held for a decade[200].

Today, IBM is at it again: making predictions about the future demands made of technology, by the planet, and all of us on it. Except this time, the predictions are not quick sound bites from the company's executives, but rather the cornerstone of the IBM brand-led 'Smarter Planet' initiative[201].

It's fairly well documented that IBM has very successfully reinvented itself from a machinery company, to one that consults and sells solutions (powered by their computer power and know-how), but with Smarter Planet, the IBM brand is going even further and being seen to lead the charge on what we must collectively do to bring about sustainable living in the ever-growing number of cities on the planet. Everything about Smarter Planet points to a brand that recognises the power of many of our Social Equity Traits, and understands the long-term importance of using them to define a brand strategy around the 5Is. Just a cursory wander around the initiative's website illustrates the commitment the brand has to building social capital around a wealth of issues and opportunities: IBM even badge their initial forays into these areas as 'IBM's conversations'[202], covering areas such as banking, cities, energy, food, oil, rail, retail and even work. The opportunities for shared thinking and engagement from this point on are clear, with the IBM brand becoming a media hub for all cutting-edge conversations and their hopefully positive outcomes. In line with our idea that true Social Equity Brands occupy a central space in a richly connected, engaged and trusting environment, IBM's Smarter Planet initiative plants the brand in just such a position. Whilst the conversation could not have started without the brand driving the *Ignition* process, it is now at a point where the brand embodies just one pool of expertise, with it taking on a dual role of enabler and convener.

Smarter Planet demonstrates the brand's commitment to the concepts that underpin our Social Capital Strategy process: *Inclusiveness* in terms of framing the fundamental challenges we face for all of humanity; *Interest* in terms of looking beyond our 'economic' value and instead at quality of life and broader wellbeing; *Imagination* in terms of the way the brand frames the dialogue and makes a series of colossal issues not only relevant to a wide audience, but potentially solvable by that audience; *Ignition* in terms of being central to the conversations getting underway; and *Interconnectedness* in terms of how the brand is leveraging its work with clients to collectively find solutions not only to the challenges we anticipate tomorrow, but to more effectively meet the challenges we face today. In short, Smarter Planet is a compelling example of the brand engaging in what we have called 'Imaginative Collaboration'.

Brand 10: Starbucks

Just shy of 300 pages in, and definitely time for a cup of coffee.

Starbucks is synonymous with coffee – or more specifically convincing all of us that £3 is an acceptable amount to pay for a cup. Contrary to what many saw as one of the first luxuries that would be cut at the glimpse of recession, it seems coffee – and the experience of drinking it – is the little luxury we allow ourselves to have, come what may in the economic climate.

To choose Starbucks as our last example of a brand that is marching towards becoming a Social Equity Brand has a delicious irony and completeness about it. Coffee has been at the centre of social capital since it was first poured into a cup. We started 268 pages ago by saying social capital has always swirled around brands – and coffee has always swirled around social capital.

Coffee houses have been the hubs of social capital development, here in the UK at least, since the late 1600s. Edward Lloyd's coffeehouse in Tower Street here in London hosted the development of the first maritime insurance market in 1688[203], as sailors, merchants and ship owners would converge on his establishment to hear shipping news. It was the beginning of Lloyds of London Insurers and Re-Insurers.

As with all forms of social capital, growth is only sustainable if the dialogue and thinking is fresh, consistent and trustworthy, which in this case it was. The result was more people coming through the door, creating higher levels of bonding, bridging and linking social capital, and so richer, more diverse and timely information and dialogue. Plus I imagine the coffee also had to be good.

So Starbucks carries a hefty responsibility to keep coffee at the centre of social capital development, and social capital development at the heart of its brand. And it seems it does.

The reason we've included Starbucks in our exploratory list of progressive brands, is not because of its commitment to Fairtrade, or health cover for its US part-time employees, or indeed the community volunteering it does (all of which are superbly important and constructive when it comes to higher social capital and more cohesive communities and society), but rather the brand-led initiative My Starbucks Idea[204]. Underpinned by a simple 'Commitment to Community', this programme encourages everyone to engage in shaping the future of the company. And because the company sees itself at the centre of, and a driving force for, strong communities, so an interest in shaping the future of the company is an interest in shaping the future of the community. Online community contributors submit ideas and suggestions, vote on them, debate and refine them further into becoming feasible initiatives, and then engage with Starbucks 'Idea Partners' who are drawn from a variety of departments within the company, and are committed to this process of inclusion, collaboration and innovation. The final step in this journey is then being able to see these ideas turned into working initiatives, powered by Starbucks and enjoyed by communities. And such is the nature of the platform and those who engage with it, it is not just the local communities that enjoy the benefits, but distant communities, united by similar social challenges.

This branded initiative – separate from all the other corporate endeavours of the parent brand – ticks many of the boxes we consider important in shaping a Social Equity Brand – not just in terms of brand characteristics, but also in terms of how those characteristics are put to such compelling use via our Social Capital Strategy 5Is. Starbucks is co-creating strong narrative; is allowing emotion to surface to good effect; is recognising consumers as citizens (and allowing them to do the same); is creating value in use via the comprehensive online environment; is stimulating dialogue and shared thinking; is striving for more balanced social capital; and is championing experience over consumption with intrinsic motivation. The result is an experience that delivers value to the user thanks to its *Inclusiveness, Imagination, Interest* and desire to *Ignite* citizen-community spirit.

Finally, the value is private too. Starbucks is enjoying considerable recognition and applause for its efforts in this area – in using its consumer-centric approach to create both private and public benefit. We feel it's achieved this through recognising that social capital has to be at the heart of its brand. Starbucks recognises social capital is its oxygen, and is working hard to ensure it – and we – have enough. It is this last quality – this recognition of the centrality of social capital to the health of the brand and its environments – that lands the brand so firmly in our opening Top Ten.

Had Edward Lloyd's coffee house still been going, who knows, maybe we'd have created a Top Eleven.

Part I Setting the scene

1 See Jon Alexander's contributions to www.conservation-economy.org.
2 For more information, see Steve Hilton's chapter in *Brands and Branding*, The Economist/Profile Books, 2003.
3 Sourced from P&G Ivory website. http://www.ivory.com/purefun_history.htm. Accessed December 2010.
4 See Nahapiet, J. and Ghoshal, S. (1998) 'Social Capital, Intellectual Capital, and the Organisational Advantage', *Academy of Management Review*, 23(2), 242–266.
5 See Marek Kohn (2008) *Trust, Self Interest and the Common Good*, Oxford.
6 Tim Ambler (1997) 'How Much of Brand Equity is Explained by Trust?' *Management Decision*, 35(4), 283–292.
7 Sourced via http://www.novelguide.com/a/discover/bls_01/bls_01_00138.html.
8 Sourced via http://money.cnn.com/magazines/fsb/fsb_archive/2003/04/01/341013/index.htm.
9 Peter White, Global Director, Sustainability, P&G. Cambridge Sustainable Leadership Conference, May 2009.
10 For more information, see Claude Hopkins (1923) *Scientific Advertising*. Reprinted in 2010 by Cosimo Inc.
11 For more information, see *Principles of Scientific Management*, 1911. Reprinted in 2008 by Forgotten Books.
12 See Haidt, J. (2001) 'The Emotional Dog and its Rational Tail', *Psychological Review*, 108, 814–834, or Feldwick, P. and Heath, R. (2008) 'Fifty Years of Using the Wrong Model of Advertising', *International Journal of Market Research*, 50(1), 29–59.
13 Vargo, S. L. and Lusch, R. F. (2004) 'Evolving to a New Dominant Logic of Marketing', *Journal of Marketing*, 68, 1–17.
14 See Holbrook, M. and Hirschman, E. (1982) 'The Experiential Aspects of Consumption: Consumer Fantasies, Feelings and Fun', *Journal of Consumer Research*, 9(2), 132–140.

15 For more information see Carol Graham (2009) *Happiness Around the World*, Oxford University Press.

16 Solomon, R. (1980) 'The Opponent Process Theory of Acquired Motivation', *American Psychologist*, **35**, 691–712.

17 Scitovsky, T. (1976) *The Joyless Economy*, Oxford University Press.

18 See Elinor Ostrom (1990) *Governing the Commons: The Evolution of Institutions for Collective Action*, Cambridge.

19 See the *Stern Review on the Economics of Climate Change*, British Government, 2006.

20 P&G Ivory Soap copy. Sourced via Broadbent (2007) *Does Advertising Create Demand?* WARC.

21 For more information, see the WBCSD 2009 Report *Sustainable Consumption: Facts and Trends*. Available via http://www.wbcsd.org/DocRoot/I9Xwhv7X5V8cDIHbHC3G/WBCSD_Sustainable_Consumption_web.pdf. Accessed December 2010.

22 *Ibid.* p. 8. World Bank database, Global Population Trends, 2008.

23 *Financial Times*, July 15, 2008 'Boom time for the global bourgeoisie'. Accessed December 2010.

24 Jackson, T. (2009) *Prosperity Without Growth? The transition to a stable economy*, UK Sustainable Development Commission.

25 Lebow, V. (1955) 'Price Competition in 1955', *Journal of Retailing*, **XXXI**, 5. © Elsevier for The New York School of Retailing.

26 Robert Kennedy campaign speech. University of Kansas, Lawrence, Kansas, March 18, 1968.

27 Commission on the Measurement of Economic Performance and Social Progress (2009). Accessed December 2010 via http://www.stiglitz-sen-fitoussi.fr/en/index.htm.

28 Easterlin, R. (2001) 'Income and Happiness: Towards a Unified Theory', *Economic Journal*, **111**, 465–484.

29 Graham, C. and Pettinato, S. (2002) 'Happiness and Hardship: Opportunity and Insecurity in New Market Economies.' In Graham, C. (2009) *Happiness Around the World*, Cambridge.

30 See New Economics Foundation. Accessed December 2010 via http://www.neweconomics.org/programmes/well-being.

31 Capra, F. and Henderson, H. (2009) *Qualitative Growth*, The Institute of Chartered Accountants in England and Wales.

32 Schwartz, B. (2000) *The Costs of Living. How Market Freedom Erodes the Best Things in Life*, Xlibris Corporation, USA.

33 *Ibid.* p. 167.

34 Schau, H. J., Muñiz, A. M. and Arnould, E. J. (2009) 'How Brand Community Practices Create Value', *Journal of Marketing*, **783**, 30–51.

35 Huxley was credited with this quote from his lecture 'The Unconscious' (delivered in the University of California, 1959 and published in *The Human Situation*, London, 1978). Sourced via Broadbent, T. (2007) *Does Advertising Create Demand?* WARC.

36 Packard, V. (1957) *The Hidden Persuaders*, David McKay, New York.
37 Toynbee, A. J. Quotation from 'Is It Immoral to Stimulate Buying?' *Printers Ink Magazine*, **279**, 43, May 11, 1962. Copyright © Printers Ink Publishing Corporation Inc.
38 Klein, N. (2000) *No Logo*, Fourth Estate, London.
39 Broadbent, T. (2007) *Does Advertising Create Demand?* WARC, London.

Part II   The 'unsustainability' of sustainability

40 From an interview given in *The Guardian*, February 21, 2010.
41 Polanyi, K. (1944) *The Great Transformation: The Political and Economic Origins of Our Time*. New edition, 2001, Beacon Press.
42 See http://www.terrachoice.com/. Accessed December 2010.
43 See http://www.terrachoice.com/Home/Portfolio/Reports. Accessed December 2010.
44 The Climate Group (2008) *Consumers, Brands and Climate Change, 2008 (UK)*. Accessed December 2010 via http://www.theclimategroup.org/publications/2008/10/31/consumers-brands-andclimate-change-2008-uk/.
45 The Climate Group (2008) *Consumers, Brands and Climate Change, 2008 (US)*. Accessed December 2010 via http://www.theclimategroup.org/publications/2008/11/4/consumers-brands-and- climate-change-2008-us/.
46 See Walmart corporate site: http://walmartstores.com/sustainability/9292.aspx. Accessed December 2010.
47 See Pepsi Refresh Everything: http://www.refresheverything.com/. Accessed December 2010.
48 See Porritt, J. (2007) *Capitalism as if the World Matters*, Earthscan, London.
49 Simon, H. A. (1956) 'Rational Choice and the Structure of the Environment', *Psychological Review*, **63**(2), 129–138.
50 See, for example, Kilbourne, W. and Pickett, G. (2008) 'How materialism affects environmental beliefs, concern, and environmentally responsible behaviour,' *Journal of Business Research*, **61**(9), 885–893. Or Pepper, M., Jackson, T. and Uzzell, D. (2009) 'An Examination of the Values that Motivate Socially Conscious and Frugal Consumer Behaviours', *International Journal of Consumer Studies*, **33**(2), 126–136.
51 Hirsch, F. (1976) *Social Limits to Growth*, Harvard University Press.
52 Schwartz, B., Ward, A., Monterosso, J., Lyubomirsky, S., White, K. and Lehman, D. (2002) 'Maximising versus Satisficing: Happiness is a Matter of Choice', *Journal of Personality and Social Psychology*, **83**, 1178–1197.
53 Abramson, L., Seligman, M. and Teasdale, J. (1978) 'Learned Helplessness in Humans: Critique and Reformulation', *Journal of Abnormal Psychology*, **87**, 32–48.
54 Max-Neef, M. A. (1991) *A Human Scale Development: Conception, Application and Further Reflections*, Apex.

55 Kahneman, D. and Tversky, A. (1979) 'Prospect Theory: An Analysis of Decision under Risk,' *Econometrica*, **47**(2), 263–291.

56 Graham, C. (2009) *Happiness Around the World*, Oxford University Press.

57 Kahneman, D., Knetsch, J. and Thaler, R. (1991) 'Anomolies: The Endowment Effect, Loss Aversion and Status Quo Bias', *The Journal of Economic Perspectives*, **5**(1), 193–206.

58 See Knetsch, J. and Sinden, J. (1984) 'The Persistence of Evaluation Disparities', *Quarterly Journal of Economics*, **102**, 691–695. Or Schwartz, B. (2005) *The Paradox of Choice. Why More is Less*, Harper Perennial, p. 71.

59 See, for example, Roese, N. J. (1997) 'Counterfactual Thinking', *Psychological Bulletin*, **21**, 133–148. Or Schwartz, B. (2005) *The Paradox of Choice. Why More is Less*, Harper Perennial, p.153.

60 Sheth, J. N., Newman, B. I. and Gross, B. L. (1991) *Consumption Values and Market Choices: Theory and Applications*, Thomson South-Western.

61 Redelmeier, D. A. and Shafir, E. (1995) 'Medical Decision Making in Situations the Offer Multiple Alternatives', *Journal of the American Medical Association*, **273**, 302–305. Sourced via Schwartz, B. (2005) *The Paradox of Choice. Why More is Less*.

62 Schwartz, B. (2005) *The Paradox of Choice. Why More is Less*, Harper Perennial, p. 136.

63 Vargo, S. L. and Lusch, R. F. (2004) 'Evolving to a new dominant logic of marketing', *Journal of Marketing*, **68**, 1–17.

64 See Claude Hopkins, *Scientific Advertising*, 1923. Reprinted in 2010 by Cosimo Inc.

65 See, for example, Court, D., Elzinga, D., Mulder, S. and Vetvik, O. (2009) 'The Consumer Decision Journey', *McKinsey Quarterly* (Online). Available at: http://www.mckinseyquarterly.com/Marketing/The_consumer_decision_journey_2373 Accessed December 2010.

66 See, for example, Bagozzi, R. P., Gurhan-Canli, Z. and Priester, J. R. (2002) *The Social Psychology of Consumer Behaviour*, Open University Press.

67 See Robert Heath. Accessed via http://www.bath.ac.uk/management/research/pdf/2005-04.pdf

68 Robert Heath (2001) *The Hidden Power of Advertising*, ADMAP.

69 IPA DataMINE (2008) *Marketing in the Era of Accountability*, IPA/WARC.

70 Haidt, J. (2007) *The Happiness Hypothesis*, Arrow.

71 This progression illustrating the growing importance of emotion was presented by Baba Shiv, Professor of Marketing, Stanford Graduate School of Business, at a conference in Barcelona, April 2010.

72 Baba Shiv, Stanford Graduate School of Business, in a lecture presented as above.

73 For a recent review of MacLean's theory, see Cory, G. A. (1999) *The Reciprocal Modular Brain in Economics and Politics: Shaping the Rational and Moral Basis of Organization, Exchange and Choice*, Plenum. New York.

74 LeDoux, J. (1998) *The Emotional Brain*, Simon and Schuster, New York.

75 Baba Shiv, Stanford Graduate School of Business, in a lecture presented as above.

76 *Ibid.*

77 Latitudes of Acceptance originate in Social Judgement Theory. See, for example, Granberg, D. and Steele, L. (1974) 'Procedural Considerations in Measuring Latitudes of Acceptance, Rejection and Noncommitment', *Social Forces*, **52**(4), 538–542.

78 For more information, see Belz, F. M. and Peattie, K. (2009) *Sustainability Marketing. A Global Perspective*, John Wiley & Sons, Ltd, Chichester.

79 For more information, see Maier, S. F. and Seligman, M. E. P. (1976) 'Learned Helplessness: Theory and Evidence', *Journal of Experimental Psychology: General*, **105**, 3–46.

80 Schwartz, B. (2005) *The Paradox of Choice. Why More is Less*, Harper Perennial, p. 209.

81 Myers, D. G. (2000) 'The funds, friends and faith of happy people,' *American Psychologist*, **55**, 56–67 (referenced in New Economics Foundation (NEF, UK) (2009) *The Happy Planet Index 2.0*).

82 New Economics Foundation (NEF, UK) (2009) *The Happy Planet Index 2.0*, NEF, London.

83 As above – Section 8, p. 39.

84 Williams, R. (Archbishop of Canterbury, UK) 'Out of the abyss of individualism' *The Guardian*, February 21, 2010. Accessed December 2010 via http://www.guardian.co.uk/commentisfree/belief/2010/feb/21/individualism-virtue-public-discourse.

Part III The elixir of life – literally

85 Wellman, B. (1988) 'The Community Question Re-evaluated.' In *Power, Community and the City* (Ed. P. Smith) Copyright © 1988 by Transaction Publishers. Reprinted by permission of the publisher.

86 Quoted in Kohn, M. (2008) *Trust, Self Interest and the Common Good*, Oxford, p. 82.

87 De Toqueville, A. (1835 and 1840) 'Democracy in America'. Quote from Putnam (2000) *Bowling Alone*, p. 118.

88 Baum, F. (2000) 'Social Capital, Economic Capital and Power: Further Issues for a Public Health Agenda', *Journal of Epidemiology & Community Health*, **54**, 409–410. Referenced in Harper, R. (2001) *Social Capital: A review of the literature*, Social Analysis and Reporting Division (ONS), p. 6.

89 Lynch, J., Due, P., Muntaner, C. and Davey Smith, G. (2000) 'Social Capital – Is it a good investment strategy for public health?' *Journal of Epidemiology & Community Health*, **54**, 404–408. Referenced in Harper, R. (2001) *Social Capital: A review of the literature*, Social Analysis and Reporting Division (ONS), p. 6.

90 Putnam, R. (2000) *Bowling Alone*, Simon and Schuster, US.

91 Hanifan, L. J. (1916) 'The Rural School Community Center,' *Annals of the American Academy of Political and Social Science*, **67**, 9. Copyright © 1916. Reprinted by permission of Sage Publications.

92 Bourdieu, P. (1986) 'The Forms of Capital.' In Baron, S., Field, J., Schuller, T. (eds) (2000) *Social Capital – Critical Perspectives*, Oxford University Press.

93 Cote, S. and Healy, T. (2001) *The Well-being of Nations. The role of human and social capital*, Organisation for Economic Co-operation and Development (OECD), Paris.

94 *Ibid.*

95 Coleman, J. (1990) *Foundations of Social Theory*, Harvard University Press, Cambridge, MA.

96 Ashworth, T. (2000) *Trench Warfare 1914–1918: The Live and Let Live System*, Pan, London.

97 This example is given in Boutilier, R. (2009) *Stakeholder Politics. Social Capital, Sustainable Development and the Corporation*, Greenleaf.

98 Boutilier, R. (2009) *Stakeholder Politics. Social Capital, Sustainable Development and the Corporation*, Greenleaf, p. 66.

99 Krishna, A. (2001) 'Moving from the Stock of Social Capital to the Flow of Benefits: The Role of Agency', *World Development*, **29**(3), 925–943 (sourced, Boutilier, 2009).

100 Nahapiet, J. and Ghoshal, S. (1998) 'Social Capital, Intellectual Capital, and the Organisational Advantage,' *Academy of Management Review*, **23**(2), 242–266.

101 Heath, R. and Feldwick, P. (2008) 'Fifty Years of Using the Wrong Model of Advertising', *International Journal of Market Research*, **50**(1), 29–59.

102 This diagram appears in Boutilier, R. (2009) *Stakeholder Politics. Social Capital, Sustainable Development and the Corporation*, Greenleaf, p. 106.

103 Fukuyama, F. (1995) *Trust: The Social Virtues and the Creation of Prosperity*, Simon and Schuster, p. 26.

104 See Kohn, M. (2008) *Trust, Self Interest and the Common Good*, Oxford.

105 *Ibid.*

106 See, for example, Putnam, R. (2000) *Bowling Alone*; Nahapiet, J. and Ghoshal, S. (1998) *Social Capital, Intellectual Capital, and the Organisational Advantage*; Kohn, M. (2008) *Trust, Self Interest and the Common Good*; and Fukuyama, F. (1995) *Trust: The Social Virtues and the Creation of Prosperity*.

107 Putnam, R. (2002) 'Social Capital: Measurement and Consequences', paper presented to OECD conference. Sourced via http://www.oecd.org/dataoecd/25/6/1825848.pdf.

108 For more information on Equity Bank and its commitment to creating what it calls the 'African Success Story', see http://www.equitybank.co.ke/.

109 Equity Bank statistics sourced via http://www.guardian.co.uk/world/2009/jan/02/equity-bank-kenya-james-mwangi. Accessed December 2010.

110 This point regarding the 'faithful' definition of credit is similarly made by Anthony Seldon in *Trust* (p. 94), Biteback, 2009 in the broader context of the financial crisis.

111 Edelman Trust Barometer 2010. See http://www.edelman.co.uk/trustbarometer/.

112 See Edelman Trust Barometer 2010 pdf, p. 5. charts 7 and 8. Accessed via http://www.edelman.co.uk/trustbarometer/files/edelman-trust-barometer-2010.pdf. Accessed December 2010.

113 For more information, see http://www.havasmedia.com.

114 Professor Bill Barnett, Stanford GSB. Presented as part of a conversation within the Stanford GSB's BSES (Business Strategies for Environmental Sustainability) programme. October 2009.

115 O'Neill, O. (2002) 'A Question of Trust.' BBC Reith Lectures 2002, Cambridge.

116 Granovetter, M. (1973) 'The Strength of Weak Ties', *American Journal of Sociology*, **78**, 1360–1379.

117 Putnam, R. (2000) *Bowling Alone*, pp. 324–325.

118 *Ibid.* Ch. 17, pp. 296–306.

119 *Ibid.* Ch. 18, pp. 307–318.

120 Jacobs, J. (1961, reprint 1992) *The Death and Life of Great American Cities*, Vintage Books.

121 Mill, J. S. (1861) 'Considerations on Representative Government,' referenced in Putnam, R. (2000) *Bowling Alone*. Accessed December 2010 via http://www.gutenberg.org/ebooks/5669.

122 Smith, A. (1776, reprint 1986) *The Wealth of Nations*, Penguin.

123 See Putnam, R. (2000) *Bowling Alone*.

124 *Ibid.* Ch. 20, pp. 326–336.

125 Marmot, M. G., Rose, G., Shipley, M. and Hamilton, P. J. (1978) 'Employment Grade and Coronary Heart Disease in British Civil Servants', *Journal of Epidemiology & Community Health* (formerly the *British Journal of Preventative & Social Medicines*). Although the initial study focused solely on 17 500 male civil servants (from 1967 onwards), the follow-up study (Whitehall II) focused on 10 300 civil servants, of which 3000+ were women. Whitehall II started in 1985, with the results still being released. The data support the findings of the original Whitehall I.

126 Shively, C. A. and Clarkson, T. B. (1994) 'Social Status and Coronary Artery Atherosclerosis in Female Monkeys', *Arteriosclerosis and Thrombosis*, **14**, 721–726. Sourced via Kohn, M. (2009) *Trust*, Oxford.

127 Kawachi, I., Kennedy, B. P. and Wilkinson, R. G. (1999) *The Society and Population Health Reader (1) Income, Inequality and Health*. New Press, New York. Sourced via Kohn (see above).

128 Putnam, R. (2000) *Bowling Alone*. See Ch. 22.

129 *Ibid.* Ch. 22, p.355.

130 O'Neill, O. (2002) 'A Question of Trust.' BBC Reith Lectures 2002, Cambridge.

Part IV Towards social equity brands

131 Kasser, T. (2002) *The High Price of Materialism*, Bradford/MIT.

132 National Geographic & GlobeScan (2009) *Greendex 2009*. Accessed December 2010 via http://environment.nationalgeographic.com/environment/greendex/.

133 Philip Pullman in *The Guardian* (February 21, 2010). Accessed December 2010 via http://www.guardian.co.uk/commentisfree/2010/feb/21/three-virtues-delight-liberty.

134 Albert, S. and Whetten, D. (1985) 'Organizational Identity', *Research in Organizational Behaviour*, 7, 263–295. Sourced via Balmer, J. M. T and Greyser, S. A. (2003) *Revealing The Corporation*, Routledge.

135 Aaker, J., Fournier, S. and Brasel, S. A. (2003) 'When Good Brands Do Bad', Stanford GSB Research Paper Series.

136 Ritzer, G. (1999) *Enchanting a Disenchanted World: Revolutionizing the Means of Consumption*, Pine Forge Press, Thousand Oaks.

137 McAlexander, J. H, Schouten, J. W. and Koenig, H. F. (2002) 'Building Brand Communities', *Journal of Marketing*, 66, 38–54.

138 See, for example, Vargo, S. L. and Lusch, R. F. (2004) 'Evolving to a New Dominant Logic of Marketing', *Journal of Marketing*, 68, 1–17.

139 *Ibid.*

140 This example is well made by Rachel Botsman in *Collaborative Consumption: What's Mine is Yours*, Harper Business, 2010.

141 Orsato, R. (2009) *Sustainability Strategies. When does it pay to be green?* Insead Business Press/Palgrave Macmillan.

142 *Ibid.*

143 See, for example, http://www.brighthub.com/environment/green-living/articles/54244.aspx. Accessed December 2010.

144 See Rachel Botsman's speech at TEDSydney on Collaborative Consumption. http://www.ted.com/talks/rachel_botsman_the_case_for_collaborative_consumption.html. Accessed December 2010.

145 For a good overview of some of the emerging models (and the general state of panic within the industry), see Danielle Sacks's feature in *Fast Company*: 'Mayhem on Madison Avenue', November 17, 2010. http://www.fastcompany.com/magazine/151/mayhem-on-madison-avenue.html. Accessed December 2010.

146 Smith, N. C., Palazzo, G. and Bhattacharya, C. B. (2010) 'Marketing's Consequences: Stakeholder Marketing and Supply Chain CSR Issues.' Working Paper, WBCSD. Geneva.

147 For more details, see: http://www.msc.org/. Accessed December 2010.

148 AISE is the EC washing and detergent initiative. See http://www.aise.eu/infoday06/downloads/material/Bender.pdf for more information. Accessed December 2010.

149 See Belz, F. M. and Peattie, K. (2009) *Sustainability Marketing. A Global Perspective*, John Wiley & Sons, Ltd, Chichester.

150 Kotler, P., Roberto, N. and Lee, N. (2002) *Social Marketing: Improving the Quality of Life*, Sage.

151 Grinstein, A. and Nisan, U. (2009) 'Demarketing, Minorities and National Attachment', *Journal of Marketing*, 73(2), 105–122.

152   For more information on the origins of brand management, and specifically the links presented in literature between the marketing mix and early brand strategy, see Tilde Heding and Charlotte Knudtzen's *Brand Management: Research, Theory and Practice*, Routledge, 2009.

153   *Ibid*, pp. 29–47.

154   Borden, N. (1964) 'The concept of the marketing mix.' In *Science in Marketing*, G. Schwartz (ed.), John Wiley & Sons, Inc., New York.

155   McCarthy, E. J. (1960) *Basic Marketing: A Managerial Approach*, Irwin.

156   See, for example, http://www.edfenergy.com/media-centre/press-news/edf-energy-and-toyota-launch-uk-trials-of-plug-in-hybrid-vehicle.shtml. Accessed December 2010. Or http://www.businessgreen.com/bg/news/1802160/edf-outlines-vision-smarter-london. Accessed December 2010.

157   For more information, see http://www.betterplace.com/. Accessed December 2010.

158   Anthony Tjan from HBR – 3 minute rule: http://blogs.hbr.org/tjan/2010/01/the-threeminute-rule.html. Accessed December 2010.

159   Williams, R. (Archbishop of Canterbury, UK) 'Out of the abyss of individualism,' *The Guardian*, February 21, 2010. Accessed December 2010 via http://www.guardian.co.uk/commentisfree/belief/2010/feb/21/individualism-virtue-public-discourse.

160   Robert Kennedy campaign speech. University of Kansas, Lawrence, Kansas, March 18, 1968.

161   For more information, see http://www.campaignforrealbeauty.com/. Accessed December 2010.

162   For more information on Lego's army of 120 000 self-proclaimed volunteer engineers and designers, go to http://www.legofactory.com.

163   Equity Bank statistics sourced via http://www.guardian.co.uk/world/2009/jan/02/equity-bank-kenya-james-mwangi. Accessed December 2010.

164   See Pepsi Refresh Everything via http://www.refresheverything.com/. Accessed December 2010.

165   See Boutilier, R. (2009) *Stakeholder Politics. Social Capital, Sustainable Development, and the Corporation*, Greenleaf, for a more comprehensive review of how to conduct social capital stakeholder research.

166   The five sources of competitive value reference the work of Jonathon Porritt in *Capitalism as if the World Matters* (revised edition, 2007) and, more broadly, work from Forum For The Future (London).

167   For more information on the relationship between the component parts (but not in the context of brands or brand-led communication), see Boutilier, R. (2009) *Stakeholder Politics. Social Capital, Sustainable Development, and the Corporation*, Greenleaf.

168   Rowley, T. J. (1997) 'Moving Beyond Dyadic Ties: A Network Theory of Stakeholder Influences', *Academy of Management Review*, 22(4), 887–910.

169   Wallerstein, I. (1979) *The Capitalist World Economy*, Cambridge University Press. Wallerstein introduces the idea of core–periphery relationships. A summary is given

in Boutilier, R. (2009) *Stakeholder Politics. Social Capital, Sustainable Development, and the Corporation*, p. 113.

170 Boutilier, R. (2009) *Stakeholder Politics. Social Capital, Sustainable Development, and the Corporation*, Greenleaf, p. 115.

171 Metcalfe, B. 'Metcalfe's Law: A network becomes more valuable as it reaches more users', *Infoworld*, October 2, 1995. Accessed via Hendler, J. and Golbeck, J. (2008) 'Metcalfe's Law, Web 2.0 and the Semantic Web', *Web Semantics: Science, Services and Agents on the World Wide Web*, 6(1), 14–20.

172 For more information, see http://www.johnkao.com. Accessed December 2010.

173 See Heding, T. and Knudtzen, C. F. (2009) *Brand Management: Research, Theory and Practice*, Routledge.

174 *Ibid.* p. 29.

175 *Ibid.* p. 151.

176 *Ibid.* p. 181.

177 *Ibid.* p. 207.

178 Fisk. P. (2006) *Marketing Genius*, Capstone.

179 *Ibid.* p. 79.

Part V   Broadcast off, dialogue on

180 For more information on Danone's efforts around wellbeing, health and sustainability, see http://www.danone.com/?lang=en. Accessed April 2011.

181 For more information, see http://www.sustainable-living.unilever.com/. Accessed April 2011.

182 Guy Champniss moderated a plenary session at the 2011 WBCSD Liaison Delegate Conference, 'Triggering Transformation', in Montreux, Switzerland. The theme of the session was the power of brands and collaboration to bring about transformative consumer behaviour change. Paul Polman, CEO Unilever, was joined by Chris Burgess of Vodafone and Robert ter Kuile of PepsiCo.

183 For more information, see http://www.refresheverything.com/index. Accessed April 2011.

184 WBCSD Liaison Delegate Conference, Montreux, Switzerland, April 2011. For more information, see http://foodfrontiers.pepsicoblogs.com/2009/11/world-food-prize-keynote-address/. Accessed April 2011.

185 For more information, see http://walmartstores.com/sustainability/9292.aspx. Accessed April 2011.

186 For more information, see http://www.sustainabilityconsortium.org/. Accessed April 2011.

187 For more information, see http://www.equitybank.co.ke/. Accessed April 2011. See also http://www.guardian.co.uk/world/2009/jan/02/equity-bank-kenya-james-mwangi. Accessed January 2011.

188 For more information, see http://www.vodafone.com/content/dam/vodafone/about/sustainability/reports/vodafone_sustainability_report.pdf. Accessed March 2011.

189 For more information, see http://worldofdifference.vodafone.co.uk/. Accessed January 2011.

190 For more information, see http://www.safaricom.co.ke/index.php?id=250. Accessed March 2011.

191 Chris Burgess, speaking as part of the WBCSD Liaison Delegate Conference, on the importance of strong brands for sustainable development goals. Montreux, Switzerland, April 2011.

192 For more information, see http://www.toyota.com/ideas-for-good/. Accessed March 2011.

193 *Ibid.*

194 For more information, see http://www.ecomagination.com/. Accessed March 2011.

195 For more information, see http://www.ge.com/visualization/appliances_energyuse/index.html. Accessed December 2010.

196 Further information on GE's MarkNet initiative can be found via http://www.forbes.com/2010/07/27/ge-twitter-facebook-marketing-engagement-cmo-network-steve-liguori.html. Accessed December 2010.

197 For a very perfunctory headline and obituary, see http://www.nytimes.com/learning/general/onthisday/bday/0217.html. Accessed March 2011.

198 For more information, see http://www-03.ibm.com/ibm/history/documents/pdf/faq.pdf. Accessed March 2011.

199 For more information, see http://groups.google.com/group/net.misc/msg/00c91c2cc0896b77. Accessed April 2011.

200 For more information, see Gordon Bell's comments, at http://research.microsoft.com/en-us/people/gbell/default.aspx. Accessed January 2011.

201 For more information, see http://www.ibm.com/smarterplanet/uk/en/ and http://www.ibm.com/smarterplanet/us/en/?ca=v_smarterplanet. Accessed March 2011.

202 For more information, see http://www.ibm.com/smarterplanet/us/en/communication_technology/perspectives/index.html. For UK specific activity, see also http://www-03.ibm.com/press/uk/en/pressrelease/32456.wss. Accessed March 2011.

203 For more information on the origins of Lloyd's of London – originally Edward Lloyd's coffee house–see http://www.lloyds.com/Lloyds/About-Lloyds/Explore-Lloyds/History. Accessed December 2010.

204 For more information, see http://www.starbucks.com/coffeehouse/community/mystarbucksidea. Accessed December 2010. For additional commentary, see http://www.psfk.com/2010/10/ed-cotton-starbucks-has-an-idea-factory-mystarbucksidea-com.html. Accessed December 2010.

INDEX